Tradition and Transformation in Anglo-Saxon England

DEBATES IN ARCHAEOLOGY

Series editor: Richard Hodges

Against Cultural Property John Carman
The Anthropology of Hunter Gatherers Vicki Cummings
Archaeologies of Conflict John Carman
Archaeology: The Conceptual Challenge Timothy Insoll
Archaeology and International Development in Africa Colin Breen & Daniel Rhodes
Archaeology and Text John Moreland
Archaeology and the Pan-European Romanesque Tadhg O'Keeffe
Beyond Celts, Germans and Scythians Peter S. Wells
Combat Archaeology John Schofield
Debating the Archaeological Heritage Robin Skeates
Early European Castles Oliver H. Creighton
Early Islamic Syria Alan Walmsley
Gerasa and the Decapolis David Kennedy
Image and Response in Early Europe Peter S. Wells
Indo-Roman Trade Roberta Tomber
Loot, Legitimacy and Ownership Colin Renfrew
Lost Civilization James L. Boone
The Origins of the Civilization of Angkor Charles F. W. Higham
The Origins of the English Catherine Hills
Rethinking Wetland Archaeology Robert Van de Noort & Aidan O'Sullivan
The Roman Countryside Stephen Dyson
Shipwreck Archaeology of the Holy Land Sean Kingsley
Social Evolution Mark Pluciennik
State Formation in Early China Li Liu & Xingcan Chen
Towns and Trade in the Age of Charlemagne Richard Hodges
Tradition and Transformation in Anglo-Saxon England: Archaeology, Common Rights and Landscape Susan Oosthuizen
Vessels of Influence: China and the Birth of Porcelain in Medieval and Early Modern Japan Nicole Coolidge Rousmaniere
Villa to Village Riccardo Francovich & Richard Hodges

Tradition and Transformation in Anglo-Saxon England

Archaeology, Common Rights and Landscape

Susan Oosthuizen

B L O O M S B U R Y
LONDON • NEW DELHI • NEW YORK • SYDNEY

Bloomsbury Academic
An imprint of Bloomsbury Publishing Plc

50 Bedford Square
London
WC1B 3DP
UK

175 Fifth Avenue
New York
NY 10010
USA

www.bloomsbury.com

First published 2013

British Library Cataloguing-in-Publication Data
A catalogue record for this book is available from the British Library.

ISBN: HB: 9781472507273
ISBN: epub: 9781472509475
ISBN: epdf: 9781472505361

Printed and bound in Great Britain

Contents

List of Figures

Figures

Acknowledgements

I am most grateful to the colleagues who have generously made their work available for reproduction here, particularly Professor Brian Roberts and Dr Stuart Wrathmell (Figures 3, 5, 9, 10 and 11, and the underlying map on Figure 12). Professor Martin Millett, Professor Simon James and the Royal Archaeological Institute were kind enough to allow reproduction of the reconstructed Anglo-Saxon hall at Cowdery's Down (Figure 6(a)). The University of Cambridge Committee for Aerial Photography in the person of the Librarian, Mr Alun Martin, provided copies of two air photographs reproduced here in Figures 2 and 7, and gave permission for their reproduction. Ms Sarah Wroot and Dr Dora Kemp assisted with the production of other figures, the former generating Figures 8 and 12, and the latter Figures 1, 4 and 6. The University of Cambridge McDonald Institute for Archaeological Research made a generous grant towards the cost of Dr Kemp's illustrations. I am grateful to them all.

Invisible behind the screen of the words in this book lie innumerable debts to colleagues and students who have over the past five years and more patiently discussed the ideas presented here, being good enough to argue with the conclusions and to challenge the flaws. I hope that they will forgive the absence of individual thanks. Two cannot, however, escape without mention. Professor Graeme Barker has been supportive and encouraging throughout – the appearance of this volume in print is a visible consequence of his knowledge and generosity. Mr Christopher Taylor will find as much to argue as to agree with in the preceding pages. His many publications, his creativity in developing new interpretations, his checks on wayward arguments, and his precision in dealing with complex and contradictory evidence have inspired many landscape historians, of whom I am one. This book is the better for such stimulus, while its flaws and misapprehensions remain incorrigibly my own.

As my family have forbidden me to mention them, I shall not say anything about the deep obligation that I owe to their support, nor shall I say that without them these ideas would never have developed or this book have been written. I hope that they are satisfied with the omission.

Prologue

This book asks whether the fundamental social values underpinning the collective governance and management of medieval fields and pastures were an Anglo-Saxon innovation or whether they represented the contribution of an older prehistoric tradition to the making of the British landscape in the centuries after the end of Roman administration in about AD 410. It does so through the case study of rural landscapes in the long eighth century between the later seventh and mid-ninth centuries AD. In particular, it focuses on rights over common grazing, thought to have originated during the fifth and sixth centuries, and on rights over open arable fields, believed to have first appeared around the mid-ninth century. There are no documents on which we can draw, only the silent testimony of the landscape itself.

The argument that follows offers a speculative paradigm for exploration through future research. That paradigm is presented here as an argument, whose premises, evidence and conclusions are explicitly stated. None should be construed as a certainty, but as a proposition to be analysed, challenged, confirmed, extended or overturned by later research.

Although touching on the elites of Anglo-Saxon England, the principal focus of this book is the peasantry, free and dependent. It begins by exploring the origin of collective organisation of, first, pasture and then arable, and moves on to an evaluation of the contribution of middle Anglo-Saxon lords in stimulating innovation in the organisation of agricultural landscapes. The final chapter offers two complementary interpretations for the origins of the medieval landscape. On the one hand it explores long-term continuities in customary forms of social organisation across much of Britain, made visible in the slow evolution of irregular medieval field systems and the persistence of common pasture. On the other, it suggests that re-organisation of traditional arable landscapes in central southern

England between about AD 700 and 1300 might constitute a negotiated compromise between traditional forms of collective governance and new systems of lordly management of inland demesnes. The result, it is suggested, was the emergence of the highly-organised regular open fields visible in central, southern England by the mid-twelfth century.

1

Introduction

Governance of common pool resources through common property regimes (CPrRs)

The central questions of this book are, first, whether medieval rights of common pasture – exercised over large and small areas across England, each carefully defined, and some still persisting in places like the New Forest (Hants.) and Westwood Common in Beverley (Yorks.) – were an Anglo-Saxon innovation or part of a continuing prehistoric tradition. The second question focuses on the contribution of common rights to the evolution of arable open fields. Definitions of common rights and the characteristics through which they can be identified are therefore critical to the arguments and discussions that follow.

Rights of common depend on concepts of property in which exclusive groups of co-owners gain and share equitable bundles of property rights over areas of resource – known to economists as **common pool resources**.[1] Common pool resources are managed within collective institutions called **common property regimes** (CPrRs) which are structured to ensure the long-term sustainability of a resource, the maximisation of its output, and its equitable distribution among those with a right to its exploitation. Those with common property rights are right-holders; in modern English, stakeholders. The acronym CPrR recurs throughout the text that follows, standing for the structures of rights allocation, governance, regulation and management through which right-holders managed the common pool resources over which they shared rights of common.

CPrRs over common pool resources share generalisable formal structures for organising access to rights, governance, sustainability, equity of output, and regulation. Such arrangements define the rights of right-holders, defend them against infractions of their rights, and control the exploitation of the resource in order to ensure the continuing stability of such ecological resources.[2] CPrRs occur across all countries and in all periods, frequently co-existing with social hierarchies of varying degrees of depth and rigidity. They were found throughout medieval England, for example, even though social relationships between individuals and groups in that period were deeply unequal, stratified and relatively inflexible.

Economists have established a limited number of straightforward characteristics through which CPrRs can readily be identified.[3] First, rights to common pool resources are legal rights over property, enforceable by sanction. It follows that the boundaries to a common pool resource must be known and protected for such property rights to be exercised within a framework of law. The boundaries of medieval commons were known and carefully maintained whether fairly limited, lying within and exploited by right-holders drawn from a single parish, or vast, like the enormous acreages of the Cambridgeshire peat fens, intercommoned by innumerable manors of the medieval abbeys of Ely, Ramsey, Thorney and Crowland. The legal status of rights of common as rights of property is of central importance since it underpins the graduated system of enforceable sanctions for infractions of the rules through which rights are protected, as well as mechanisms for resolving disputes.[4]

Second, rights over common pool resources represent 'a structured ownership arrangement within which management rules are developed, group size is known[, limited] and enforced, incentives exist for co-owners to follow accepted institutional arrangements, and sanctions work to ensure compliance'.[5] That is, access to a resource is restricted to a known and exclusive group of right-holders, whether small or large, and rights of common cannot be said to imply a free-for-all on an open resource.

Third, governance, regulation and exploitation are underpinned by principles of equity among right-holders the practical expression of which is an expectation that all right-holders will participate in decision-making, that there will be regular meetings of the group, and that decision-making is based on consensus across the group as a whole – that is, that changes to regulations require the assent of all right-holders.[6] In the early thirteenth century the great jurist Henry de Bratton explained that 'unwritten law and custom' was derived from what had been 'approved by the consent of those who use them and confirmed by the oath of kings, *they cannot be changed without the common consent of all those by whose counsel and consent they were promulgated*'.[7] It is easy to imagine, if this were not the case, the damage that one cussed right-holder could cause by deliberating staying away from a meeting in order to argue that, as he had not agreed to an amendment either of a principle or of the detail of its implementation, any change agreed in his absence could not therefore apply to him.

Fourth, it would be enormously time-consuming (and tedious) for non-literate right-holders to establish each year from scratch such principles and the detailed rules (by-laws) based on them, especially since agreement demanded the assent of all right-holders. The customs through which regulations found practical implementation are therefore recorded in oral traditions, generally requiring only amendment of the minor details of their implementation from year to year rather than substantive restructuring of the principles themselves.[8] The experience of a student from Norfolk demonstrated this clearly: she had moved into a village in which so few people now exercised their common rights that the parish council leased the common to a local farmer. During discussions at parish council meetings it became clear that the dates between which the lessee was able to move his cattle onto the common were well-known to all parties, but there was nothing in writing because 'everyone knew' what the rules were. That is, these customs and practices were still being transmitted in the early twenty-first century from one generation to the next through the recitation of collective oral memory.

Fifth, CPrRs offer transparency of both governance and management in which all right-holders are able to monitor the proper application of regulations and the possibility of breaches. The organisation of irrigation systems in the Andes within CPrRs, for instance, ensures that knowledge of the mechanism for the distribution of scarce water supplies is embedded across the community: 'People's rights … are qualitatively equal, in that everyone is subject to the same roles and procedures, which they know well. Indeed, everyone in the village knows not only how to irrigate a terrace but also how to operate the entire system … [and] knowledge of the rules is evenly distributed throughout the community'.[9]

And finally, CPrRs are governed by the principle of the 'moral economy', that is, the equitable distribution of a resource between all right-holders. At Cockermouth (Cumbria), tenants in 1326 were forbidden to 'dig more turves than they can conveniently and sufficiently use for burning' (that is, they were not allowed to extract peat for sale), while everyone with a turbary could monitor the volume of peat extracted by others.[10] The fundamental principal is that no right-holder should profit from a common right at the expense of other right-holders beyond satisfying the subsistence needs of his household.

The customs and practices which governed medieval English commons conformed precisely to these principles, that is, they were structured within CPrRs.[11] The distribution of rights to common was restricted to an exclusive group – those who occupied freehold land – although their rights could be delegated to their sub-tenants. Rights and their customary applications had legal status, and their record in collective memory was so important that, as late as the twelfth and thirteenth centuries AD, both judges and peasants regarded public recitations of collective memory as more reliable than the written records of statute law.[12] Governance and regulation were undertaken in regular meetings in which all right-holders were expected to participate, and decisions were reached through consensus. In the early twelfth century, 'all freemen, both householders in their own right and those in the service of others' were expected to attend the hundred courts, held twice each year.[13] Meeting places were most frequently on neutral sites in open country, often near boundaries 'in areas which were shared between communities', giving physical expression to equality of participation between right-holders.[14] Representatives were elected by right-holders to monitor activity, and were empowered to impose sanctions for infractions. The moral principle was exemplified in restrictions on the extent to which medieval rights of common pasture could be exercised, which frequently stipulated that a right-holder could only graze as many beasts as he could support on his own homestead during the winter (animals 'levant and couchant').[15]

CPrRs provided right-holders with important social benefits that extended far beyond the immediate exploitation of an area of pasture. Gifts or favours of (say) hay, wool or cheese derived from their access to the commons, or help at particular times of year, for example, with lambing, calving or with sick beasts provided opportunities for individuals to create and respond to obligations of reciprocity. Such personal connections strengthened the formal and informal relationships that bound individuals to their communities and located them within social hierarchies. They were often expressed in feasting, official celebrations and ceremonial events like those of the tenth-century 'hundredman and those in charge of tithings ... [who] dine together and supply themselves as they think fitting'.[16] Men all over medieval England set up fraternities governed by CPrRs within their communities to establish networks of reciprocal support in hard times like loss of livestock, robbery, accident or death. Such structures for collective organisation were so universal that 'all over western Europe the character of communities in the central Middle Ages was rooted and grounded in older traditions, traditions which simply assumed the existence, rights and duties of collectivities large and small: responsibilities were owed collectively to collectives and decisions of every sort were made by groups'.[17] CPrRs were embedded in early medieval and later social custom.

The landscape

The principal sources of evidence for this book are the fields and pastures of medieval Britain, especially those under collective control in which almost everyone had an interest and an influence, whether as labourer, tenant or owner. The ways in which people use a landscape reflect the importance they place on the ownership of land, whether several or collective, their beliefs about which places are particularly significant to individuals and/or communities, and their approaches to managing the exploitation of physical qualities of the terrain to maximise the productivity of different areas.[18] It is a truism, then, that large tracts of most landscapes are human artefacts.

Yet if landscapes are artefacts, they are particularly complex ones. Extrinsic limitations on their layout and development are especially obvious: the effects of climate change are quietly proclaimed by deserted medieval settlements on Dartmoor and other marginal uplands; changing sea-levels affected the management of the medieval Somerset Levels (Harrison 2011). Intrinsic (but not necessarily immutable) qualities of topography, soil and drainage provide other restrictions on available choices. Opportunities for human exploitation are further restricted by the limits of tolerance of herds and flocks, or of species of cereal, in different geographical conditions. The undrained Cambridgeshire peat fens offer an extreme example: before large-scale early modern drainage, the duration and intensity of flooding in the lower-lying areas could be managed through judicious construction of banks and ditches, but only the most desperate, foolhardy or plainly insane would consider ploughing such areas for grain. Cultural factors offered yet another steer – technological change, for instance, could have profound implications for land use: the introduction of the heavy plough is believed to have been integral to the extension of Anglo-Saxon cultivation to heavy clay soils.

The processes through which landscapes are created and amended, redrawn or gradually evolve tend, however, to be invisible to us. This may be because those responsible for such changes, whether transformative or gradual, were not literate or did not live in literate times; but as often it is because such men, even when they were able to read and write, did not see the value of recording their day-to-day management of the land. Hypothetical reconstruction of lifetimes spent in agricultural communities and engaged in agricultural production goes some way to stimulating the kinds of questions that might be asked about the way in which social relationships might be played out in the landscape. If it were possible, for instance, to undertake time-lapse aerial photography of past communities over decades or even centuries across greater and lesser landscapes from one season and one year to the next it might be possible to map the interaction of people and their landscapes over the entire span of their lives. The movements of some individuals across the landscape – of different length and in different directions, of greater or lesser frequency – depended not only on season but also on age, gender and status, wealth, occupation, political and administrative demands, and family networks. People sometimes walk singly, for example to fetch water; at other times collectively, as in beating the bounds or attending a marriage or funeral. Bringing cows in for milking or going to church involve regular, predictable journeys; others are intermittent – travelling to market, or responding to an emergency. Some are undertaken throughout a lifetime while others, like courting, are generally more likely to be undertaken within a short, intensive period. Driving herds to pasture, or going out to plough involve informal journeys whose timing and route will depend on what else an individual is doing that day. In contrast, people who joined the progress of a manorial lord or attended the *ffyrd* would travel along a route carefully designed to make the best impression on those who came to watch. A landscape whose layout did not facilitate interactions to support the practical necessities of making a living, fulfil people's hopes and fears for their own lives and for their relationships with each other, as well as their duties and their emotional attachments, would have to be remodelled to make living through the complexity of each day as easy as possible. There was a good reason why 'all roads' for medieval kings and churchmen 'led to Rome'. 'All roads' for local men may not have led to Rome, but will certainly have been focused on the places and people most important to them. An analysis of the ways in which landscapes were occupied and used over time might, then, reveal a great deal about the ways in which they express and preserve social relationships, and it is the social relationships behind agricultural production that are the principal interest of this book.

That time-depth adds a further complexity. Only a vanishingly few landscapes are static at any time, let alone for any period. The relative importance allocated to features and activities within them from one period to the next stimulate constant changes, slow and fast; some features remaining stable while others are lost, amended or changed beyond recognition. For example, fresh track ways might emerge to connect existing villages with new centres; in the same period some centuries-old routes might go out of use; but others might persist, their alignments remaining stable or shifting by large or small increments without the paths themselves being abandoned. The same influences can be seen in the well-known dictum that because it is physically easier to work within or to adapt older boundaries and ditches into new layouts than it is to destroy them altogether, the persistence of older, abandoned features can sometimes be striking in later landscapes. Medieval headlands, for example, survive as low banks in modern deep-ploughed fields, while Bronze Age property boundaries (reaves) can still be seen on Dartmoor.

The physical context which landscapes provide for the emotional business of daily life thus makes for a strong attachment between individuals and the areas within which they live, and underpins the identification of specific locations within collective memory.[19] The importance of such places can be transient, informal and very personal, like the (identifiable) willow along the Cam to which my mother-in-law vainly clung after losing her punt-pole; my father-in-law laughed so much after she was gently lowered into the river that she (briefly) broke off the engagement. Over the longer term, communal traditions of the significance of specific places are transmitted from one generation to the next in the narration of oral traditions embedded in overlapping family histories, myths, genealogies, land-grants, and in customary practices. It is important for everyone to know where the boundaries of the vill are; it is as important for them to know the churches to which they owe which tithes.[20] Boundaries, husbandry, gifts of property, agricultural produce given as gifts or renders, rights over land, physical management of different parts of the landscape, and infringements of traditional regulations associated with it – each provides a prompt to collective memory.[21]

The physical world of the landscape both contributes to and records cultural development – 'it shapes our sensory experiences, our emotional responses, our social organisation, our political structures, and our understanding of the world', and we shape it under the same influences in turn.[22] If the distinctive features of collective organisation in the early medieval landscape could be identified, perhaps something might be revealed about middle Anglo-Saxon social relations expressed in the continuities and transformations in agricultural production over the period of the long eighth century.

Method

The method adopted here is to locate evidence from Anglo-Saxon England in the wider context of what Fernand Braudel, the eminent French historian, called the '*longue durée*'. By setting a period within its wider time-frame, he argued, historians could determine which of its elements were part of an unchanged inheritance from the past, which traditional elements had been modified – to a greater or lesser extent – and how, and therefore (perhaps most importantly) what the major innovations were of the period under study.[23] To take two examples: a small group of early Anglo-Saxon textiles called three-shed twills are quite atypical of the cloths produced by sixth-century Germanic migrants into England. Past scholars have concluded that this form of weaving was invented after their assimilation into 'the Anglo-Saxons', suggesting that it may have been an expression of emergent

'Anglo-Saxon' identity. More recent research has revealed that, actually, Romano-British looms would have been ideal for producing this kind of cloth, and it now seems more likely that perhaps these twills were, in fact, woven by Late British women who continued to use traditional technologies and techniques to produce indigenous forms of cloth long after every else about them appeared to be 'English'.[24] Similarly, a comparison between the flamboyant loops and curves of Anglo-Saxon interlace work on brooches, stonework and other artefacts, and Iron Age decoration preserved on mirrors and shields, indicates that continuing traditions of prehistoric and Romano-British metalworking did not disappear after the end of Roman administration in Britain, but contributed to early medieval aesthetic tastes too.[25]

Without the wider context of the *longue durée*, these long-term patterns of behaviour might be elusive and there would be a danger of interpreting artefacts as contemporary innovations when they were really derived from older traditions. In the same way, locating the Anglo-Saxon landscape in the wider context of the preceding two to four millennia may make it easier to distinguish between what was inherited and what was new in the management of pasture and arable between the mid-seventh and late ninth centuries.

The durability of tradition

How reasonable might it be to approach landscape as an artefact in which customary relationships between individuals in communities and between communities and their lords might be likely to endure over long periods? Anthropologists like Bourdieu have proposed that our fundamental attitudes to other people – how we expect them to treat us, as well as how we expect to treat them, across a wide range of contexts – are transmitted from one generation to the next through a multiplicity of unspoken attitudes and preconceptions that we mostly learn through example before adulthood.[26] Children absorb through observation and informal instruction the variations in what is considered 'polite' or 'respectful' behaviour in relation to a stranger, a parent, an aunt or grandparent, someone with authority over their family, or one of their siblings or friends. The tacit nature of the process ensures that the beliefs which underpin social relationships, what Bourdieu called *habitus*, are both deeply entrenched and resistant to change. Values and tenets stipulating 'right' and 'wrong' ways of behaving in different contexts are learned and transmitted uncritically, tending to become so inchoate as to be beyond rational discussion. They provide an explanation, for instance, for the deep indignation that can be felt about queuing by travellers. Those who expect access to a bus or a train to depend on *when* an individual arrives at the gate will be outraged by the behaviour of those who cleave as firmly to the certainty that simply *being at* the gate is all that counts. Such expectations about how people should behave are learned implicitly through example, in a process quite different from the explicit way in which, for instance, reading Latin might be taught.

Bourdieu's proposition of *habitus* thus provides an explanatory framework for the mechanisms by which communities recreate themselves from one generation to the next through the perpetuation of their values. These enduring principles tend to be generalised, simply because this attribute ensures sufficient flexibility to adapt to changing circumstance. Take, for example, the case in 1218 of Adam of Tyd from Lincolnshire. As one of the older members of his vill, he was asked in court on what authority he could claim the location of the boundaries to the pasture commons of his parish. He said that 'he had known these bounds for 40 years and more, and there were no other than these'.[27] Now, it is possible that Adam did not discuss this evidence with anyone in advance. But it is equally possible that, for several weeks before his court appearance, he and other senior members of his community deliberated on what his evidence should be. It might have been an accurate reflection of past practice, but it might as easily have included an 'adjustment', perhaps in moving the boundary in question just a little way to the advantage of the men of Tyd, and claiming the new alignment as an old one. Yet Adam did not challenge the two habitual principles that underpinned his testimony – that legal rights were maintained through custom and practice recorded in recitations of collective memory, and that they applied to the boundaries about which he was being asked. This example illustrates how such generalised principles can survive over very long periods, while still allowing the adjustment of minor details of their implementation as circumstances change. By contrast, an hypothetical example illustrates how fragile *habitus* based on inflexibility might be: say that a small group was formed on the basis of two rules – that no one could join it, and that any sexual relationship between men and women was entirely forbidden. The group would disappear within a generation unless one or the other rule were amended: either to permit outsiders to join the group, whether under open or qualified rules of access, or to allow sexual relationships, whether under open or qualified conditions. This means that long-enduring habitual values tend to be highly generalised, providing successive generations with the flexibility to amend the details of their implementation without substantial amendment to the underlying principle.[28] No one would claim, for instance, that the specific meaning to local communities of the White Horse at Uffington (Berks.) has remained unchanged since the horse was initially scratched out of the chalk four thousand years ago. Yet the regular maintenance of the monument over a period spanning four millennia shows how important it has been, and remains, to successive generations of local communities.[29] To take another example: high-status Iron Age households were rapidly assimilated into Roman society after the conquest by Claudius in AD 43, and by about AD 100 their households were fairly exclusively furnished with Roman pottery wares. They appeared to be utterly Romanised, at least as far as the things that they owned and/or used were concerned. Yet it seems that they were using groups of Roman cups, jars and jugs in exactly the same drinking rituals traditionally practiced by their Iron Age ancestors. The members of households who participated, directly or indirectly, in these events knew when they would be practised, what would be needed in the way of equipment, and how they would be performed. It didn't seem to matter to them whether an Iron Age or Roman 'drinking vessel' was used; what *did* matter was that the ritual took place at the appropriate time and in more or less in the same way.[30] Here the detail of *habitus* was adapted by individuals to fit new circumstances but the underlying values of their social interaction remained unchanged.[31]

The public recitation of collective memory plays a central role in perpetuating habitual values, particularly in non-literate societies where there is no other mechanism for recording decisions concerning communal decisions for managing CPrRs. Early documents record the 'wise and old men' and 'better men' of seventh- and eighth-century Wales who, like Adam of Tyd, acted as witnesses to legal transactions within a radius of about 10 miles of their homes.[32] The existence of such customs can sometimes be inferred from archaeological evidence: although large numbers of people were buried between about AD 475 and 650 in an area of open pasture at West Heslerton (Yorks.), there was very little intercutting by later burials of earlier graves – perhaps by then largely invisible on the ground. The excavators suggested that this could only have been the result of 'careful maintenance, perhaps supported by its layout passed down by oral tradition' within families and the wider community over the period of just under two hundred years in which the cemetery was in use.[33]

The continuous construction and reconstruction by communities of their collective memory of customary rights depended on public recitation in order to achieve continuity of consensual approval from right-holders, whether in relation to the exercise of or boundaries to rights of common in relation to any common pool resource.[34] Regular public performance of shared memory provides reinforcement of existing customs as well as offering an opportunity to communities to make incremental adjustments to them by agreeing as a group to 'remember' minor adjustments as part of their 'traditions'.[35] The use of Old English to record boundary clauses in (otherwise Latin) charters of the long eighth century is a case in point. Gearey has argued that the vernacular was deliberately used to ensure that, for example, when estate bounds were recited, they could be understood and ratified by peasant audiences, illiterate and ignorant of Latin, both as the record of past performance and as the basis for agreeing a 'script' for future recitals.[36] Repetition, verbal contrasts, musicality and predictive phrasing helped to embed oral texts in the minds of speakers and listeners. Even those without a knowledge of Old English will be able to identify techniques to assist memory in the alliteration, rhetorical contrasts, repetitive structures, and sing-song rhythms of an eleventh-century charter in which King Edward the Confessor confirmed specific rights over an estate he had previously granted to his Abbey at Westminster:

> *Eadward kyng gret wel mine/ biscopas 7 mine eorlas 7 ealle mine ðegnas on þam scyrum þær Sancte Peter into Westmynstre hafað land/ inne 7 menn freondlice. 7 ic kyðe eow þæt ic hæbbe gegyfen hym on eallum hys lande* ***saca 7 socna***, ***toll 7 team***, *infangeneþeof 7 flymenefyrmþe, griðbrice 7 hamsocne 7 foresteall 7 ealle oðre gerihtu* ***inne tid 7 ut of tid***, ***binna burh 7 butan burh***, ***on stræte 7 of stræte swa full 7 swa forð swa*** *hi me sylfon fyrmest on handan stodon. 7 ic nelle geþafian þæt ænig mann hæbbe ænigne onsting ofer hys land ne ofer hys menn* ***be strande ne be lande ne on wuda ne on felda*** *buton se abbod 7 þa gebroðru to ðæs mynstres neode. God eow ealle gehealde, Amen.*[37]

Such boundary clauses provide a vivid portrayal of the importance to collective memory of the spoken word to early medieval CPrRs, whose right-holders attended meetings in order to hear their rights described in language whose cadences and aesthetic forms were familiar from earlier events. How old were these structures by the time of the emergence of the middle Anglo-Saxon kingdoms in the seventh and eighth centuries AD? Common property regimes over pasture and arable, examined through the lens of *habitus* in the context of the *longue durée*, form the focus of the next sections, exploring the social traditions which ploughmen and herdsmen brought with them in planning and managing the layout and organisation of their fields and pastures over the long centuries before the emergence of the middle Anglo-Saxon kingdoms.

Notes

1 Earle 2000: 51; Ciriacy-Wantrup and Bishop 1975: 714. Very often such resources are environmental: pastures, marsh, woodland, water and so on. Common property regimes can govern intangible institutions as well as physical entities: the University of Cambridge is a common pool resource rights over which are vested in its 'community of scholars'; the British National Health Service is a common pool resource in which right-holders all those with rights of domicile in Britain are stakeholders.
2 Earle 2000: 41.
3 The classic text is Östrom 1990.
4 Ruttan 1998; Östrom 1990: 90; Netting 1976; Lu 2001: 428.
5 Lu 2001: 428, my addition.
6 Östrom 1990: 38.
7 Bracton vol. 2: 22, and vol. 2: 21, my emphasis.
8 Ruttan 1998: 59, 62; Lu 2001: 428.
9 Trawick 2001: 13.
10 France 1954: 42.
11 Ault 1954, 1960, 1965.
12 Bedell 1999; cf. Minc 1986: 42.
13 Downer 1972: 102–3, 8, 1.
14 Pantos 2003: 47.
15 Neilson 1925: 483; Neilson 1942: 57.
16 Pantos 2003: 47; Reynolds 1984: 68.
17 Reynolds 1984: 15. See also Reynolds 1984: 5; for fraternities see Richardson 2005.
18 Cf. Boivin 2008.
19 DeMarrais et al. 1996: 16; Giddens 1984: 132; Gosden and Lock 1998: 4; Earle 2000: 39; Dobres and Robb 2005:162; Owoc 2005: 258; Robb 2010: 513–14.
20 Robb 2010: 502. See also Dobres and Robb 2005: 162.
21 Boivin 2008: 9.
22 Ibid.: 181.
23 Braudel 1981: 560, my addition. See also ibid.: 18.
24 Owen-Crocker 2007.
25 Laing 2007: 55.

26 Bourdieu 1977; Robb 2010.

27 Neilson 1920: xxxv–xxxvi.

28 Robb 2010: 500, also 497–8; Giddens 1984: 30; Boivin 2008: 56.

29 Huntingford 1957; Gosden 1994: 49–51; Gosden and Lock 1998; Schwyzer 1999.

30 Pitts 2010: 144. See also Gearey 1999: 173.

31 cf. Evison 1997: 9.

32 Davies 1978: 14. Druids were repositories of symbolic knowledge of omens and other beliefs in early medieval Ireland, while heroic tales, histories and epics were composed and transmitted by poets and bards (Jackson 1964: 23–56; Wormald 1986: 159–60).

33 Haughton and Powlesland 1999: 78.

34 Gosden 1994: 146; Giddens 1984: 376.

35 Innes 1998: 34.

36 Gearey 1999, 185. See also Wormald 1986: 161, and 1999: 172.

37 Anglo-Saxon Charters, S 1126, accessed July 2011, my emphases. See Swanton 1993: 43–4 for the translation of an almost identical charter. See also DeMarrais et al. 1996: 68.

Part One

Tradition

2

Common pasture

Much of the charm of the English landscape lies in the variety of colour and texture contributed by its many forms of pasture: salt marsh intersected by mazes of winding creeks; freshwater marsh and fen; the thin grasses of the chalk downs; upland moors of bluegrass or heather; riverside meadows; and wood pastures punctuated by pollard or standard trees, or sometimes interrupted altogether by woods or scrub. The range reflects not only the complex interaction of soils, drainage and relief but also centuries of management by generations of graziers to meet a range of needs and demands.[1] Pasture was, of course, an integral aspect of the medieval landscape, whether small-scale meadows of the arable-intensive areas or huge areas of grazing on the uplands of northern and south-western England. Although, of course, much was held in severalty, the principal focus of this chapter is pasture governed as a common pool resource by a number of husbandmen under a system of common rights. Such places, once grazed by Anglo-Saxon and, later, medieval sheep and/or cattle still survive at places like Danbury and Hatfield (both Essex), Thorington (Suff.), Longham (Norf.), Whaddon (Cambs.), Catherton Common (Salop.), and Eggleston (Co. Durham), whether whole or in part.[2] This chapter explores the possibility that there was long-term continuity into the early medieval period of collective structures for the management of grazing as a common pool resource.

Long-term continuities in the management of pasture

Prehistoric or Romano-British pastures have been identified across England, usually on the basis of one or both of the following criteria: they usually support very little (or no) archaeological evidence of settlement or arable farming in any period, or (sometimes 'and') there is palynological evidence that they lay predominantly under grass for much of the prehistoric and Romano-British periods. Dunstone Down, Shapley Common, and Cosden Hill on the upland areas of Dartmoor and the 'open grassy heaths' of Codsend Moors on Exmoor are typical examples; so, too, are the heaths of the Quantocks which reveal 'very little evidence' for Neolithic, Bronze or Iron Age settlement or field systems.[3] Overton Down (Wilts.) has been pasture for most of the past 2,500 years, despite brief episodes of cultivation in the late Bronze and early Iron Age.[4] Iron Age farmers took their cattle and sheep to graze on the uplands of the Yorkshire Wolds.[5] Similar areas of grazing lie across the plateaux of southern England from the Cotswolds to Northamptonshire and Suffolk, in low-lying regions like the Somerset Levels and the East Anglian fens, on estuarine marshlands, and on inland flood-plains of rivers like the Thames, Humber, Great Ouse, and Welland.[6]

Animal husbandry has a long history in England, with evidence of herding – especially of cattle – from the Neolithic period onwards, that is, from around 4,000 BC, and the governance of access to grazing is likely to have been as ancient. Access on its own is insufficient, since grassland needs careful management and regulation not only to support the range of micro-ecologies required by different species of domesticates (and the subgroups within them), but also to assure its long-term sustainability.[7] A mosaic of grazing types is required to support cattle – herded since at least 4000 BC – and sheep (whose numbers rose steadily from the Bronze Age onwards, perhaps mirroring the growing acreages of arable that needed to be manured), especially since grassland cannot necessarily be accessed continuously throughout the year.[8] Damp ground is unhealthy for sheep in summer; cattle crop less closely than sheep and cannot, therefore graze with them; dairy cattle and young animals are particularly sensitive to changes in the quality of grass; the need to grow winter fodder closes meadows until around midsummer; mineral content and nutritional value varies from one area to the next; seasonal flooding can limit access; new grass is susceptible to trampling; pastures need time to recover from grazing; and so on. As important in an economy based principally on mixed agriculture is the necessity to ensure that land is not so overexploited as to become useless in the future; at a minimum, subsistence requires that next year's herds and those of the years, decades and centuries to follow will also need to be fed.

Some uplands, marshes and meadows have only ever been used for pasture. On some, ecological evidence indicates that the mosaics of grassland species they contain remained relatively stable for long periods of a millennium or more before the Middle Ages when they were recorded as subject to rights of common. Because environmental systems are not naturally static, such stability can only have been the result of continuous, long-term and deliberate management. On the Cheviot Hills, for example, late Iron Age farmers 'were … using high quality, species-rich grassland as a pastoral resource' whose character remained relatively unchanged until the mid-eighteenth century.[9] On Bodmin Moor, 'the vegetation of the moor seems to have been very similar [from the Iron Age] throughout the first millennium AD, with predominantly pastoral land use, plus some grassland management for hay'.[10] Similar long-term stability of sophisticated land-management techniques over the past millennium from the medieval into the post-medieval period has been identified in Cambridgeshire, Norfolk, and the north of England.[11] O'Connor has suggested that 'maybe, in at least some cases, that constancy was deliberate, and what we are detecting (and largely ignoring) is quite deliberate management of the landscape to maintain that landscape as it ought to be'.[12]

The long-term success of animal husbandry from the Neolithic through the prehistoric millennia and into the Middle Ages depended on knowledgeable management of land and animals, and that in turn cannot have been undertaken in social isolation. It is a truism to comment on the interplay between economy and social relations. Animals and the products derived from them contributed to renders and the sale of surplus. Such large numbers of cattle were slaughtered at seasonal round-ups at Neolithic causewayed enclosures – over 1,000 at Harrow Hill (Sussex) – that they are believed to represent contributions from whole communities rather just one or two households or individuals.[13] Some Middle Iron Age hillforts in Wessex appear to have been centres for the collection and stockpiling of agricultural produce, especially of corn and wool.[14] More difficult to demonstrate archaeologically are the formal or informal gifts in kind or labour, both within and beyond immediate family or household, that play a role in establishing reciprocal supportive networks between households. Such gifts might simply take the form of help with shearing, calving or in treating a sick beast; alternatively, they might be gifts in kind, perhaps of wool or cheese at times of celebration, or provided to support someone in need. In the Middle Ages such gifts maintained a customary moral economy in which communities gave to those who were poor or indigent, or might become so, and in so doing ameliorated the risk that they themselves might be friendless in times of need. They are common forms of assistance in rural communities of all periods for just these reasons.[15]

Cattle were an enduring icon of affluence and status – expressed in currency, in feasting and in gift-exchange – from the prehistoric into the Romano-British periods, and long thereafter, although the ratios of cattle to sheep varied from region to region and from period to period.[16] They provided traction for ploughs and carts, and dairy products, meat, leather and horn. Livestock on the Cheviots seem to have been treated as 'moveable wealth' allowing farmers from the prehistoric into the medieval periods 'the flexibility to maintain the grazing regime through periods of social and political upheaval'.[17] The contribution of cattle to indices of wealth and status in an 'integrated livestock economy' persisted into medieval England and Ireland with some regional variation.[18] Crabtree has commented on the importance of cattle in East Anglian assemblages: the number of cattle on middle Anglo-Saxon sites appears to have remained relatively constant even where sheep husbandry was predominant and where a shift to wool production saw an increase in the proportions of sheep to cattle.[19] As late as the tenth century English law codes were still predominantly focused on penalties for cattle-raiding, even though arable cultivation was much more important across most of southern England by then.[20]

The cultural significance of cattle in the post-Roman period is vividly exemplified in feasting on cuts of beef on high status middle Anglo-Saxon sites, the use of elaborately decorated drinking horns (which could hardly be less suited to the purpose) in banqueting assemblages, and the origin of the Anglo-Saxon word for 'inheritance' in *orfe*, 'cattle'.[21] Beef was the most frequently eaten red meat at West Stow, even though there were more sheep than cattle on the site, and meat came from adult cattle rather than from disposable calves.[22] The role of sheep in maintaining the productivity of arable land had been recognised from at least the early Iron Age and can still be discerned in the medieval distinction between 'field sheep', folded on arable land for dunging, and wool-producing 'wethers' which grazed on richer pastures.[23] Cattle in particular appear to have been an important signifier of status over the *longue durée* of the three millennia before AD 1100.

What were the systems of ownership and governance over the pastures on which these flocks and herds were kept over those 3,000 years? The remainder of this chapter examines this question through four sub-questions:

1 Were there any similarities in layout between land known to be managed through medieval rights of common and areas used for grazing before about AD 400? If there were none, then the likelihood of continuity is lessened;
2 Is there any evidence for the existence of rights of property in grazing before about AD 400? Property rights over grazing are integral to the management of common pool resources discussed in the previous chapter;

3 If rights of property over grazing existed in prehistoric and Roman Britain, were they exercised in severalty or collectively? If pastures were owned and exploited by individuals rather than by communities acting in common, then rights of common could not have existed before the early Middle Ages;
4 And, if there was collective access to areas of grazing before about AD 400, how likely is it that such access was governed as a common pool resource?

Typologies of medieval and earlier commons

However diverse their ecology and whatever their extent, pastures grazed in common by medieval communities tended to share the same characteristics as areas of prehistoric and Roman grassland. There were concomitant long-term continuities in the ecology of grasslands and in the importance of animal husbandry which sometimes resulted in a continuous history of grazing over a millennium or more.[24]

Grasslands used for common grazing in the Middle Ages are typified by a number of characteristics. First, like Weasenham Moor (Norf.), they tended to be devoid ('empty') of settlement or arable fields.[25] Secondly, they often (although not always) underlay or were the focus of territorial boundaries, being shared or divided between communities: the great marshy pasture at Otmoor (Oxon.), for instance, was intercommoned by the seven parishes which ringed it, while the long-lost mere at Rymer Point (Suff.) was commonly owned by nine surrounding parishes.[26] Sometimes (thirdly), they were bounded by continuous earthworks, hedges or walling – like the turf bank and ditch that skirts Southampton Common (Hants.); and sometimes by rights of way, such as those that preserve the early boundaries of a once-vast green at Haslingfield (Cambs.).[27] On large areas of upland grazing, such barriers frequently took the form of a substantial bank and ditch called a 'head dyke', 'spinal linear' or 'terminal reave', which ran more or less along the contours of hills and downs often (but not always) some way below the summit. The 'top walls' running along the boundaries of the Swaledale moors are a well-known example.[28] On lowland plateaux and valley floors, boundaries to commons could be irregular or curvilinear, often with a 'irregular concave outline' like that at Tiptrey Common (Essex).[29] A fifth criterion is a marked preference to locate settlement on the boundary between arable and pasture. The medieval settlement at Barrington (Cambs.), for instance, encircled an enormous area of pasture which now forms the village green. Commons tended to provide a focus for lanes, droves and tracks which led towards them from any number of directions.[30] And finally, entrances to areas of grazing were frequently funnel shaped, narrowing towards the exit from the common to make it easier to manage cattle and sheep as they were herded onto rights of way.[31] Boxted Heath (Essex) is a typical lowland common: its irregular outline fossilises inroads by arable fields and private enclosures, it is empty of settlement (which tends to cluster around its verges), and it is the focus of rights of way from all directions, many of which enter it through widening funnels.[32] The medieval cattle (and sheep) which grazed 'horn under horn' on common pastures were found on such landscapes.[33]

Prehistoric or Romano-British pastures demonstrate the same characteristics. They are frequently described as 'empty zones', occupied neither by settlements nor fields (Figure 1(a)). Like their medieval successors, such places were often bounded or enclosed: Bronze Age 'terminal reaves' that define the lower limits of upland pasture have survived on Dartmoor in monuments like Venford reave on Holne Moor and Saddlesborough on Shaugh Moor, and can also be seen on East Moor on Bodmin.[34] Middle or late Bronze Age linear boundaries on the Salisbury Plain Training Area could be several kilometres in length. Old Ditch West, for example, ran for more than 16 km, dividing 'land to the north, owned and worked by individual groups, and land to the south, which appears to have been a shared resource, possibly common land'.[35] A similar layout can be seen at Woolbury Fields (Hants.), where a 45-foot ditch separated 'Celtic' arable fields from neighbouring grazing, and there are other examples at Windy

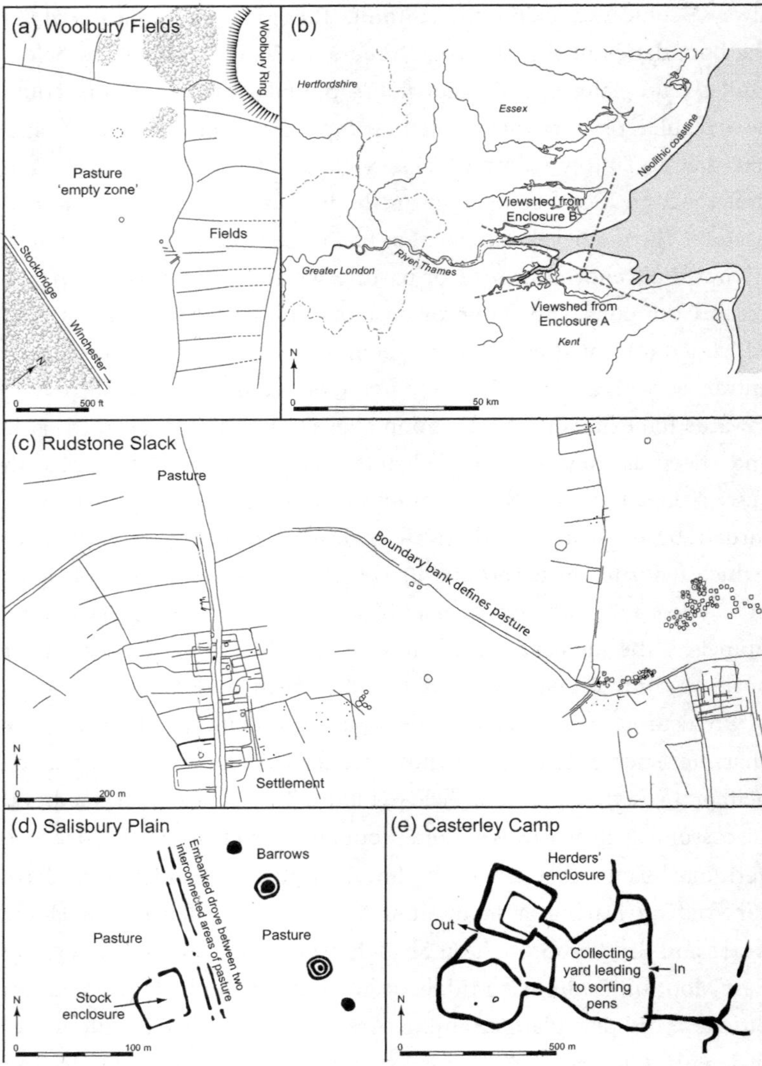

Figure 1. Ancient pastures (a) Iron Age pasture and associated fields at Woolbury (Hants.) (after Crawford 1928). (b) Territories associated with Neolithic causewayed enclosures on the Isle of Sheppey (Kent) (after Allen et al. 2008). (c) Iron Age settlements along tracks leading to funnel entrances into pasture at Rudston Slack (Yorks.) (after Stoertz 1997). (d) Iron Age stock enclosure at Milston Down on Salisbury Plain, alongside a linear boundary (after McOmish et al. 2002). (e) Iron Age stock enclosure at Casterley Camp (Hants.), for sorting sheep during annual autumn round-ups (after Cunliffe 2010).

Dido, Danebury (all Hants.), Gussage Hill (Dorset), Thickthorn Down (Wilts.), and Bignor (Sussex).[36] Substantial late Bronze or early Iron Age 'head dykes' have been identified on the Yorkshire Wolds at places like Wetwang Slack, and on the Dales at Bishopsdale.[37] Many of these boundaries retained their function for a thousand years or more – Old Nursery Ditch, which extends for more than 11 km across Charlton Down (Wilts.), was constructed in the late Bronze or early Iron Age, and over a millennium later still formed the boundary between arable and pasture for at least five Romano-British communities.[38]

Sometimes large areas of grassland lay within a curvilinear bank, as at Newbottle (Northants.) where a huge cattle pasture measuring at least 750 m by 2 km was laid out in the Iron Age, part of its boundary fossilised in that of the medieval parish of Carlton.[39] Banks and/or ditches separated Iron Age and/or Romano-British fields and settlements from grazing at Chysauster (Cornwall), Rockbourne Down (Dorset), Hambledon (Bucks.), on the Suffolk claylands, and on the Cambridgeshire fens, where a fence-line excavated at Must Farm appears to have been put up for 'keeping stock in and 'the wild' out'.[40]

Prehistoric and Romano-British settlements were frequently situated on the boundaries between enclosed fields and open pasture, just as they were in the Middle Ages. At Bishopsdale, one of the 'vast grazing areas for cattle and sheep' on the Yorkshire Dales, prehistoric farms lay along the 'head dike between the enclosed field and the open moorland', just as they did at Sweetworthy, Codsend and Withycombe Hill on Exmoor, at Rudston North, Garton Slack and Wetwang Slack on the Yorkshire Wolds, and at Orcheston Down on Salisbury Plain.[41] Iron Age and then Romano-British farmsteads and their associated fields lay just outside the periphery bank of the enormous pasture at Newbottle (Northants.), whose entrance widens into a funnel.[42]

Areas of prehistoric and Romano-British grazing were also a focus for local routes. On the Yorkshire Wolds, 'a number of these empty zones are approached by tracks' as, for example, to the north of Rudston.[43] Linear tracks and access lanes, originally prehistoric, led from Romano-British settlements at Charlton Down, Upavon Down and Compton Down (Wilts.) to pasture south of Old Nursery Ditch on Salisbury Plain; similar lanes ran north through early co-axial field systems on Lockeridge Down and Totterdown (also Wilts.) to the linear boundary which separates them from pasture, from Romano-British fields onto downland at Chisenbury Warren (Wilts.), and from Romano-British farmsteads to meadows and upland pastures at Biddenham (Beds.).[44] Extensive Romano-British pasture along the upper clay plateaux of the Bourn Valley in west Cambridgeshire was 'traversed by a wide network of intermeshing drove-ways'; and further north, large-scale Romano-British stock-raising on the Cambridgeshire fen has been inferred from the numerous animal stockyards and paddocks visible on air photographs of the fen-edge, at places like at March and Apes Hall, Littleport.[45]

Funnel-entrances to tracks leading from Bronze and Iron Age pasture were as typical of prehistoric and Romano-British pasture as they were on medieval commons. Those at Blealands Nook, North Dalston and Rudston (Yorks.) offer 'the strong impression … that here [Iron Age] drove ways controlled the movement of herds of animals between pastures and paddocks, and through cultivated or inhabited areas' (Figure 1(c)).[46] There are other Iron Age examples at places like Harlestone and Chapel Brampton (both Northants.), and perhaps Romano-British instances on the curvilinear greens of clayland Suffolk.[47] By contrast, however, the sheep creeps of Bronze Age Dartmoor – narrow openings in a terminal reeve – allowed animals from each holding to move straight onto and off the moor.[48]

In summary, then, prehistoric and Romano-British pastures demonstrated similar characteristics of layout to medieval common pastures: they were generally devoid of occupation, and were frequently defined by banks, walls, hedges or other features. Settlements and field systems tended to cluster around their margins, and they provided a focus for track ways which opened into pastures through funnels.

Territorial rights

This is a long way, however, from establishing the proposition that prehistoric and Romano-British cultivators utilised and managed their grazing lands in the same ways as their medieval successors. In many cases, of course, artefacts used for the same purposes by different cultures can share same characteristics, especially if the purpose itself may be quite narrowly defined. The general *idea* of spears, for example – a straight handle with a pointed end – is the same the world over, varying principally in detail of material and finish rather than in the basic principles of plan or structure. Yet other apparently identical artefacts may have been created for quite different reasons to fulfil quite different functions.[49] An Anglo-Saxon loom weight, for instance, is very similar in size and design to South African prehistoric bored stone axe heads, yet they are completely different in function, geography, cultural origin, and period. The question explored in the remainder of this chapter is, therefore, whether prehistoric and Romano-British pastures and medieval commons shared not only long-term continuities of layout but also of collective rights of access and of management in common.

All rights over land depend on concepts of property that allow claims to 'exclusive rights to things' within agreed and/or enforced physical limits (boundaries).[50] Rights of common depend on concepts of property in which limited groups of co-owners gain and share equitable bundles of private property rights over areas with marked boundaries.[51] Geographic definitions of territory both limit the area within which rights may be exercised and permit the identification of groups and subgroups of right-holders. Outsiders remain unenfranchised and have no rights within the territory unless granted by special ordinance. Beyond their territory, the converse will apply – our groups and subgroups will have no rights unless agreed by those who are right-holders in those other territories. If common rights to grazing were exercised before AD 400, then they could only have been exercised if territories had already been defined.[52]

It is an archaeological commonplace that most of England had been divided into territories controlled by different groups by the middle of the Neolithic period (and possibly long before), even if boundaries were somewhat dynamic in practice.[53] Marking of boundaries is a direct and straightforward assertion of rights of property and was undertaken perhaps as early as the Mesolithic, since Neolithic groups appear to have maintained sites already identified as special in some way by 4000 BC.[54] Neolithic long barrows dominate downland and pasture at Broom Heath, Ditchingham (Norf.), Therfield Heath, Royston (Herts.), and Silk Hill on the Salisbury Plain Training Area (Wilts.).[55] Bronze Age stone circles, rows or standing stones marked significant aspects of territory on pasture throughout those parts of England where stone is easily available; Brown Willy (Cornwall) or Codsend Moors (Exmoor) provide just two examples.[56] In Bronze Age Wessex barrow cemeteries were constructed on 'traditional grazing grounds' to which flocks and herds were brought in the summer.[57] Both Neolithic long barrows and Bronze Age round barrows are believed to have bee constructed on 'summer grazing lands for cattle and sheep from different territories', perhaps invoking the protection of ancestors to ensure access to and control of pastures underlying territorial boundaries.[58]

By about 1600 BC territorial boundaries themselves began to be marked as middle Bronze Age dykes were constructed across ridges or along watersheds apparently to (re-)apportion upland pastures between different territories.[59] Rippon Tor and Wind Tor (both Dartmoor), Dead Woman's Ditch or Cothelstone Hill (both Quantocks), Sidbury, Orcheston Down and Cold Kitchen (all Wilts.), Butser Hill and Quarley Hill (all Hants.), and Garton Slack (Yorks.) are just a few of many examples.[60] Their 'sheer scale' and distribution – like those at Snail Down and Tidworth Down on Salisbury Plain (both Wilts.) – indicate 'that the primary function was a form of socially determined land division' defining 'the limits of territorial or functional blocks of land'.[61] In river valleys, long alignments of pits marked territorial boundaries on flood meadows: alignments excavated at Wollaston (Northants.) divided the Nene valley floor into regular blocks and were continuously maintained from the Bronze Age until well into the Romano-British period.[62] Similar alignments have been identified at Grendon (Northants.), Ketton (Rutland) and along the Ouse Valley.[63] Although the form of monument signifying control of pasture varied from one region and one period to the next, the underlying concept remained constant: a normative, visible claim of control over grazing.

Historians of the medieval period interpret areas of intercommon as relics of large polities that were progressively subdivided, and perhaps the same was true in the prehistoric period.[64] Some areas of pasture – perhaps 'ancestral heartlands' – appear to have been shared between a number of territories, like the uplands of north and east Dartmoor which were divided between at least five Bronze Age groups by long boundary markers leading from the edge to the centre of the pasture, all apparently under the authority of a regional controlling elite.[65]

Intercommoning and transhumance are often linked, sending movements of flocks and herds over long distances to and from shared areas of summer grazing.[66] A group which sends its cattle and/or sheep for months at a time to distant pastures, perhaps shared with other communities, perhaps detached from its own territory, must be sure of its rights to do so, depending on 'social order, large-scale investment, the establishment of safe and recognised' routes.[67] Otherwise its members risk not only losing their animals *en route* to and from the grazing lands, but also when they have reached their goal. There is a growing body of archaeological evidence to demonstrate the practice of transhumance over the prehistoric *longue durée*: Neolithic flocks and herds came in the spring to the chalkland slopes of Salisbury Plain, the Marlborough Downs, and places like Hambledon Hill (Dorset) from the Hampshire basin in the east, and the low lands of Dorset and Wiltshire to the west (Figure 2).[68] The analysis of strontium isotopes in the teeth of Bronze Age cattle reveals that the animals travelled seasonally between the Pennines and the Yorkshire Wolds.[69] Iron Age and Romano-British graziers brought their herds and flocks to summer grazing along the marshes of the Severn estuary, at places

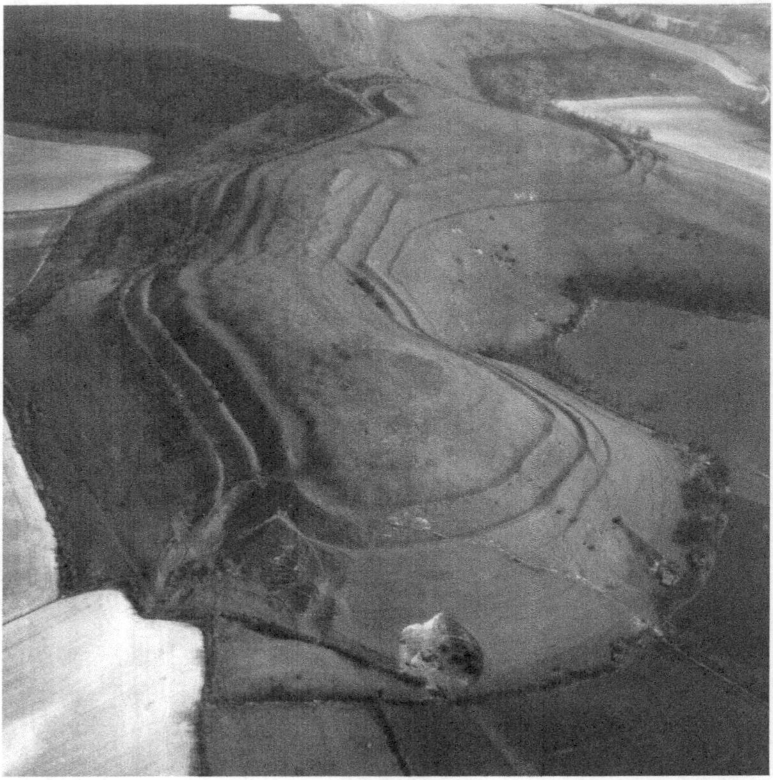

Figure 2. Neolithic and Iron Age earthworks at Hambledon Hill, (Dorset). (Reproduced with permission, Cambridge University Committee for Aerial Photography, CFN66, 1978).

like Goldcliff (Gwent), and Hallen and Northwick (both Glos.), and to meadows along the Nene in Northamptonshire, in the same way that the peat (and, later, the silt) fens of East Anglia provided a focus for transhumant flocks and herds from at least the Bronze Age into the Romano-British period and later.[70] Like the evidence for territorial boundaries, and their frequent association with areas of grazing, the practice of transhumance suggests that, by the Neolithic period at the latest, enforceable rights of access to known areas of pasture had been negotiated and agreed both within territories and with groups across whose land animals were driven outwards in the spring, and returning in autumn.

Access: collective or individual?

Nonetheless, ancient rights to pasture sheep and cattle within defined areas do not necessarily signify that such grazing was itself collectively governed and managed. Pasture might be exclusively owned by individual households or formally subdivided between households. While collective access is a precondition of common property – commons are not open access; they are available only to those who collectively own rights of pasture on them and are most frequently subject to 'rights of equal access and use' – the flocks and herds of each household may have been kept separate in some way once on the pastures, even where access was collective.[71] Landscapes in which grazing was allocated to or owned by a single household or individual, has been identified at Henllys (Gower), where access to a large pastoral enclosure was controlled by a single Romano-British farmstead; and at Roystone Grange (Derbys.) which appears to have been in the sole occupation of a single family, household or kinship group from the Neolithic into the Romano-British periods (see Figure 4(c)).[72] The formal subdivision of large areas of pasture between households can be seen on Iron Age meadows along the Nene in Northamptonshire and along the Thames at Farmoor (Oxon.), where grazing was divided into blocks, each associated with a single household.[73]

Yet alongside evidence for several grazing there is also consistent evidence for collective access to substantial areas of open pasture. There are no signs before the Middle Ages of partitioning of Exmoor, Dartmoor, the Wiltshire and Hampshire Downs, or the Yorkshire Wolds between individual households. At Wetwang Slack (Yorks.), for example, each Iron Age and (later) each Romano-British holding fronted onto to tracks that led to the upland moors, ensuring unrestricted entry for the animals of each farmstead (see also Figure 1(c)).[74] Nor is there any indication of preferential admission to pasture from the Iron Age and, later, Romano-British settlements and fields that lay around the perimeter of the enormous curvilinear pastoral enclosure at Newbottle (Northants.).[75] At Chalton (Hants.) large downland pastures appeared to have been common to a number of settlements from the Iron Age through the Romano-British and into the early Anglo-Saxon periods; while the huge early Iron Age wood pasture at Minchinhampton (Glos.), survives today even though 'wood-pastures are less stable ecologically and socially than coppices'.[76] Cattle and sheep could move freely along drove ways between holdings and pasture on the chalk downs of Salisbury Plain from Romano-British settlements at Upavon Down or Compton Down (Wilts.).[77] Each of the communities cultivating the five Romano-British field systems on Charlton Down (Wilts.) sent their stock to the same area of open downland to the south, while the multiple small Romano-British settlements in Raunds (Northants.) shared grazing across eight small valleys.[78] Lack of evidence for controlled or preferential access, or for the subdivision of pastures between households, suggests that collective rights of access to pasture had already been established as one of the norms underpinning pastoral husbandry by the Neolithic period.

Collective governance and management of pasture

Territorial rights over and collective access to pasture do not, however, necessarily imply that grazing was also collectively governed and managed. Each household might, for example, send its flocks and/or herds to shared pasture under the direction of its own herder, as (for example) happens when sheep are hefted.[79] On the other hand, if farmsteads did combine their sheep and/or cattle in communal flocks and herds for the summer months, as was traditional in early medieval Ireland and in medieval England from Kent to Warwickshire and in the north, then issues of collective management and governance of grazing become more relevant.[80] Such arrangements would immediately offer economies of labour, since 'a handful of men [or young people] can herd the animals of an entire village, milk them and produce cheese in bulk'; the remaining members of the community can then focus on the heavy work of haying, harvest and ploughing which is so urgent in summer.[81] The practice was ancient and universal. By the first century BC, the Roman scholar, Marcus Terentius Varro, noted that 'in the wood pastures (*saltus*) it behoves one to have young men and usually armed men, while on the farm boys or even girls may tend the flock. Those who use the distant feeding grounds should require their shepherds to feed their flocks together all day, but at night to remain each one with his own flock. They should all be under the supervision of one flock-master'.[82] The possibility of the collective seasonal management of sheep and cattle in communal herds across the *longue durée* is explored below through three related topics: enclosures for the seasonal management of stock, communal arrangements for the protection of herds, and annual round-ups of large numbers of cattle and sheep.

The frequency with which prehistoric and Romano-British stock enclosures have been identified on areas of pasture appears to indicate at least some collectivity in the seasonal management of herds. They can be found on practically every area of prehistoric grazing, yet do not seem to have been constructed in sufficient numbers to suggest that each farmstead had its own. They appear to have been 'designed, at least in part, to aid the collection, selection and temporary corralling of livestock' in communal herds.[83] The design of circular Bronze Age pounds had been carefully refined by the early to middle Iron Age to include a single ditched enclosure, generally only between 40 m and 50 m in diameter, approached by a long drove which widened into a funnel at its farther entrance, like those at Bozeat and Evenley (Northants.), Caldecote (Cambs.), or Nettlebank Copse and Warren Farm (both Hants.).[84] They were usually located on hill-slopes at a distance from fields and settlement, near a territorial boundary, and not far from a supply of water, of which places like Shaugh Moor and Lower Hartor Tor on Dartmoor, the Trendle in the Quantocks,

Brigmerston Down and Milston Down (both Wilts.), and Berry Castle, Porlock, Voley Castle and Myrtleberry North (all Exmoor) are just a few examples (Figure 1(d)).[85] The evidence of excavation suggests that many were seasonally occupied, and they have been interpreted as a summer base for 'shepherds tending flocks of sheep and smaller herds of cattle', providing a base for cheese-making, spinning and weaving wool in the same way by small groups like the 'booleying' young people or professional herdsmen of early medieval Ireland who took the communal stock to the 'summer milking place'.[86]

In other places, the careful choice of location ensured maximum inter-visibility between pasture and large settlements or hillforts at places like Danebury (Hants.) or Rainsborough (Northants.), allowing the 'entire herd of cattle belonging to the community … [to] have been corralled in safety'.[87] A large enclosed Iron Age settlement on the fen-edge at Wardy Hill (Cambs.) was positioned to keep a watch over summer grazing on the fen, and Arbury Camp, a huge single Iron Age earthwork, was 'situated so as to dominate a large block of terrace-edge pasture' just north of Cambridge.[88] The embellishment of substantial Iron Age settlements with additional external, concentric ditches, usually at intervals of about 15 m, may also have been designed to offer additional protected outer corrals to collective herds and flocks. At Sidbury (Hants.), Old Oswestry (Salop.), Mingies Ditch (Oxon.) and Groundwell Farm (Wilts.), for example, external works provided several hectares of protected pasture, while an embanked outwork at Ruborough Camp (Quantocks) may also have been designed for safeguarding stock.[89] There is an echo in such designs of areas called *les* in early medieval Ireland: areas bounded by an earthen bank that provided enclosures around farmsteads. The *les* provided protection for livestock at night, and for the most valuable agricultural assets of the steading which included a midden, pens for calves and sheep, pig-sties, 'a souterrain for keeping dairy products and other perishable products', and 'four raised beds' for vegetables.[90] Summer corrals and carefully structured collective supervision all indicate that some herds, at least, were kept in communal groups over the summer months, frequently on large open pastures.

There is also evidence that annual round-ups of very large numbers of animals in late summer or autumn were a standard feature of pastoral husbandry from at least the Bronze Age onwards, like the 'great drives' of medieval cattle that took place each year in the peat fens. At East Fen in Skirbeck Wapentake (Lincs.) the cattle of at least 19 vills were collected together each autumn for sorting; there were so many animals that the round-up took three days and nights, and required 'a bailiff, and twenty-two men with twelve horses, supported by eight men with boats'.[91] Seasonal gatherings of large numbers of people were held at Neolithic and Bronze Age hill-top enclosures for 'sorting, castrating and culling' animals as, for example, at Hambledon Hill (Dorset), Walbury (Berks.), Norbury (Glos.) and Ivinghoe Beacon (Herts.).[92] Late Bronze Age stockyards at Fengate (Northants.) and at Deeping (Lincs.) as well as Iron Age examples at places like Casterley Camp (Hants.) have been interpreted as evidence of the annual processing of communal flocks of between 2,500 and 3,500 sheep (Figure 1(e)).[93] Focused alignments of linear ditches on the Yorkshire Wolds, like those at Burton Fleming and Thwing, were designed 'to perform a special controlling or blocking function', perhaps also for sorting and otherwise managing large Iron Age herds and flocks.[94] The small Iron Age enclosure on pasture at Suddern Farm (Hants.) appears to have been occupied seasonally in winter and early spring for culling older sheep and lambs.[95] A large volume of Iron Age horse gear and a high proportion of horse bones from which foals and young horses were absent, suggests that at Gussage All Saints (Dorset) in the New Forest 'horses were allowed to breed in the wild on the wastelands and were annually rounded up for selection and subsequent training', just as they are today.[96] Finds of horse bones with cattle bones, and an intensification in cattle and sheep rearing in the later fourth century AD, led Applebaum to suggest that 'free ranging herds were run for meat and hides' at Romano-British villas at Rockbourne Down (Dorset), Hambledon (Bucks.) and Appleton (Norf.).[97]

Lastly, growing evidence throughout prehistory for communal spring or autumn feasts at monuments set on pasture adds to the evidence from stock enclosures and large-scale autumn round-ups. At Hambledon Hill (Dorset), for example, Neolithic communities from as far away as Devon and the Severn met in spring and again in late summer for about 300 years from around 3600 BC, butchering and eating large numbers of cattle, sheep and pigs at the beginning and end of the summer grazing season.[98] An indication of the importance of such gatherings is implied by the accurate recutting of the ditch of the Neolithic causewayed camp at Hambledon Hill over periods of hundreds of years, even when its original alignment was just 'a mere undulation in the surface' of the hill, a degree of continuity of a place of assembly that can only be explained in terms of oral tradition (Figure 2).[99] Similar Neolithic causewayed enclosures were constructed around 3600 BC across southern England on large areas of open grassland to bring people together for 'gatherings, rites and feasting' at places like Uffington (Oxon.), Haddenham (Cambs.), Briar Hill and Raunds (both Northants.); they include two which lay back-to-back overlooking opposing viewsheds from the Isle of Sheppey (Kent) (Figure 1(b)).[100] The design and scale of such causewayed enclosures emphasised collective values and communal labour which gave physical expression to the identification of groups with their common areas of grazing.[101] The discovery of large volumes of animal bones at Iron Age seasonal enclosures like Nettlebank Copse (Hants.) and at Harrow Hill (Sussex) (where the skulls of more than 1,000 cattle were excavated) has been interpreted as marking 'the annual round up of livestock accompanied by bouts of communal feasting'.[102] After the party, animal bones and dung were raised in huge Iron Age middens to mark the places 'where large numbers of people gathered' to feast among enormous herds on their common pastures.[103] A massive early Iron Age midden, covering at least 2.5 ha and set within an oval enclosure on sheep pasture at East Chisenbury (Wilts.), was made up of huge numbers of mutton and lamb bones, the remains of vast feasts, culled from 'an intensity of sheep farming rivalling, perhaps, even that of the post-medieval period' and which furnished the menu.[104] Others have been identified on meadows and pastures close to long-distance routes at Runnymede and Wallingford (both Berks.), and at Potterne and All Cannings Cross (both Wilts.).[105] These substantial events seem to have been timed to coincide with the arrival and/or departure of the animals when disputes about rights to grazing and ownership of stock were most likely to occur.[106]

Over the three millennia before about AD 1100, there were, then, many places where pastures were grazed in common by flocks or herds of communities who came together for annual round-ups marked by large-scale feasting. Access by whole communities to areas of grazing whose boundaries were known and marked, which remained consistently 'empty' of fields and settlements, and whose grassland ecologies were maintained over hundreds, sometimes thousands, of years, all indicate that the possibility remains viable that such pastures were collectively governed and managed as common pool resources long before the Anglo-Saxon *adventus*,

Common pool resources?

If such areas were organised under CPrRs, how might they be recognised at such a distance and without documentary evidence?

In any common pasture, an efficient mechanism would be required both for establishing and recording regulations for rights allocation and for necessary structures and details of governance, as well as for the enforcement of regulations. It would be dauntingly time-consuming to attempt to achieve consensus on such matters among a number of right-holders on an annual basis. If agreement were reached on general principles of entitlement to rights, and on the structures for their governance and regulation, most subsequent discussions could focus on the minor details more likely to vary from year to year: admission of new members, election of representatives, amendments to dates for access, settlement of disputes, and so on. Disputes could be minimised by the active participation of all right-holders in discussions and decisions, reached on the basis of consensus. Regular formal, public assemblies would be necessary. Together, these norms match very closely those of structures for managing common pool resources. In a non-literate society, formal regulations for the collective governance and management of any resource, including pasture, could obviously not be written down. Custom and practice recollected through a spoken tradition and agreed by consensus would offer support for these principles over the longer term.

Although no absolute evidential proof for common property institutions for managing pasture as common property resources is possible for prehistoric Britain, the history of the collective management of other environmental resources confirms that such methods and structures were being practised in the fourth millennium BC. The Sweet Track in the Somerset Levels, for example, was constructed in a single year in the fifth or fourth millennium BC by two communities, working from opposite sides of the marsh, each drawing on separate stands of managed woodland and coppice.[107] The materials used in constructing a middle Iron Age house on the Glastonbury fens similarly suggest the collective management of resources: they included oak coppice cut on a 10- to 15-year cycle, hazel or willow coppice cut on a 4- to 5-year cycle, 17,000 bundles of reeds and eight cubic metres of clay.[108] Ancient managed woodland, perhaps at one time belonging to nearby Iron Age and Romano-British settlements, has been identified at Knook Down East (Wilts.) and at Rayleigh (Essex).[109]

Prehistoric pastures that survived into the medieval period and after offer physical examples of the longevity of some institutions for managing common property resources. Some, like the huge tracts of Dartmoor, Exmoor, the Wolds, the Cheviots and the Pennines are well-known, as are smaller areas which were not ploughed before the high tide of the late thirteenth century and sometimes not even then – places like Minchinhampton Common (Glos.), Uffington (Oxon.), Therfield (Herts.), parts of Salisbury Plain, and so on. In other places, the survival of Celtic elements in names for wood pastures suggests long-term continuity of pastoral land use from sub-Roman times, and perhaps long before, into the Middle Ages. Such names include Penge (*pen*, 'high' and *cēt*, 'wood') (Kent), Barnwood (*bryn* 'wood') and Maisemore (*maes*, 'plain' and *mor*, 'moor') (both Glos.), *coit maur* ('great wood', now called Selwood) (Wilts.), *Letocetum*, a large Roman wood south of Lichfield (Staffs.), the Forest of Wyre (Worcs.), woods around Bunbury and Malpas (both Ches.), and so on.[110] Their communal character is sometimes implied by their names: Somerset (*sumor*, 'summer' and *saete*, 'people, especially of Romano-British origin') records the seasonal movement of animals to and from the Somerset Levels; *Andredswald*, the Anglo-Saxon name for the Sussex and Kentish Weald was derived from *Anderita*, the Roman name for Pevensey.[111] Jones argued that the boundaries of *Burghshire* (a large early medieval estate focused on Aldborough (Yorks.)) along the upper slopes of the Nidd Valley perpetuated those not only of *Isurium Brigantum*, the fortified Roman cantonal capital of the Brigantes recorded in AD 150, but also its Iron Age predecessor, and that woods along the boundaries had provided common grazing for the region long before the Roman conquest.[112] The persistence over nearly a millennium of such institutions in some places demonstrates the feasibility of the proposition, of which the New Forest Verderers are just one example – recorded in the eleventh century for the first time, the institution itself may well be even older.[113]

There are even hints in the typically small areas of Iron Age and Romano-British ('Celtic') fields that the principles of levancy and couchancy may have been applied, which restricted the numbers of animals from each holding that had access to the commons to those that could be overwintered. Examples are almost universal, ranging from those at Warter, Kilham and Langtoft (all Yorks.), and Caldecote, Apes Hall and March (all Cambs.) to Charlton Down (Wilts.); many of which 'may have been used as livestock paddocks at various times'.[114] Such continuities are indicated too by analyses of Anglo-Saxon patterns of pastoral husbandry which demonstrate that 'the patterns of sheep exploitation at West Stow were more similar to native British patterns than to patterns of sheep use in the continental AS homelands, and the ageing evidence for cattle produces very similar results'.[115]

Over at least two millennia, the long history of grazing, the use of cattle and sheep as an index of status and wealth, consistent open access to pasture, the absence of subdivision of grassland into individual units, evidence for communal herding (and feasting) on grazing lands in the summer months, and the unbroken use of some areas for common pasture sometimes for a millennium or more, indicate a high degree of likelihood that prehistoric right-holders collectively managed and cropped at least some pastures without higher direction. General continuity over the *longue durée* of structures for the governance and management of common pool resources seems likely unless we are to postulate both the complete desertion of large tracts of countryside and a duration for that abandonment for a period long enough to allow all norms governing their past use and management to disappear from living memory. There is, as argued above, little evidence that this occurred on any wide scale. Daily, monthly and seasonal agricultural tasks relating to stock made a fundamental contribution to subsistence in all periods. A man who lost his herds or flocks, or the pastures to which he was accustomed to take them, might (if he were able to replace either) be expected to bring his past experience and that of his neighbours and peers to his conceptions of the norms, practices, and sanctions governing his future access to grazing. Inarticulate, habitual expectations governing common rights and maintained in oral traditions of customary practice provide appropriate conditions for the long-term continuity of structures for the management of common pool resources within local communities.

No one would suggest that every medieval pasture or common was managed under a CPrR over the previous two millennia. Some prehistoric areas of grazing were doubtless lost to other forms of agricultural exploitation, the regeneration of woodland, or rights of severalty; in other places, new commons may have developed. Yet, although the detail of a *particular* right of common or rights governing a *specific* pasture might change, the structures within which collective management of pasture could be undertaken under a CPrR in a non-literate society were sufficiently generalised and flexible, and (as is argued below) so embedded in social relations, that the collective management of pastoral landscapes under common rights may represent a continuous tradition from prehistoric into early medieval England and after. How pervasive were such values? Were they restricted to non-arable resources or might they also have been applied in the management of arable cultivation? It is to these questions that we turn next.

Notes

1 Denman et al. 1967: v and 10–212; Rackham 1986.

2 e.g. Beresford and St Joseph 1979: 96–7; Wade-Martins 1980b: 34; Rackham 1986: 137, 142; Warner 1987: 8; Roberts 1989: 159; Oosthuizen 1993: 93–100; Oosthuizen 2002a: 73–88.

3 Fleming 2008: 48, 54; Riley and Wilson-North 2001: 50–1; Riley 2006: 80, 206.

4 Fowler 2000: 226.

5 Stoertz 1997: 67–9, 82–3.

6 RCHME 1976: 73a; Evans 1992: 16; Gingell 1992: 151–2; Hey 2002: 193; Gardiner et al. 2002: 1–40; McOmish et al. 2002: 154; Pryor 2002: 30; Evans et al. 2009: 52; Moorhouse 2005: 303; Fulford et al. 2006: 229; Deegan and Foard 2007: 82; Luke 2008: 64–8; Cunliffe 2010: 428.

7 O'Connor 2009.

8 Whittle 2009: 81. Parker Pearson 2008: 40–1; Cunliffe 2010: 415–18.

9 Davies and Dixon 2007: 29, 38.

10 Gearey et al. 2000: 506, my addition.

11 Oosthuizen 2006; Davison 1990; Stoertz 1997.

12 O'Connor 2009: 11.

13 Cunliffe 2010: 50–2; Whittle 2009: 98.

14 Cunliffe 2010: 390–396. See also Lock 2007.

15 Cf. Richardson 2005; Thompson 1991.

16 Cf. Applebaum 1954: 103–14; Evans and Serjeantson 1988: 366; Fulford et al. 2006: 205–6; Gingell 1992: 151–2; Dawson 2000: 120; Evans 2003: 136; Cunliffe 2010: 416; Rippon 2005: 93–122; Bradley and Fulford 2008: 121; Evans with Mackay and Webley 2008: 126; Parker Pearson 2008: 40–1.

17 Davies and Dixon 2007: 43.

18 O'Connor 2011: 367; cf. Van Bavel 2010: 125: 'horses, and also horned cattle, were an important status symbol among German tribes'.
19 Crabtree 2010: 125–7.
20 Whitelock 1979. Cf. Kelly 1997: 27.
21 Hamerow 2002b: 129; Oosthuizen 2006: 111–12; Charles-Edwards 1987: 98.
22 O'Connor 2011: 368, 370, 362.
23 Beresford 1953.
24 See, for example, Rackham 1986: 343; Roberts 1989: 158–9; Rippon 2000: 147.
25 Wade-Martins 1980b: Figure 33.
26 Hoskins and Stamp 1963: 25–6; Rackham 1986: 355–6. See also Hooke 1981a: 112; Everitt 1986: 144; Ford 1987: 152; Jones 1987b: 186–8; Hooke 1992: 53–6; Lewis et al. 1997: 59; Everitt 2002: 221; Cannell 2005: 38; Warner 1987: 7.
27 Bowden et al. 2009: 31.
28 Fleming 1998b: 60–1.
29 Chapman and André 1777 (1960 edn): Plate IX; Rackham 1986: 343. See also Beresford and St Joseph 1979: 95–8; Warner 1987: 7, 11–12; Hey 2002: 47.
30 Everitt 1986; Silvester 1988: 32; Rippon 2000: 147; Corcos 2002: 117–20; Rippon 2004: 111.
31 e.g. Rackham 1986: 343; Roberts 1989: 158–9; Rippon 2000: 147.
32 Chapman and André 1777 (1960 edn): Plate IX.
33 Darby 1974: 68, 72; Neilson 1920, 1928.
34 Fleming 2008: 49, 52–3, 145.
35 McOmish et al. 2002: 64.
36 Crawford 1928: 154; Fulford et al. 2006: 229.
37 Stoertz 1997: 63; Moorhouse 2005: 307–8.
38 McOmish et al. 2002: 102–3.
39 Deegan and Foard 2007: 85, 108.
40 Evans et al. 2009: 52. See also Smith 1996: 172–4; Applebaum 1966: 101–102; Warner 1987: 7, 10–11.
41 Moorhouse 2005: 307–8; Riley and Wilson-North 2001: 50–1, 74–5, 83; McOmish et al. 2002: 62.
42 Deegan and Foard 2007: 133, 85.

43 Stoertz 1997: 69.
44 McOmish et al. 2002: 107; Fowler 2000: 65; Fulford et al. 2006: 89–90; Luke 2008: 62–3.
45 Abrams and Ingam 2008: 117. See also Hall 1987: 44; Hall 1996: 26, 159.
46 Stoertz 1997: 43–5, 71, my addition.
47 Deegan and Foard 2007: 86, 89–90; Warner 1987: 10–11.
48 Fleming 1983: 223; Fleming 2008: 90–1.
49 cf. Baker and Butlin 1973: 624.
50 Earle 2000: 40.
51 Earle 1996: 51; Ciriacy-Wantrup and Bishop 1975: 714.
52 Cf. Lu 2001: 428.
53 Bradley 1984: 12; Parker Pearson 2008: 48–9. Mesolithic hunter-gatherers appear to have moved within territories, for example, between winter base-camps on the wolds of north Lincolnshire and summer Pennines uplands in summer, cf. Milner and Mithen 2009: 71.
54 Earle 2000: 51; Whittle 2009: 86.
55 Wade-Martins 1987: 6; Darvill 1996: 85–7; McOmish et al. 2002: 50.
56 Herring 2008; Riley and Wilson-North 2001: 50–1.
57 Parker-Pearson 2009: 120.
58 Fleming 1971: 156–61; cf. Earle 2000: 51.
59 Fleming 2008: 140; cf. Spratt 1991; Sharples 2010: 46–51.
60 Fleming 2008: 65–6; Riley 2006: 47–8; Cunliffe 2010: 52–3; Stoertz 1997: 41–2.
61 McOmish et al. 2002: 63–4; Stoertz 1997: 62.
62 Deegan and Foard 2007: 82.
63 Last 2005: 333–60; Deegan and Foard 2007: 82, 84; Dawson 2000.
64 e.g. Neilson 1920: xxiv–lviii.
65 Parker Pearson 2009: 120; Fleming 2008: 66–70, 136–7.
66 Transhumance was, of course, common in early medieval and medieval England and Ireland; cf. Everitt 1986: 150–61; Winchester 2000: 80; Neilson 1920: xliv; Neilson 1928: 55; Silvester 1988: 32; Rippon 2000: 147; Riley and Wilson-North 2001: 102; Rippon 2005: 107; Kelly 1997: 43–4; Fox 2012.
67 Faith 2010: 188. See also Fox 2012. Although both Faith and Fox discuss Anglo-Saxon and medieval transhumance, the principles remain the same.

68 Fleming 1998b: 55; Cunliffe 2010: 259; Parker Pearson 2008: 47–8; Mercer 2009.

69 Parker Pearson 2008: 47.

70 Meddens and Beasley 2001: 143–85; Harding and Healy 2007: 283; Gardiner et al. 2002: 30–1; Silvester 1988: 151–6.

71 Feeney et al. 1990: 4; cf. Ciriacy-Wantrup 1975: 715.

72 Kissock and Anthony 2009; Hodges 1991: 84.

73 Deegan and Foard 2007: 82; Cunliffe 2010: 256–7.

74 Stoertz 1997: 53.

75 Deegan and Foard 2007: 133.

76 Rackham 2004: 145; Cunliffe 1973: 183; McOmish et al. 2002: 102–3; 107; Cunliffe 2010: 51; RCHME 1976: 83b.

77 McOmish et al. 2002: 92, 107.

78 Ibid.: 102–3; 107; Parry 2006: 82.

79 Hart n.d.

80 Kelly 1997: 43–4; Neilson 1920: 78; Ault 1972: 104.

81 Netting 1976: 141.

82 Harrison 1918: 255.

83 Cunliffe 2010: 246.

84 Deegan and Foard 2007: 107–8; Abrams and Ingham 2008: 119; Cunliffe 2010: 244–7.

85 Darvill 1996: 64–5; Cunliffe 2010: 52, 244–7; Riley 2006: 61–3; McOmish et al. 2002: 70–1; Riley and Wilson-North 2001: 65–9.

86 McOmish et al. 2002: 71; Kelly 1997: 44, see also 43–5. Cheese-making was undertaken in summer, between the weaning of the calves and lambs whose birth stimulated the milk that provided the raw material, and the autumn when the animals would once more be pregnant. In Italy, in the first-century BC, 'the custom is to make cheese from the rising of the Pleiades in spring to their rising in summer', that is from about the beginning of May until the beginning of November (Harrison 1918: 263).

87 Cunliffe 2010: 425; Deegan and Foard 2007: 89.

88 Evans 2003: 136, 144; Evans 1992: 20.

89 Cunliffe 2010: 428, 255, 314–17; Riley and Wilson-North 2001: 55; cf. Kelly 1997: 364.

90 Kelly 1997: 365. See also pp. 363–7.

91 Cunliffe 2010: 427; Fulford et al. 2006: 229; Neilson 1920: xiii. See also Darby 1974: 68, 72.

92 Cunliffe 2010: 379–82; Mercer 2009. See also Payne, Corney and Cunliffe 2006: 156.

93 Cunliffe 2010: 379–82, 427. See also Pryor 1996: 318–21 and 2002: 27, though this interpretation remains controversial.

94 Stoertz 1997: 73–7, also 52–3; McOmish et al. 2002: 52; Abrams and Ingham 2008: 119; Hall 1996: 26; Hall 1987: 44.

95 Sharples 2010: 74.

96 Cunliffe 2010: 428.

97 Applebaum 1966: 102.

98 Mercer 2009: 41–3.

99 Mercer cited in Fleming 2008: 152.

100 Mercer 2009: 38–43. See also Allen et al. 2004: 235–322, 279; Harding and Healy 2007: 280–1; Whittle 2009: 98.

101 cf. DeMarrais et al. 1996: 15–19; Whittle 2009: 98.

102 Cunliffe 2010: 247, 424–5.

103 Sharples 2010: 53.

104 McOmish et al. 2002: 73, 60.

105 Sharples 2010: 52, 308.

106 cf. Darvill 1996: 30–1; Pryor 2002: 20; Jones 2007; Lock 2007.

107 Coles and Coles 1986: 55–6, 77, 85, 105.

108 Sharples 2010: 204–5.

109 Rackham 2010: 41, 68 and 1988: 18, 75; McOmish et al. 2002: 97.

110 Everitt 2002: 216; Finberg 1955: 37; Gelling 1992: 64; Costen 1988: 41; Rackham 1988: 25; Higham 2004: 30; Ford 1987: 148.

111 Hoskins and Stamp 1963: 7, 24; Fleming 1998b: 56; Neilson 1928: 3.

112 Jones 1987a: 29–30. Recent archaeological investigation at the site of Aldborough appears to confirm Jones' interpretation, Wainwright 2011. See also Thirsk 1973: 245–6.

113 The Verderers of the New Forest, http://www.verderers.org.uk/ [accessed August 2011]; Dallas 2010; Birtles 1999.

114 Hall, 1987: 44. See also McOmish et al. 2002: 52; Stoertz 1997: 52–3; Abrams and Ingham 2008: 119; Hall 1996: 26.

115 Crabtree 1989: 212.

3

Arable laid out in open fields

In almost every part of medieval England at least some arable lay in open fields – from the 'champion' two- and three-field landscapes of the central southern counties to the 'ancient' landscapes where open fields were smaller in scale than in the midlands, frequently alongside arable fields held in severalty, but nonetheless still present (Figures 3 and 5).[1] The defining physical characteristic of an open-field layout was its subdivision between two or more cultivators in a form that allowed easy access between and across their holdings. At the extremes, there were places (especially in the west of England) in which there was little or no open-field land and other places, as frequently found (particularly across central southern England), where arable was only cultivated in open fields. In between, there was enormous variety – and change over time – in the proportion of arable in each vill that lay in open fields and the proportion that was held in severalty. Holdings within open fields were frequently laid out in long strips of land (also called selions) that contained anything between a fraction of an acre to one, two or more acres. Sometimes the subdivisions of a cultivator's holding were concentrated in two or more blocks, sometimes each strip of each holding lay intermingled among those of other cultivators.[2] There is a fallacy that *all* selions were ploughed to create a permanent central ridge bounded on either side by a furrow. Instead, ridge and furrow tends to be restricted to clay soils where it assisted drainage. Many cultivators on lighter soils, while still ploughing in strips, nonetheless managed their cultivation to prevent ridging. Unridged selions can still be seen in open fields around Soham (Cambs.) and the Isle of Axeholme (Lincs.) that were never enclosed, either privately or by Parliamentary Award.[3]

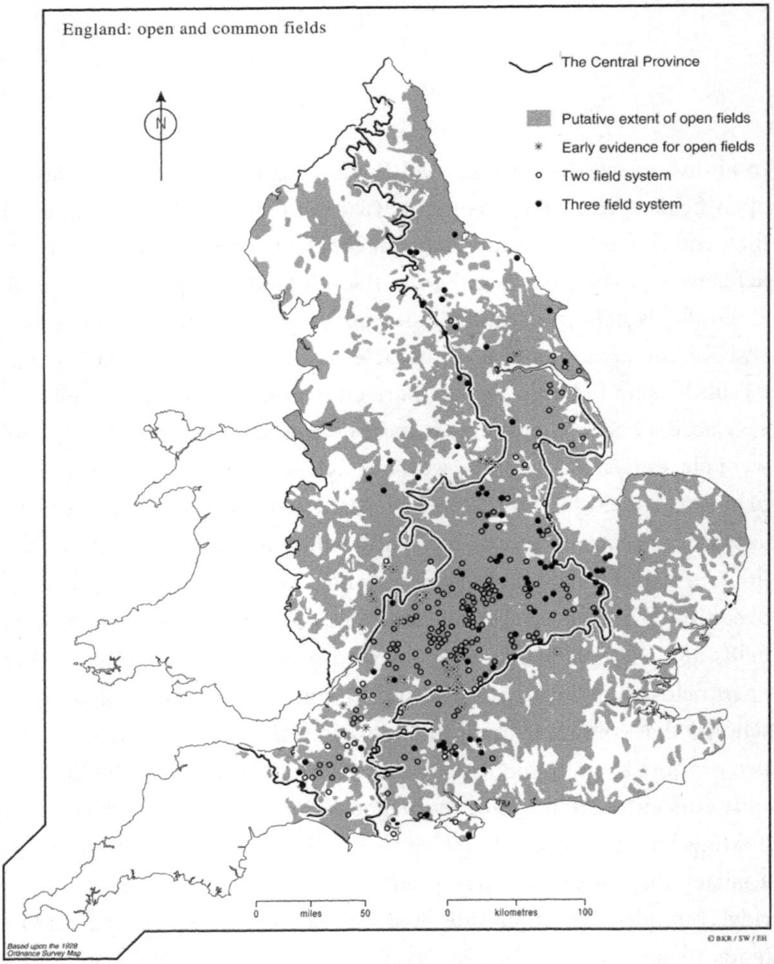

Figure 3. Open fields under narrow CPrRs (note that the range in densities refers to the work of different scholars, rather than to variations in the numbers of these field systems in each region). (Reproduced with permission from Roberts and Wrathmell 2002).

This chapter is principally concerned with the history of collective management of arable open fields, that is, with open-field systems. The quality of 'open-ness' itself implies a minimal degree of such collectivity. Even where all aspects of cultivation, fallowing and grazing are undertaken in severalty on each holding, cultivators will still need to agree some form of equitable governance and regulation to prevent and/or respond to infractions.[4] Open fields were therefore always more than just a form of layout and men with holdings in them were always members of a limited group of stakeholders with limited or extensive collective rights in them of governance and regulation. In a seminal paper, Bailey has proposed that open-field systems can be divided between those over which there was a relatively limited range of collective rights and in which all or most activity was undertaken in severalty or (referred to here as 'narrow CPrRs'), and those over in which there was an extensive range of collective rights (referred to here as 'wide CPrRs') and in which most cultivation was undertaken cooperatively.[5] That distinction provides a central focus for the discussions that follow, both in this and other chapters.

Historiography of collective cultivation

From the later nineteenth century until about 40 years ago three premises provided a consistent foundation for research on open-field systems, each principally based on documentary evidence. Such premises were firmly located within a wider literature in which the extent of late Iron Age occupation of Britain was still to be demonstrated and the density and sophistication of peasant Romano-British culture remained to be discovered; Anglo-Saxon timber buildings and artefacts were largely unknown, particularly as the early period was frequently aceramic and mostly unmonetarised.

The first premise was that Anglo-Saxon migrants found a virgin landscape, relatively empty, certainly underexploited, in which there was plenty of opportunity for new settlement. Based on limited documentary sources for the early period, and especially on the writings of Gildas and Bede, the second premise was that the indigenous Romano-British population were almost entirely annihilated and/or displaced in areas of Anglo-Saxon colonisation. The migrants were thus free to arrange matters to suit themselves, both in terms of social organisation and in the physical layout of the landscapes they took over. The third premise, that open fields were an Anglo-Saxon introduction, was based on interpretations of one of the clauses in the law code of King Ine of Wessex (688–694) which stipulated that 'If *ceorls* have a *common* meadow or other land divided into shares to fence and some have fenced their portion and some have not and [if cattle] eat up their *common* crops or grass, those who are responsible are to go and pay to *the others, who have fenced their part*, compensation for the damage that has been done there.'[6] Amid general consensus that the clause referred to newly imposed regulations put into place as part of the process of colonisation, Vinogradoff explained that 'the formation of intermixed holdings and open-field customs in the case of settlements and plots gradually develop[ed] out of more or less complete isolation' in the 'tribal period'.[7]

These three premises framed a long-standing consensus that open fields were an innovation of Anglo-Saxon settlers in an empty countryside from which the indigenous population had all but disappeared. Yet the debate has not been entirely one-sided. Seebohm struck the first blow. While agreeing that 'in the seventh century the fields of Wessex were … open fields', he also contended that all English field systems – including open fields – were derived from Romano-British antecedents. His argument was based on the observations that, although there were open fields in areas settled by 'Anglo-Saxons', there were also open fields in Wales, where the migrants did not penetrate; similarly, there were no open fields in some areas of early settlement, like Kent; furthermore, although open fields could be found in some of the homelands from which the settlers originated, they were absent in others.[8] To paraphrase Debby Banham, the Anglo-Saxons did not introduce open fields everywhere they went and other people must have laid out open fields in areas beyond.[9]

Gray could not have disagreed more brutally, attacking Seebohm for offering 'the thread of an hypothesis which interested the author more than did the presentation of facts'.[10] Nonetheless, although he admitted that 'in a general way … the furlongs of open field arable field cultivated in accordance with Celtic runrig presented an aspect not very different from that of an English midland township', he also argued that any similarities were superficial and the two systems had quite different origins.[11] Instead, he suggested, the English fieldscape had evolved from three separate points of origin: in the south-west, west and north-west where Rome had had little influence, enclosed and open fields developed from prehistoric ('Celtic') fields; the grid-like landscapes of south-east England, where irregular open-field systems lay alongside fields cultivated in severalty, had evolved from Romano-British arable practices; and only the regular two- and three-field systems of the English midlands were an introduction *ab novo* by Anglo-Saxon migrants.[12]

Maitland agreed, asserting that 'we dare not argue that this [i.e. Ine's] law is a general law for the whole of Wessex. It may refer only to some newly settled and allotted districts', although he was prepared to concede some continuity of field patterns in the south-west.[13] The Orwins concurred: 'at present we can say no more than that the division of the land for agriculture in Britain today seems to derive from two widely different systems, the little square fields of the Celtic system, so called and the big open fields of the so-called Saxon system' … 'open-field farming system … introduced into Britain by Germanic settlers'.[14] T. A. M. Bishop added colour to the thesis, making a strong case for the evolution of regular open fields by assart as settlements expanded into the wilderness.[15] Analysis of the distribution of holdings between open-field furlongs at Leighton Bromswold (Hunts.) exemplified his hypothesis: the smallest, oldest furlongs were divided between a few, original holdings; larger, later furlongs resulted from colonisation of the remaining waste as numbers of cultivators rose.[16] Finberg, Hoskins and Stenton, the great economic historians of the twentieth-century, all agreed that open fields were an introduction that followed, directly or indirectly, from the Anglo-Saxon migrations of the fifth and sixth centuries.[17]

New research in the 1960s and 1970s rendered each premise increasingly problematic. Two seminal papers by Joan Thirsk acknowledged the problem that open fields could be irregular *or* regular in both layout and management.[18] She proposed that their distinctive distributions revealed a chronological relationship between them – that in the post-Conquest centuries regular open-field systems had evolved from irregular open-field systems. This work had a powerful effect on the debate and by 1973 a major study of open fields concluded that 'it can therefore no longer be claimed that in the fifth and sixth centuries the Anglo-Saxons brought with them to England a ready made and mature two- or three-field system'.[19] Instead, an evolutionary model was proposed: arable cultivation on the basis of infield-outfield 'soon evolved into more intensive field systems in areas of relatively high population pressure'.[20]

Although prescient, such views found little acceptance, particularly in the face of strong archaeological evidence from Northamptonshire.[21] Here, open-field strips and furlongs overlay abandoned middle Anglo-Saxon farmsteads and hamlets. Pottery sherds thrown away during the lifetime of these settlements appeared to indicate that 'the furrows of the strip fields cannot be earlier than the ninth century'.[22] Comparable or slightly later dates were suggested for the origin of similar fields in Holderness (Yorks.).[23] It was widely accepted that large-scale open-field systems were laid out across substantial tracts of landscape from the ninth century onwards, cutting across and destroying pre-existing field boundaries in a single event across each parish of ruthless landscape replanning. From an epicentre somewhere in the English midlands, it was argued, open fields gradually spread west and east, erasing the remains of prehistoric or Roman cultivation, irrelevant in the face of new systems of organisation for arable holdings.[24] The consensus was thus revised (although not fundamentally re-examined) explicitly to exclude the evolutionary model: open-field systems *were* of Anglo-Saxon origin, but dated from the period between the ninth and eleventh centuries. In Northamptonshire, 'one looks [in vain] for many extensive systems of Roman or prehistoric fields that could convincingly be converted to a recogniseable furlong pattern'.[25] Rackham, too, considered that 'there is not the slightest evidence that open fields existed in the Roman period'.[26] Just over a decade later, Lewis, Dyer and Mitchell-Fox concurred that open fields were an innovation of the later Anglo-Saxon period, as did Hooke, who suggested that 'the open fields, themselves, in some form, would have been present in many regions by the later Anglo-Saxon period'.[27] And, if field layouts were entirely new, it followed that the systems of collective organisation which underpinned them must be new too.

The subversion of the premises underpinning the debate gathered pace, however, particularly under pressure from archaeological evidence. Ecological and environmental archaeology has shown not only that the landscape was almost fully cleared by the end of the Iron Age, but also that it has remained largely open since. Air photography and excavation have revealed a growing number of places in which prehistoric and/or Romano-British ditches and banks underlay divisions within medieval open fields, indicating long-term persistence of many field layouts and no large-scale abandonment of farms and hamlets.[28] Analysis of population trends has suggested that there may have been as many as 3 to 4 million people living in Britain by the late fourth century AD. If many 'Anglo-Saxons' were actually of Romano-British descent it could only follow that there was widespread demographic continuity into the fifth and sixth centuries and that late British populations continued to occupy the post-Roman landscape. The 'cleansing' of indigenous Romano-Britons from sub-Roman Britain could not have occurred to any substantial degree. Not only was most of the early Anglo-Saxon landscape not 'virgin', but many areas were never abandoned. Late British cultivators continued to occupy their ancestral farms and fields which continued to be cultivated or grazed well across the Anglo-Saxon centuries. The three premises of the argument that open-field systems owed nothing to the past seem to fail at more or less the same time.

This is, then, an appropriate point at which to take another look at the origins of open fields and in particular of the collectivity that appeared to be such a distinctive, Anglo-Saxon, feature of their management. The problem is explored in more detail below through four sub-questions:

1 Is there any evidence for the persistence of earlier field layouts into the Anglo-Saxon and medieval periods? If all or most prehistoric/Romano-British field layouts were abandoned in the two or three centuries after AD 400, then continuity in the management of arable cultivation becomes less likely.
2 Even if some fields at least continued to be cultivated within the same boundaries throughout the first millennium AD, they might nonetheless have been exploited in completely new ways. To what extent, then, was there any continuity in arable management, plough technology and cropping?
3 What is the evidence for that the open layout of arable fields was new in the Anglo-Saxon period?
4 The last question explores the history of collective management of arable, setting Anglo-Saxon cultivation within the wider context of the *longue durée*.

The survival of prehistoric and Romano-British field layouts into the Anglo-Saxon period

The possibility that some aspects, at least, of open-field systems may have originated in the management of land before about AD 400 could only be entertained if there were at least some continuity in the occupation of fields across the fourth to the seventh centuries. If there was no continuity, then the origins of open-field systems must be entirely Anglo-Saxon. That question is explored here.

On the face of it, the possibility that Romano-British arable fields survived into the Anglo-Saxon period appears slim. From the later fourth century, grain producers had to contend with a concatenation of adversity which badly affected the prospects of growing surplus grain for sale. Steadily worsening climatic conditions meant that summers became yet colder and wetter, reaching a nadir in around AD 500 – land became more difficult to plough, the days on which ploughing was possible became fewer and even where crops survived to maturity they were often unable to ripen.[29] The physical conditions for producing grain above subsistence level became more difficult. Demographic decline – perhaps the result of a series of plagues and possibly of malnutrition – led to a fall in demand for grain, since there were fewer mouths to feed. At the same time, widespread economic collapse meant that coins, especially those of low denomination, became valueless and rapidly went out of use and most of the markets to which cultivators had been accustomed to take their surplus became moribund. Anarchic political conditions made it difficult to assure protected conditions for transactions or a safe passage to market, even if one could be identified. Most cultivators reverted to subsistence farming, producing only enough grain for their own needs or for limited local exchange. Pollen evidence indicates that large areas of former arable were converted to pasture. In the countryside on which medieval Stafford was later to be founded, for example, there was 'a return to basic subsistence and herding' in the fifth and sixth centuries, while heavy clay fields at Yarnton (Oxon.) were converted to grass, leaving only low-lying lighter soils in the flood-plain of the Thames under the plough.[30] Similar evidence for a reduction in the area of arable has been found at Haddon and other sites near Peterborough (Cambs.), Mucking and Springfield Lyons (both Essex), Barton Bendish, Witton, Hales and Loddon (all Norf.) and West Stow (Suff.).[31] As late as the tenth century, charters for Anglo-Saxon estates recorded pasture on the Berkshire downs where the earthworks of abandoned prehistoric fields can still be seen in grassland today.[32]

But although there were some places where regenerated woodland gradually obliterated Romano-British fields – for example, in Rockingham Forest, large tracts of the Weald and the more marginal uplands of Exmoor – it was relatively rare for fields to be abandoned altogether and Murphy has concluded that few 'large tracts of countryside reverted to woodland … in the post-Roman period, though on a local level some regeneration no doubt occurred'.[33] Pollen records from Devon and west Somerset show little change in ground cover between the fourth and sixth centuries, indicating 'continuity in an essentially pastoral landscape'.[34] The landscapes at Yarnton and Barton Court (both Oxon.), Micklemere and Pakenham (both Suff.) and Colchester and Springfield Lyons (both Essex), all remained open perhaps because much former arable continued to be grazed.[35]

At the same time, even where trees and scrub did eventually replace arable fields, it is not always straightforward to attribute this change to the difficult conditions of the post-Roman centuries. Arable land at Biddlesden in Whittlewood was abandoned to mixed woodland during the fourth century AD, well before the end of Roman administration, while the advance of woodland over arable did not even begin in parts of Northamptonshire until the sixth century, when climatic conditions were actually beginning to improve and political stability was returning in the emergent Anglo-Saxon kingdoms.[36]

On the other hand, it is clear that in many places property rights over prehistoric and Romano-British fields were forgotten or became irrelevant in the fifth and sixth centuries. In those places, even where silted-up ditches, patchy hedgerows or degraded banks survived, new boundaries were laid out along quite different alignments when ownership was once more extended over these areas. On Salisbury Plain in Wiltshire, for example, by the seventh century at least some prehistoric and Romano-British field boundaries had become sufficiently faint on the ground or irrelevant in local tradition to be ignored by tithing boundaries of that date.[37] At Overton Down (Wilts.) almost an entire field system survived, but continuity in its usage is more debatable.[38] Medieval open fields in Faxton (Northants.), Maxey, Cambridge (both Cambs.) and southeast Essex were laid out on completely new alignments across the abandoned remains of earlier landscapes.[39] Innumerable other examples have been identified in Wiltshire, Hampshire, Berkshire, Cambridgeshire, Essex,

Northamptonshire, Nottinghamshire, Derbyshire and beyond.[40] And even where the ridges of medieval cultivation fit into 'the framework of much older lynchets that had fossilised patterns of Roman fields modifying prehistoric ones' – as at West Chisenbury and Fyfield Down (both Wilts.) – it is impossible to say whether they were continuously ploughed or whether husbandmen, reoccupying an abandoned landscape, simply re-used existing boundaries they could see on the ground.[41]

There are, however, a growing number of places across southern and central England where prehistoric and Roman field layouts continued to be occupied throughout the Anglo-Saxon period. The middle Anglo-Saxon settlement at Catholme (Staffs.) was built on the northern part of Romano-British farmland which may either have 'passed entire into Anglo-Saxon hands' or simply have continued to be held by 'a local British population which had never gone away'.[42] Landscapes at Yarnton (Oxon.) and Mucking (Essex) remained unchanged throughout the fifth century, while the Anglo-Saxon settlement at Barton Court (Oxon.) was framed by the 'grid of ditched paddocks or closes' of an earlier Roman villa estate.[43] Similar evidence has been found at Sutton Courtenay (Berks.).[44] Romano-British fields at Church Down in Chalton and Catherington (both Hants.), Bow Brickhill (Bucks.) and Havering (Essex) all continued to be ploughed into the seventh century.[45] A survey of parts of Northamptonshire by the Royal Commission on Historic Monuments concluded in the late 1970s that 'Part of a system older than the common fields, into which the furlongs were fitted and from which the layout of the common fields emerged' may have survived in places like Castle Ashby and Walgrave.[46]Topographical evidence suggests that a pre-Roman field system at Caxton (Cambs.) was simply absorbed into a medieval open-field layout, while prehistoric or Romano-British ditches underlie medieval headlands or strip boundaries at Wylye (Wilts.), Wharram Percy (Yorks.) and Caldecote, Hardwick, Teversham and Duxford (all Cambs.) (Figure 4(a)).[47]

Physical continuity could sometimes be extensive. The medieval field layout at Strettington (Sussex) was respected by, and probably

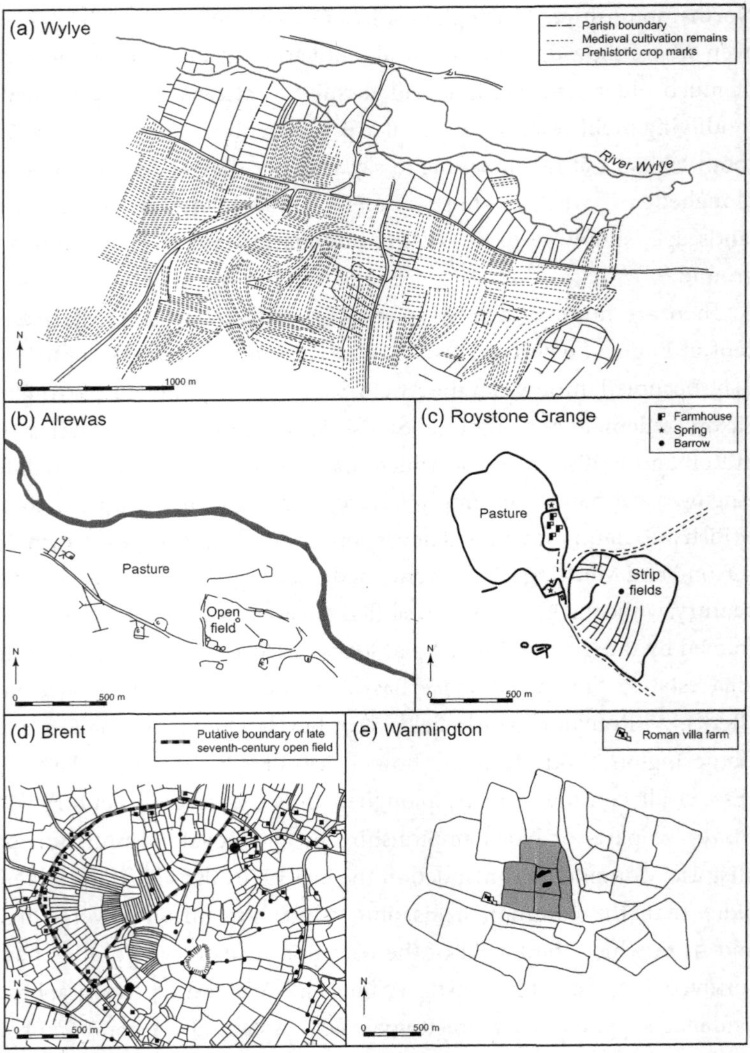

Figure 4. Ancient fields (a) Wylye (Wilts.): prehistoric field boundaries (surviving as crop- and soilmarks) reused in medieval furlong boundaries (after Hooke 1988). (b) An Iron Age curvilinear arable field located in an area of riverside pasture at Alrewas (Staffs.) (after Smith 1978–79). (c) Romano-British curvilinear arable field subdivided into strips, Roystone Grange (Derbys.) (after Hodges 1991). (d) Curvilinear open field subdivided into strips at Brent (Som.), recorded in a late seventh-century charter (after Rippon 1998). (e) Warmington (Northants.): Romano-British fields around a villa farmhouse and later integrated into medieval open-field furlongs (after Upex 1987).

predated, some parish boundaries which were almost certainly in place by the seventh century: one tracks the alignment of a prehistoric dyke, while another follows the line of a Roman road.[48] Existing prehistoric or Roman fields at Sutton Walls (Herefords.), Compton Beauchamp (Oxon.), Burton Lazars (Leics.), Lichfield (Staffs.), Castle Ashby and Walgrave (both Northants.), Tadlow (Cambs.), Goltho (Lincs.) and Wharram Percy (Yorks.) continued to be cultivated throughout the Anglo-Saxon period and were simply incorporated into medieval open fields.[49] The same process can be observed at Haddon, Orton Longueville, Elton and Warmington near Peterborough in Cambridgeshire and Grantham (Lincs.) (Figure 4(e)).[50] Rectilinear – probably Iron Age – field layouts survive across large areas of Buckinghamshire, central, western and southern Hertfordshire and at places in Suffolk like the Elmhams and Ilketshalls.[51] Continuous post-Roman agricultural usage is believed to explain the persistence of large-scale landscapes like the 'system of sinuous and roughly parallel lands and boundaries' at Scole and Dickleborough (both Norf.) and in prehistoric alignments fossilised in medieval furlong boundaries in the Bourn Valley (Cambs.).[52] It seems that, in many cases 'centuries of piecemeal alteration (...) preserved the essential orientation of field layout but not in every case the original boundaries'.[53] It is possible, then, that some prehistoric and Roman fields continued to be cultivated across the Anglo-Saxon centuries and, if this were to be the case, then the possibility that some features of later open-field systems may have had their roots in earlier systems of arable management is at least a viable hypothesis for exploration.

Methods of cultivation: similarities and differences

Persistence of some prehistoric and Romano-British field boundaries into the Anglo-Saxon centuries does not, of course, imply continuity of the ways in which they were cultivated. Even if the hedges and ditches that surrounded earlier fields continued to be utilised in

Anglo-Saxon England, it is possible that collective cultivation of arable may have been an Anglo-Saxon introduction. How similar, then, were the techniques of agricultural production in the long eighth century – when open fields are believed to have been introduced – with those of prehistoric and Roman Britain?

The most common form of arable management before about AD 400 was infield-outfield cultivation. The arable core (the infield) of a holding was continuously cultivated from year to year without a fallow season. The outfield was largely used for pasture but small areas were taken into arable cultivation for just a few years at a time, before being returned to grass, often for decades.[54] Small arable fields thus shifted around the outfield from one year to the next, while the infield was used for producing arable crops every year. Soil impoverishment on the infield was an inevitable result, unless some form of fertiliser could be added to it each year. Farmyard manure, collected from animals kept close to the settlement between late autumn and early spring, to which the household waste could be added, provided an obvious solution to the problem. The practice was ubiquitous by the Iron Age and has been identified at Shapwick (Som.), Raunds (Northants.), Barton Bendish, Hales and Loddon (all Norf.) and Strethall (Essex) and elsewhere.[55] Household refuse, including bits of broken pottery, and manure from overwintered animals was collected in farmyard middens and spread each year on the infield. More intensive muck-spreading on the infield has been inferred from finds of bits of broken pottery: there tend to be more finds of each period across the infields nearer a settlement and fewer further away.

There is little doubt that infield-outfield cultivation continued to be practised throughout the early and middle Anglo-Saxon periods. Early Anglo-Saxon outfields have been identified at Chalton (Hants.), Raunds (Northants.) and Eton Rowing Lake and Dorney (both Berks.), even though they make their first documentary appearance only in the tenth century 'Heath Fields' recorded at places like Chieveley and Donnington (Berks.).[56] Increased densities of middle Anglo-Saxon pottery signifying infield cultivation have been plotted at

Shapwick (Som.), Barnsley Park (Glos.), Higham Ferrers (Northants.), Chellington (Beds.), Peterborough (Cambs.) and at Congham, Barton Bendish, Witton and Hales and Loddon (Norf.).[57] Each middle Anglo-Saxon settlement in the later medieval parish at Raunds (Northants.) had its own infield, ranging from about 100 to 200 acres, set in a larger area of outfield/pasture.[58] More importantly, infield-outfield cultivation continued to form the basis of arable management at Raunds in the *later* Anglo-Saxon centuries: ninth- or early tenth-century pottery scatters show intensive manuring of the same infields, now apparently lying within the boundaries of open-field furlongs. Even if new boundaries were laid out, the form of arable management remained the same.[59] Similar evidence for differential manuring in the later Anglo-Saxon period has been observed at Whittlewood (Northants.) and Whittlesford (Cambs.) and elsewhere.[60] Crop rotation continued to be managed within infield-outfield systems throughout the Anglo-Saxon period, just as it had done since at least the Iron Age.[61]

On the other hand, general stability in arable management was accompanied by a sustained attempt to increase the productivity of cereal output within this more traditional framework. The production of grain surpluses which far exceeded the requirements of subsistence is implied by the burgeoning number of seventh- and eighth-century watermills that have been excavated.[62] Place-names indicate that estates designated centres of directed, specialised arable production at locations like Barley ('barley clearing') (Lincs.), Reydon ('rye hill') (Suff.), or Waddington ('wheat hill') (Middx.). Crops at Yarnton (Oxon.) – for example – were threshed, winnowed and probably fine-sieved before they were stored.[63] Improvements in yields were, it seems, achieved by increasing the area under the plough, changes in crop varieties, innovations in plough technology, and in the introduction of sustained strategies for maintaining soil fertility.

There is widespread evidence for an extension of the acreage of arable land in the long eighth century and beyond. Pollen evidence from lowland Devon, Stafford and from Yarnton (Oxon.) shows a marked intensification of cereal growing in the seventh and eighth centuries, while the area of arable was extended at Chellington (Beds.) in the same period.[64] The area of arable at Witton (Norf.), doubled from about 100 acres in the sixth century to 200 acres in the seventh and eighth centuries and had doubled again by the eleventh century.[65] The process did not occur simultaneously across the country and some regional variation is implied by a peak in cereal production at Stafford in the mid-seventh century, while arable intensification only began at Yarnton (Oxon.) in the mid-ninth century, and several generations later at Whittlewood and other places in Northamptonshire.[66]

There was at the same time a substantial shift in the most frequently cultivated species of wheat. Spelt (*triticum spelta*, a bread wheat) and emmer (*triticum dicoccon*, a rivet or durum wheat), the most commonly planted cereals of prehistoric and Roman Britain, were rapidly supplanted during the long eighth century by *triticum aestivum* and rivet wheat (*triticum turgidum*). These were not new varieties; the change was, rather, in their new dominance on the arable fields of middle Anglo-Saxon England.[67] Although spelt and emmer were lower-yielding, they had had the advantage of being less prone to damage from pests when stored in the ear and were particularly useful in making ale. Flour ground from the newer wheats, on the other hand, produced soft, well-risen loaves; and *triticum turgidum*, useful in mixed grain loaves, had the additional benefit of a particularly tall, strong stalk that was useful for thatching. Barley (*hordeum sp.*) became the second most important grain crop, compensating for the shift from brewing to baking wheats.[68] Oats and rye were more often grown too (the latter grown on its own for the first time, rather than mixed with other grains and useful, too, for its long straw), and legumes may have been grown as a 'green manure'. Flax and hemp were produced on an industrial scale to support the manufacture of linen at places like Barton Court and Yarnton (both Oxon.), Brandon (Suff.), Flixborough (Lincs.), or West Heslerton (Yorks).[69]

Jones has suggested that the new crops are a 'direct record of the ecological impact of the transition from ard cultivation to deep ploughing' with the heavy plough.[70] The wooden crook-ard – perhaps including a stone or (later) iron tip on the share – had been in use since the Neolithic period. Because it scratched, but did not turn, the earth, the ard needed to be taken twice across each field, the second time at right-angles to the line of the first.[71] The marks left by such cross-ploughing record the continuing use of this technology into and after the Roman period. The introduction of the heavy plough on the estates of wealthier Romano-British landowners was probably the most dramatic agricultural innovation for millennia.[72] Its magic lay in its ability to turn the soil: the share cut the land vertically; the coulter, attached in front of the share, cut the earth horizontally; together they cut the soil to a depth which obviated the need for cross-ploughing, and which contributed to maintaining soil fertility by sealing manure and stubbles into the plough-earth.[73] The attachment of a mouldboard allowed the ploughman to produce a ridge of soil to one side of the share and a furrow in the land to the other.[74] The heavy plough also made it easier to cultivate heavier, but more fertile, clays.[75] On the other hand, it was an expensive investment: it required a team of six to eight oxen (each with a limited working life), substantial timbers and solid iron work. Whether the heavy plough disappeared from England at the end of the Roman period or continued in use over the following two or three centuries has been a matter for intense debate.[76] The discovery of iron implements which may be middle Anglo-Saxon coulters at St Neots (Hunts.), Westley Waterless (Cambs.), Thetford (Norf.), Nazeing (Suff.) and Flixborough (Lincs.) may indicate a degree of continuity, and the possibility is supported by the discovery of mouldboards and iron ploughshares in early medieval Irish contexts.[77] At Yarnton (Oxon.), the use of the mouldboard plough enabled the return of arable cultivation to the claylands on higher ground, a process which was at its most intense in the eighth and ninth centuries, while at Pennyland (Bucks.) 'deep cultivation' was practised.[78] The heavy plough can also be seen in the aratral curve of some of the track ways around the middle Anglo-Saxon settlement at Catholme (Staffs.).[79] The iron coulter recently excavated at Lyminge (Kent), sealed under a deposit of the first half of the seventh century AD, adds to growing evidence for the persistence of the heavy plough, although perhaps only on the lands of the very wealthiest landowners.[80] Perhaps an expansion in the usage of the heavy plough in the long eighth century mirrored investment in capital-intensive technology on newly formed extensive estates.

New crops and the more widespread adoption of mouldboard ploughs were accompanied by more intensive methods for maintaining soil fertility. Annual manuring had been practised on the infields since before the Roman period, but from the seventh century AD onwards the extension of arable fields over a greater area, combined with demands for predictable surpluses of grain, required more formal attention to soil fertility. In addition to planting nitrogenous legumes, three other strategies were also adopted: improvements in the quality of manure produced over winter, attention paid to the quality of dung from sheep folded on arable, and the inclusion of a fallow season in crop rotations.

The midden was a valuable resource in contemporary early medieval Ireland, where it was important enough to be located within the protective boundaries of the inner farmyard.[81] A substantial increase in the pollen of henbane, a weed specific to middens, suggests that Anglo-Saxon farmers also took deliberate steps to increase the volume and improve the quality of manure that they spread on their infields before ploughing.[82] The quality of manure produced by cattle and sheep stalled over winter depends on the quality of their winter fodder. Although hay for overwintered stock had been produced since at least the Bronze Age, hay meadows managed specifically for the production of grass seem to have been an introduction of the long eighth century. Meadows bounded by substantial banks and deliberately managed for the production of grass were created by farmers at places like Yarnton (Oxon.), Dorney and Eton Rowing Lake (Berks.); a late Anglo-Saxon example has been recognised at West Cotton (Northants.).[83]

A second, related, innovation may have been the deliberate inclusion in open-field layouts of discrete areas of grazing where sheep could be pastured by day before being folded on the arable at night. Their dung would thus add new fertility to the soil, rather than simply recycling that already locked in stubbles or fallows. Campbell has characterised the folding system of eastern Norfolk as 'one of the most effective methods of fertilising the land', which the sheep 'tathed with their dung and urine', and whose structure was improved by the treading of their light hooves.[84] Such a system may explain the structure of a middle Anglo-Saxon field system across the lower northern slopes of the Bourn Valley (Cambs.), whose furlongs were separated by long strips of common pasture up to 54 yards wide.[85]

The origins of a fallow season in open-field crop rotations remains controversial, although Millett has suggested that 'there is strong evidence from southern Britain of a full crop rotation in the later Roman period'.[86] There is some inconclusive evidence for the replacement of perennial weeds by annual varieties at middle Anglo-Saxon Yarnton (Oxon.) and later Saxon Raunds (Northants.), which might be interpreted as evidence of fallowing, but the inference remains controversial.[87] On the other hand, the argument against fallowing depends on the assumption that infields were heavily manured each year in order to avoid the concomitant loss of land available for growing a crop (and hence of output) that fallowing would inevitably entail. This assumption may not be sound as there are good examples, for instance from the medieval Breckland, of the inclusion of fallows as a flexible component of crop rotations on infields there. It is just as possible that fallowing had been an integrated part of approaches to the management of infields long before the later Anglo-Saxon period.[88] Yet even if crop rotations and fallowing on open fields were practised on prehistoric and Roman fields, it cannot be inferred that such fields were collectively managed. On the medieval manor of Westerham (Kent) 'irregular and heterogeneous rotations on many fields, the transference of even more or less regularly cultivated fields from one season to another, and the tendency of nearly every field to revet, at frequent intervals and for varying periods, to an uncultivated state – these practices could only have been adjusted with great difficulty, if at all, to communal methods and interests in the management of arable and pasture'.[89] If many arable fields continued to be cultivated on an infield-outfield system throughout (and after) the Anglo-Saxon period, did the intensification of production – managed through the extension of arable acreages, changes in crop species, plough technology and approaches to soil fertility – nonetheless accompany a further innovation in the long eighth century: arable laid out in *open* fields?[90]

Arable laid out in open fields: morphology

Anglo-Saxon cultivators appear to have adopted two general field layouts in setting out large, apparently 'open' fields: curvilinear or rectilinear, which are dealt with here in turn, before moving on to explore whether such layouts were new or traditional in the post-Roman landscape.

Large curvilinear fields were a distinctive feature of middle Anglo-Saxon landscapes, covering anything between 30 acres and 200 acres.[91] Based on an irregular circle or oval and enclosed by a substantial hedge, bank and/or ditch, they have been identified at Withy (Som.), Daventry, Kislingbury, Hardingstone Hall, Raunds, Higham Ferrers and Wollaston, (all Northants.), Whaddon, Litlington and Balsham (all Cambs.), Wenhaston and Hinton (Suff.), Walpole St Andrew and West Walton (both Norf.), Grewelthorpe (Yorks.), Crosby Ravensworth (Cumb.) and Cockfield (Co. Durham).[92] While these fields were often subdivided, their internal divisions did not offer physical barriers to movement across the enclosure and they seem therefore to have lain 'open', either shared between a (generally small) number of men or representing the core demesne (inland) of an estate.[93] Oval fields divided between a relatively small number of men have been identified at places like Cutcombe (Som.) a single open field bounded by enormous banks was divided between the five farms of the parish, while an arable oval was shared by four cultivators at Tunley (Lancs.).[94] They may provide a contemporary physical example of the 'common ...

share-land' of King Ine's Laws discussed above, which was interpreted by both Finberg and Fox as a field in shared ownership, bounded by a single hedge.[95] Pollen evidence from a sub-circular open field at Brent (Som.), nearby, appears to demonstrate the presence of cultivated open fields at the same time that the arable estate there was granted to Glastonbury Abbey in AD 693; it remained divided into strips into the nineteenth century.[96] Inland arable on manorial and freeholding demesnes was frequently laid out in rough ovals or rounded rectangles and cultivated in severalty.[97] At Aston Magna (Glos.), for example, 'all the demesne land surrounded by a dyke outside' by 904 has been identified with a small oval enclosure of between 20 and 30 acres near the site of the medieval manor.[98] Middle Anglo-Saxon demesnes at Kislingbury, Hardingstone Hall, Raunds, Higham Ferrers and Wollaston (all Northants.) lay in a compact block; that at Wollaston may already have been of some antiquity, since it included the sites of a Roman villa and an early Anglo-Saxon settlement.[99] Similar examples have been identified at Withy (Som.), Daventry (Northants.), Whaddon, Litlington and Balsham (all Cambs.), and Grewelthorpe (Yorks.).[100] A 'long, curving ring-fence boundary … which forms the nucleus of the manorial demesne' and which enclosed about 200 acres in each cases have been identified at a number of places in Suffolk, including Wenhaston Old Hall and Hinton Hall.[101] Costen and Faith have suggested that place-names including the element 'worthy', found across England from Devon to Lancashire, might record a subset of such oval enclosures at places like Sweetworthy (Som.), perhaps giving physical form to the homesteads of *ceorls* which had to be 'fenced winter and summer' in late seventh-century Wessex to prevent stray animals from getting into their crops, and similar layouts are visible at Yadsworthy (Devon), Abbot's Worthy (Hants.), and Quarrington (Lincs.).[102]

Centuries before, a large oval Iron Age field was laid out at Alrewas (Staffs.) which continued to be cultivated within the same boundaries into the medieval period (Figure 4(b)); others can be found at the Bronze Age site at Park Brow (Sussex) and Iron Age Grateley South

(Hants.); Atkins suggested that the medieval curvilinear fields at Tunley and Wrightington (both Lancs.) may have also had prehistoric origins.[103] Large curvilinear fields have tended to survive best where stone walls have preserved the heavy labour of land-clearance on land which has not been cultivated since the prehistoric period, at places like Skomer Island and St David's Head (Pembs.), Zennor (Cornwall), or Sheepstor (Devon).[104] There was a large curvilinear field at the Romano-British farmstead at Roystone Grange (Derbys.) and another at High Knowes (Northumb.) (Figure 4(c)).[105] (It is worth noting that such forms were common in a number of contexts in landscapes of all periods, for example in bounding settlements, pastures, defended sites or places of ritual.[106] Eleventh-century and later examples survive at Puxton (Som.), South Radworthy (Devon), Tetsworth (Oxon.), Hathersage (Derbys.), Hunsterson in Wybunbury (Ches.), Wheldrake (Yorks.), Cockfield (Co. Durham) and Waitby (Westm.).)[107] There was then, nothing new in the morphology of post-Roman curvilinear fields.

The second form of layout for Anglo-Saxon fields was large-scale and fundamentally geometric, its character vividly described by Warner: 'it is as if a net were lowered gently over the landscape so that where it fell on flat ground the linear pattern of the net remains more or less unchanged, but where it fell on uneven ground the pattern of the net became deformed or distorted by the topography'.[108] Such field layouts reflect the large-scale partition, heavily influenced by the local topography, of considerable areas of land and have been identified across England.[109] Romano-British fields at Chalton (Hants.), for example, were abandoned in favour of an entirely new arrangement of rectilinear open fields in the ninth century.[110] At Dorchester (Dorset), a large, open-field, perhaps created in the eighth century, was so 'extensive and regular that it is clear that it results from a deliberate act of planning'.[111] It was made up of long, slightly wany, parallel field divisions running from east to west, that predated the medieval open fields. An eighth-century date has also been proposed for a similar and equally large, open field at Sherborne (Dorset).[112] Both are very like an enormous open field running for seven miles from west to east across four parishes south-west of Cambridge which may have been set out between about AD 700 and 850.[113] Seminal work in Northamptonshire suggested that many regular open-field layouts there were laid out from the eighth century onwards, and the boundaries and ditches that formed the framework of a regular open field at Kempston (Beds.) appear to be of the same period.[114] Late Anglo-Saxon examples can be found across England from Berkshire and Oxfordshire to Yorkshire.[115]

Yet such roughly rectilinear designs are virtually identical to those underlying 'co-axial' prehistoric and Romano-British fields which subdivided the landscape into long narrow units from valley to plateau at intervals of about 200 m. The subdivision of these long units resulted in a characteristic 'chequer-board' layout. Bronze Age examples survive in the low stone walls called reaves that run up to open pastures around the summits of the uplands of Dartmoor; they lead down to the western edge of the peat fens around Fengate (Cambs.) and Deeping (Lincs.); others cluster around the uplands of Mynydd Carn-ingli (Pembs.).[116] There are Iron Age examples on the vales of Hertfordshire around Broxbourne and Wormley, on hill slopes at Grassington (Yorks.), at Chysauster (Cornwall), Steeple Langford (Wilts.) and almost continuously from St Neots to Cambridge (Cambs.).[117] Those at Lye Hole in Somerset and at March (Cambs.) appear to have been laid out in the Romano-British period.[118]

Morphologically, then, the layout of prehistoric and Roman curvilinear and rectilinear field patterns is similar to that underlying medieval open fields. The geometry of furlong patterns at Lichfield (Staffs.), Burton Lazars (Leics.) Goltho (Lincs.) and Orton Longueville and Caxton (both Cambs.) is not obviously different from the medieval fields so extensively mapped across Leicester by Hartley or across Northamptonshire by Hall – yet the former were structured, to a greater or lesser extent, on prehistoric or Roman fields, and the latter were supposed to be new.[119] Similarly, the curvilinear enclosures at Aston Magna and Alrewas are virtually identical in both plan and scale.

The innovations of middle Anglo-Saxon agricultural production appear to have been undertaken within traditional structures of crop management and, in some cases, of field layout. On the other hand, there is only a limited range of practicable field shapes and, even if there were continuities in expectations of that way in which arable land 'should' be laid out, completely new structures for managing cultivation within those fields might have been introduced. To what extent, then, was the collective management of arable in subdivided fields *the* innovation of the long eighth century? This question has two facets: whether fields were subdivided between a number of cultivators in such a way that there was easy access from one holding to the next – that is, holdings lay within open fields; and, even if there were open fields, whether they were managed under a CPrR.

The identification of open fields

The cultivation of arable land within a CPrR is generally believed to have been introduced at some time between the late seventh and tenth centuries and its identification conventionally relies heavily on documentary evidence. As Taylor has observed, 'without historical evidence ridge-and-furrow, for example, would be totally meaningless beyond the certainty that it was formed from a technique of ploughing. [Archaeologists] would never realise the complex pattern of landholding, communal cultivation and social organisation just from the physical remains themselves.'[120] Yet documentary evidence for the early part of that period is extremely limited, and even after the later seventh century, when charters, hagiographies, annals and other accounts become more common, they have little to say about the organisation of cultivation. Let us, then, experiment. Say that there was no documentary evidence for the organisation of arable cultivation in the Middle Ages. Evidence from air photography, archaeological excavation and environmental research would demonstrate that the hedges and ditches which defined arable land also enclosed large areas. It would be immediately obvious both on the ground and on air photographs that these extensive fields were subdivided into long, narrow units, each separated from its neighbour on either side by a shallow furrow and (on clay soils) each ridged towards the middle. In larger areas of arable, such units might be grouped into blocks bounded by particularly substantial banks – interpreted as headlands, a form still utilised by contemporary farmers.

There would be great debate about the social organisation of such fields. The subdivision of a large, enclosed area into smaller units might be held to imply some degree of co-ownership (although it would be impossible to say whether units were held in bundles or whether tenure was distributed across the field). If the possibility of shared ownership were admitted, then cooperation between cultivators would be essential because of the requirement to protect growing crops from stray animals and from damage or depredation by other holders. A conclusion to consideration of these problems would thus, necessarily, be weighted towards the view that such areas of arable were likely to have been managed on the basis of (at very least) a minimal communality of governance in which rights to holdings, access, maintenance of outer boundaries, and regulation of infringements were collectively controlled. These suggestions provide a way forward into a generalised investigation into the origins of open fields. We might, on the other hand, expect *details* of the management of tenure and cropping and the links of both to social organisation to continue to elude us. The argument can be applied to the prehistoric and Roman curvilinear and rectilinear field layouts already explored to ask whether there is any evidence that they may have been laid out and subdivided in such a way as to constitute open fields?

There are many undivided prehistoric and Roman co-axial fields enclosed by sufficiently substantial hedges or ditches to make it very likely that they were cultivated in severalty, like the hedges around Bronze and Iron Age fields excavated on the site of Terminal 5 at Heathrow (Middx.).[121] Yet in other places, some prehistoric and Romano-British fields were quite large and Fowler has suggested that 'in such treeless landscapes, the visual aspects of such layouts may well have been 'open'' (although something that looked open may not have been managed as an open field).[122] The large – apparently open – curvilinear fields laid out at Park Brow (Sussex) and High Knowes (Northumb.) in the Bronze Age, at Alrewas (Staffs.) and Grateley (Hants.) in the Iron Age, and at the Romano-British farmstead at Roystone Grange (Derbys.) have been discussed above, together with other prehistoric examples from Pembrokeshire, Cornwall and Devon.[123] The smallest units of co-axial prehistoric fields may have been 'plots' grouped into larger 'fields' for cultivation, in the same way that furlongs in medieval open fields were grouped for cropping purposes, thus forming an open field within a rectilinear lay out.[124] Such arrangements offer a practical explanation for the 'halos' of intensive manuring that mark the infields of prehistoric and Romano-British settlements.

On the other hand, the existence of an open field does not in itself necessarily imply communal management. Each open field might be held in severalty, in the same way as those defined by the early Middle Ages as an inland or a *worthig*. Only if arable were divided between two or more cultivators would collective approaches to arable management become an issue.

The earliest known documentary reference to fields subdivided between two or more cultivators is the clause in the late seventh-century laws of King Ine of Wessex already cited. The 'common … share-land' of the clause was interpreted by Finberg and, later, Fox as a field in shared ownership which was bounded by a single hedge for whose upkeep all holders of land within the unit were responsible.[125] Only if the field were open could collective responsibility for the maintenance of the boundary explain the damage that a stray cow might make to *common* crops of corn or grass. Eighth-century Irish laws record similar custom and practice in stipulating that fences around fields should be stock-proof.[126] Yet the clause in Ine's law can neither be identified as a new way of organising arable in open fields nor claimed as an old one. There are no earlier English documents with which to compare it, nor do we know whether it was intended to address problems of compensation and culpability because they were perennial, or because they were new. The practice was sufficiently widespread across early medieval Britain to suggest the possibility that it may not have been a recent innovation: Kelly has noted that in eighth-century Ireland it was 'normal practice for four low-ranking farmers – probably relatives – to plough in co-operation' within an infield-outfield system close to their dwellings, in which the infield was subdivided between them in such a way as to lie open to them all; similar practices were common across Wales in the same period.[127] Just these kinds of landscapes may have been described in charters like that for Ardington (Berks.) in the tenth century where 'the open pasture is common and the meadow is common and the arable is common', or that for Tidenham (Glos.) in AD 956 whose tenants contributed to the 'acre fencing' which separated open arable from pasture.[128]

The subdivision of arable land specifically into strips is apparently attested in documentary evidence only by the tenth century, and the texts are often more ambiguous than they appear at first sight.[129] Where a charter of 1016 at Bishopton (Warwicks.), for example, recorded 'every third acre of beanland on Bishop's hill', it is difficult to know whether the clerk intended simply to record the grant of a third of the arable, or whether he really did mean the exchange of every third strip in an open field.[130] There is more solid ground for identifying selions in 956 at Charlton (Berks.) where the arable had 'no fixed bounds because the acres adjoined other acres', a description confirmed in 982 when other land granted there was not 'demarcated on all sides by clear bounds because to left and right lie acres in combination with one another'.[131] Here it seems that open fields had certainly been subdivided by the mid-tenth century.

Archaeological evidence from Northamptonshire and Yorkshire takes the evidence for strip holdings back to the eighth or ninth centuries and suggests that they may predate subdivision into furlongs.[132] Small rectilinear fields in Somerset, probably dating from the seventh and eighth centuries, were subdivided by low banks into 'long, narrow, curving, strip-like subdivisions', as were eighth- or ninth-century fields at West Walton and Walpole St Andrew (Norf.).[133] There are indications that strips were an intrinsic part of the structure of the large middle Anglo-Saxon field layout in the Bourn Valley (Cambs.)

where they were respected by an early tenth-century boundary.[134] The most enigmatic evidence of all comes from Milfield (Northumb.), where evidence for eighth- or ninth-century arable cultivation has been found in close association with traces of undated ridge and furrow.[135]

The subdivision of an arable field could be identified in archaeological evidence if the boundaries between its internal sub-units were sufficiently permanent to have been constructed as (or formed over time as) ditches or banks. The implication of such survivals is that the boundaries between sub-units were important enough to be refreshed over a considerable period, and might be more likely to represent the partition of the field between a number of cultivators than evidence for temporary boundaries. A holder in severalty might find it useful to group sub-sections of an arable field within impermanent boundaries in order to grow winter- or spring-sown crops, or to fence off areas temporarily under fallow. In eighth-century Ireland, for example, impermanent 'bare fences' proof against livestock were made of rods woven between stout stakes and topped with blackthorn to make an arable on the outfield, or pasture on the infield.[136] It is more difficult to develop a rationale for a field is owned and cultivated by one individual to be subdivided into relatively small semi-permanent units like selions.

Where an arable field has been divided into selions, the explanation that each one represents a different holding is easier to defend (although, as the example of Tunley (Lancs.) has demonstrated, this is not the only way to divide an open field between a number of men).[137] There is evidence of strip cultivation throughout prehistoric and Roman Britain. Prehistoric, perhaps Bronze Age, strips have been identified on St David's Head (Pembs.) and in Northumberland.[138] Iron Age examples have been excavated at Sawtry (Cambs.).[139]

Sizeable curvilinear Roman fields on the Gwent levels were subdivided by narrow ditches into long narrow strips between 16 m and 21 m wide and up to 600 m in length – each ditch deep enough to mark a boundary, but shallow enough to allow access across them. They are believed to have distinguished the holdings of different cultivators in open fields.[140] Strips in the contemporary open field at Roystone Grange (Derbys.), were about 40 metres wide (Figure 4(c)).[141] At Frocester (Glos.), excavation revealed early post-Roman strip cultivation on a different alignment from the ridge and furrow of later medieval fields.[142] Other Roman strip fields have also been identified at Jevington (Sussex), Twyford Down and King's Worthy (Hants.), Bathhampton Down (Glos.), Great Wymondley (Herts.), as well as in Somerset, Dorset, Nottinghamshire, Lincolnshire and, perhaps, at Burnham Market (Norf.).[143] It seems, then, that the subdivision of large areas of open arable between a number of holders may not have been new in Anglo-Saxon England.

The management of open fields under CPrRs

The partitioning of an open field between two or more holdings had immediate implications for each holder's right peaceably to enjoy his holding even if all agricultural activities were undertaken in severalty: rights of tenure in the field, access to holdings, and protection against damage to crops from stray beasts could all be affected by the behaviour of other owners or their tenants. Principles of equity and transparency in the exercise of their rights required each right-holder to be an active participant in decision-making, agreement by consensus, regular meetings to deal with practicalities, enforceable rights and the application of sanctions, as well as agreed mechanisms for dealing with disputes and damage. In a non-literate society, traditional practices and customs could only have been recorded in collective spoken memories in whose recollection all right-holders were participant. In effect, then, the subdivision of a field into two or more holdings in an open layout would have required governance and management within a CPrR. Fox, for example, concluded that the clause in Ine's laws described the division of an open field into holdings such that each holder was responsible for a stretch of the boundary in order to prevent damage from cattle.[144] Another example can be seen in Carolingian open fields in Westfalia, Saxony, Lechfeld and the Hassegau (Germany), where each holding was equally divided between the two or three open fields of the vill, in which it was represented by single strip.[145] In these examples, governance and management was almost certainly undertaken within a narrow CPrR, since all agricultural activities were undertaken in severalty within each holding.

It follows then, that if at least some prehistoric and Roman arable was laid out in open fields subdivided between a number of cultivators, then they were probably managed within a CPrR. It is impossible at this distance in time to do more than guess at the narrowness or width of common rights that holders were able to exercise within such early open fields. The most cautious (and most likely) interpretation is that they were managed within a narrow CPrR, each man undertaking all aspects of cultivation or fallowing on his holding in severalty. To this extent, at least, such early field systems share many characteristics of layout with irregular medieval open fields managed within a narrow CPrR. Such medieval arable tended to be subdivided into any number of fields of varying sizes; individual holdings tended to be irregular both in area and in their distribution across the open fields; demesne holdings tended to be concentrated in compact blocks outside the open fields; and finally, these open fields lay mingled among enclosures, pasture and woodland.[146]

In conclusion, then, it seems at least possible that the practice of laying out arable land in open fields subdivided between a number of cultivators *may* have been a familiar tradition in Britain for centuries before Germanic migrants arrived. The Anglo-Saxon descendants and/or successors of prehistoric and Romano-British farmers worked within existing fields, often centuries-old, sometimes open in layout and some of those open fields were subdivided into strips. Such traditions, persisting and evolving over the *longue durée*, of arable cultivation under narrow CPrRs may have continued to influence the organisation of arable cultivation in the sub-Roman centuries.

Yet it is worth emphasising that the kinds of arable landscapes in which these customs can be identified were small in scale. The open, curvilinear enclosures described above were not large and certainly nothing like the extensive areas of open arable that were later found in many parts of medieval England. The small fields within rectilinear field systems that survived as open-field furlongs at Leighton Bromswold (Hunts.), Etton and Haddon (both Northants.) could only have been subdivided between a few cultivators.[147] Each form lay alongside enclosed fields of arable and pasture held in severalty, interspersed among commonable woods, pastures and meadows. Nor were they immutable. There were innovations in agricultural management and practice in such traditional landscapes during the long eighth century and it is to these that we turn next.

Notes

1 Roberts and Wrathmell 2002: 124 and 144; Fox 1981.
2 See Hall 1996: 80 Plate VII.
3 As early as the first century BC, Roman farmers were advised to ridge their fields only after the seed had been sown (the 'third ploughing'), ploughing without mouldboards at other times, Harrison 1918: 130–1.
4 cf. Bailey 2010: 157.
5 Ibid.: 56, who also provides a masterful critique of the confused terminology used in discussing these forms.
6 Whitelock 1979: 403, my emphasis.
7 Vinogradoff 1908: 277: 476.
8 Seebohm 1883: 110, my addition; also 179–80: 410–11: 437–8.
9 The citation is from a pre-publication copy generously provided by Dr Banham of a paper now published as Banham 2009.
10 Gray 1959 edn: 5.
11 Ibid.: 199.
12 Ibid.: 418.
13 Maitland 1897: 237, my addition, see also 112, 115 and 220.
14 Orwin and Orwin: 1938: 3: 23–4.
15 Bishop 1935–6: 26–40.

16 Roberts 1989: 49–51,
17 Finberg 1972: 416–17; Hoskins 1988: 45; Stenton 1971: 280.
18 Thirsk 1964, 1966.
19 Baker and Butlin 1973: 625.
20 Ibid.: 656.
21 Addyman 1964: 24; Hall 1995: 129–30.
22 Hall 1995: 130.
23 Harvey 1980, 1983, 1984, 1985.
24 Roberts and Wrathmell 2002: 145; Taylor 2002.
25 Hall 1981: 44.
26 Rackham 1986: 172. See also Maitland 1897: 338, 365; Hoskins 1988: 45–7; Stenton 1971: 280; Hooke 1998: 114–15; Fowler 2002: 270.
27 Lewis et al. 1997: 107–8; Hooke 1998: 106.
28 Millett 1990: 185; Hamerow 1997: 33.
29 Payne 2007: 54.
30 Carver 2010: 59, 65; Hey 2004: 40–1.
31 Upex 2002: 89; Murphy 1994: 37; Rogerson et al. 1997: 20, 23; Lawson 1983: 75; Davison 1990: 18–19.
32 Hooke 2011: 316.
33 Murphy 1994: 37. See also Dark 2000: chapter 5; Foard 2001; Rippon et al. 2006: 49. See also Rackham 1986: 74.
34 Rippon et al. 2006: 49.
35 Hey 2004: 40–1; Miles 1984: 25; Murphy 1994: 25–7 and 37.
36 Jones and Page 2006: 56; Taylor 1983: 121.
37 McOmish et al. 2002: 111.
38 Fowler 2000: Figure 6.11.
39 Brown and Foard 1998: 74; Addyman 1964: 24; Hall and Ravensdale 1974; Rippon 1991.
40 McOmish et al. 2002: 111; Hooke 1988: 64, 130; Cunliffe 1973: 183–8; Hall 1982a: 54–5; Campbell 1994: 65; Oosthuizen 2005; Unwin 1983: 344.
41 McOmish et al. 2002: 111; Fowler 2000: 235–7.
42 Losco-Bradley and Wheeler 1984: 105; Hamerow 2002a: 128.
43 Hey 2004: 37–9; Hamerow 1993: 94; Miles 1984: 14, 16.
44 Hamerow et al. 2007: 115.

45 Cunliffe 1973: 183–8; Lewis et al. 1997: 92; Bradley et al. 1999: 251; Gaimster and Bradley 2002: 242.

46 RCHME 1979: lxii.

47 Oosthuizen 1998 and 2006: 81–3; Hooke 1988*a*: 123–5 and 1988b: 131; Beresford and Hurst 1979: 82; Taylor and Fowler 1978: 159; Hurst 1984.

48 Nash 1982: 42.

49 Sheppard 1979: 33; Brown 1996: 43; Bassett 1981: 93–121 and 1985: 32–4; RCHME 1968: xxx.

50 Upex 2002: 87–94; Gaimster and Bradley 2001: 294–5.

51 Bull 1993: 16; Williamson 2010: 144–52; Rackham 1986: 158.

52 Williamson 1987; Oosthuizen 2006: 68–90; Hooke 1988a: 123–5; Brown 1996: 43; Bassett 1981: 93–121 and 1985: 32–4; McOmish et al. 2002: 111; Fowler 2000: 235–7; Nash 1982: 42; Sheppard 1979: 33; RCHME 1979: lxii; RCHME 1968: xxx; Oosthuizen 1998; Taylor and Fowler 1978: 159; Upex 2002: 87–94; Williamson 1987; Gaimster and Bradley 2001: 294–5; Beresford and Hurst 1979: 82.

53 Williamson 1987: 425, my addition.

54 See also this chapter, above.

55 Rogerson et al. 1997: 15: 17; Williamson 1984 and 1986; Cunliffe 2010: 413; Davison 1990: 13, 17; Fowler 2002: 209.

56 Cunliffe 1973: 185; Parry 2006: 93; Hiller et al. 2002: 65; Hooke 1981a: 206–10.

57 Aston 1999: 27; Brown and Taylor 1993: 106; Upex 2002: 84 and 90–4; Rogerson et al. 1997: 19–20; Lawson 1983: 75–7; Davison 1990: 18–19; Webster 1967; Fowler 1975; Brown and Foard 1998: 78; Davies 2010: 104–5.

58 Parry 2006: 93, 96.

59 Ibid.: 93, 133, 276; Hall 1982a and 1982b. Infield-outfield cultivation continued to be practised across medieval England, inside as well as outside the Central Province including Kent, Staffordshire, Nottinghamshire, Norfolk. Suffolk, Lincolnshire and Yorkshire: Baker 1965: 89–90.

60 Jones and Page 2006: 93; Taylor and Arbon 2007: 38; Roberts and Wrathmell 2002. See also e.g. Aston 1988: 97; Rippon et al. 2006: 58–64.

61 See Bishop 1938: 41 for examples of crop rotations on both infields and outfields.

62 Rahtz and Meeson 1992: 156; *British Archaeology* 1995: 5. Moreland 2000: 103; Fowler 2002: 176; Blair 2005: 253, 256. See Chapter 4, below.
63 Gelling 1984: 260, 306, 319; Faith 1997: 47–8. Hey 2004: 361
64 Rippon et al. 2006: 49–53; Hey 2004: 48–9; Brown and Taylor 1993: 109.
65 Lawson 1983: 74–5
66 Carver 2010: 65; Brown and Foard 1978: 82; Hey 2004: 54, 265; Jones and Page 2006: 93.
67 Moffett 2011: 349–50
68 Ibid.: 348–9, 351–2.
69 Hamerow 2002b: 153; Bradley and Gaimster 2000: 299; Murphy 1994: 34–5; Miles 1984: 25; Hey 2004: 48; Carr et al. 1988: 375; Haughton and Powlesland 1999: 143–71.
70 Cited in Fowler 2002: 213–14.
71 Taylor 2000: 24–6.
72 Millett 1990: 202.
73 Stevens 1966: 111.
74 Kelly 1997: 471.
75 Baker and Butlin 1973: 634.
76 Cf. Hill 2000.
77 Langdon 1988: 88–9; Loveluck 1998: 156; Hill 2000: 11; Kelly 1997: 469–70.
78 Hey 2004: 48–9, 362–4; Williams 1993: 86.
79 Losco-Bradley and Kinsley 2002: 29.
80 *British Archaeology* 2011: 7. See, for example, Hill 2000, Fowler 2000: 184.
81 Hey 2004: 49; Kelly 1997: 364.
82 Hey 2004: 49. Cf. Cato (234–249 BC): 'Plan to have a big compost heap and take the best of care of the manure. When it is hauled out see that it is well-rotted and spread. The Autumn is the time to do this' (Harrison 1918: 40). It was common practice on Roman villa estates at Bignor (Sussex), Thistelton Dyer (Rutland), Pitney (Som.) and Stanwix (Cumbria) and Applebaum calculated that more than 200 tons each year was produced in this way at Bignor (1966: 101–2).
83 Hey 2004: 48, 362; Hiller et al. 2002: 57; Campbell 1994: 76. The contribution of manure to agricultural productivity – and the

connection between common rights of pasture and arable cultivation – was noted by John Denson, a yeoman husbandman from Waterbeach (Cambs.) who explained in 1824 that the 'goodness [of the poor quality of clay soils in his parish] is principally owing to the quantity of manure made by the number of cattle, which was kept by the occupiers and proprietors of common-right before the late inclosure', – which manure, in most cases, found its way to the arable land (Denson 1991: 60).

84 Campbell 1983: 32.

85 Oosthuizen 2006: 108.

86 Millett 1990: 202.

87 Hey 2004: 48–9, 362; Campbell 1994: 77–81; Parry 2006: 35–6.

88 Postgate 1962: 88–96; Postgate 1973: 300–3.

89 Bishop 1938: 43–4.

90 e.g. Hamerow 2002b: 152–5.

91 Rippon et al. 2006: 66–7; Atkin 1985; Roberts and Wrathmell 2002: 96–115).

92 Rippon 1994: 243–5; Brown 1991: 78; Hall 1984: 51–2; Hall 1988: 114–15; Hall 1983: 117–19; Shaw 1991: 16–17; Oosthuizen 1993: 95–7, 1996: 28, 2002a and 2002b; Warner 1987: 30, 33; Silvester 1988: 69, 95; Roberts 1985: 25; Roberts 1996: 26; Roberts 1981: 145–61. Rippon 1994: 243–5; Shaw 1991: 16–17; Silvester 1988: 69, 95; Roberts 1996: 26; Roberts 1981: 145–61.

93 Rippon 1994: 244.

94 Aston 1988: 94–5; Atkin 1985; Roberts and Wrathmell 2002: 96–116.

95 Finberg 1972: 416–17; Fox 1981: 87–8.

96 Aston 1988: 94–5; Atkin 1985; Roberts and Wrathmell 2002: 96–116. Rippon 1994: 243–5; Anglo-Saxon Charters, S238, accessed August 2011.

97 Finberg 1972: 416; Faith 1997: 170–4; Yorke 1995: 268.

98 Faith 1997: 171–2, my addition.

99 Hall 1984: 51–2; Hall 1988: 114–15; Hall 1983: 117–19.

100 Rippon 1994: 243–5; Brown 1991: 78; Hall 1984: 51–2; Hall 1988: 114–15; Hall 1983: 117–19; Shaw 1991: 16–17; Oosthuizen 1993: 95–7, 1996: 28, 2002a and 2002b; Silvester 1988: 69, 95; Roberts 1985: 25; Roberts 1996: 26; Roberts 1981: 145–61.

101 Warner 1987: 30, 33.

102 Costen 1992a; Costen 1992b: 221; Faith 2006: 9. See also Faith 1997: 32–4, 1998 and 2009; Whitelock 1979: 403; Loveluck 2005: 239; Hodges 1989: 238; Oosthuizen 1993; Carr et al. 1988; Hamerow 2002b: 62 and 90–3; Roberts and Wrathmell 2002: 181.

103 Smith 1978–9: 12; Drewett et al. 1988: 135; Cunliffe 1993: 221; Atkin 1985: 179.

104 Darvill 1996: 232–4, 65; Hoskins 1988: 25.

105 Hodges 1991: 84; Topping 2008: 343–8.

106 e.g. Cunliffe 1993: 93–5: 141–4 and 168–82; Drewett et al. 1988: 135: 149–51. See also Stoertz 1997: 57.

107 Atkin 1985; Bond 1985: 115; Riley and Wilson-North 2001: 97; Rippon 1998, 2002 and 2007; Rippon et al. 2006: 66–7; Roberts 1981: 149, 1985: 25 and 1993; Sheppard 1966; Roberts and Wrathmell 2002: 96–115.

108 Warner 1996: 49–52.

109 Hooke 1988a; Pocock 1968; Harvey 1980; 1983; 1984; 1985; Powlesland 1986: 165.

110 Cunliffe 1973: 183–8.

111 Keen 1984: 236.

112 ibid.: 210, 221, 230.

113 Oosthuizen 2006: 91–113.

114 Hall 1982a: 46; Brown and Taylor 1993.

115 Hooke 1988a; Pocock 1968; Harvey 1980; 1983; 1984; 1985; Powlesland 1986: 165; Campbell 1994: 65; Keen 1984: 236; Hall 1982a: 46; Gaimster and Bradley 2003: 221; Oosthuizen 2006: 91–113.

116 Fleming 2008; Pryor 2002; Driver 2007: 122; Hall and Coles 1994: 78

117 Williamson 2010: 186–7; Darvill 1996: 62–4; Crawford 1928: 162–4; Hinman, pers. comm. 2011; Abrams and Ingam 2006; Oosthuizen 2006.

118 Fowler 2002: 145; Taylor 2000 edn: 54.

119 Bassett 1980–1; Brown 1996; Bassett 1985; Upex 2002; Oosthuizen 1998; see for comparison, for example, Hartley 1983, 1984, 1989; Hall 1995.

120 Taylor 1981: 16, my addition.

121 cf. Lewis et al. 2006: 104–12.

122 Fowler 2002: 158.

123 Smith 1978–9: 12; Drewett et al. 1988: 135; Cunliffe 1993: 221; Darvill 1996: 232–4 and 65; Hoskins 1988 edn: 25; Hodges 1991: 84; Topping 2008: 343–8.

124 Fowler 1983: 102.

125 Finberg 1972: 416–17; Fox 1981: 87–8.

126 Kelly 1997: 372–8, 140–2.

127 Ibid.: 371, 241, 245, 445; Jones 1981: 205–7; Ó'Corráin 2005: 553.

128 Fox 1981: 84; Roberts and Wrathmell 2002: 131. There is an early reference to common land at Cofton Hackett (Worcs.), in 849, but it might describe arable or pasture: Hooke 1981b: 58.

129 References to acres or headlands do not in themselves amount to evidence for strips, any more than they do today.

130 Hooke 1998: 121.

131 Hooke 1981a: 206–7. See also Hooke 1988a: 125,

132 Hall 1981, 1982a, 1982b, 1983, 1984, 1988, 1995; Harvey 1980, 1983, 1984, 1985.

133 Rippon et al. 2006: 59 and 66; Silvester 1988: 95, 69.

134 Oosthuizen 2006: 99–107.

135 Bradley and Gaimster 2000: 299.

136 Kelly 1997: 374–6.

137 Unless the labour and crops were also shared in common. This seems unlikely in many cases and the arguments are dealt with more fully in Chapter 5.

138 Murphy 2001: 94; Topping 1989: 161–79; Topping 2008; Cunliffe 2010: 414.

139 Richard Newman: pers. comm. 2009.

140 Rippon 1996: 50, my addition.

141 Ibid.: 31; Hodges 1991: 79; Applebaum 1972: 90–5; Arnold 1984: 57; Williamson 2003: 81; Applebaum 1966: 105.

142 Price 2000: 242.

143 Rippon 1996: 31; Hodges 1991: 79; Applebaum 1972: 90–5; Arnold 1984: 57; Williamson 2003: 81; Applebaum 1966: 105.

144 Fox 1981: 87. Roberts and Wrathmell (2002: 135) cite an eighteenth-century Swedish law which is virtually identical and whose meaning matches Fox's interpretation.

145 Droege 1970: 287; Nitz 1988a: 156 and 1988b: 252–62, though see Matzat 1988: 141 for another view.

146 Bailey 2010: 17–24; Campbell 1981b: 25 and 115; Bailey 2007.

147 Roberts 1987: 49–51; Upex 2002.

Part Two

Transformation

4

Innovations in agricultural management

'Ancient' and 'champion' England

The distinction is often made in England between 'ancient' landscapes of small-scale, hedged fields and dispersed hamlets and the wide views of the open arable, 'champion' landscapes in which settlement is generally nucleated, and which coincides with field systems managed under wide CPrRs, like those preserved in the extensive medieval cultivation remains around the deserted village of Baggrave (Leics.) (Figure 7). 'Champion' England is generally found in a broad zone running from north-east Wiltshire to Yorkshire (now termed the 'Central Province').[1] The two landscapes were certainly present by the later Middle Ages. Generally speaking, open-field systems managed under wide CPrRs exhibited three distinctive characteristics which resulted from the management of the arable within them as a common property resource: the inclusion of a fallow season in crop rotations during which cultivators exercised full rights of common pasture; the systematic management of crop rotations across the arable as a whole; and the equitable subdivision of arable into units for cropping and the equitable distribution of holdings across each unit. Those under narrow CPrRs showed a marked tendency to cultivation in severalty and widespread irregularity in almost every aspect of layout and management.

The differences between ancient and champion England were documented in the mid-sixteenth century by William Harrison,

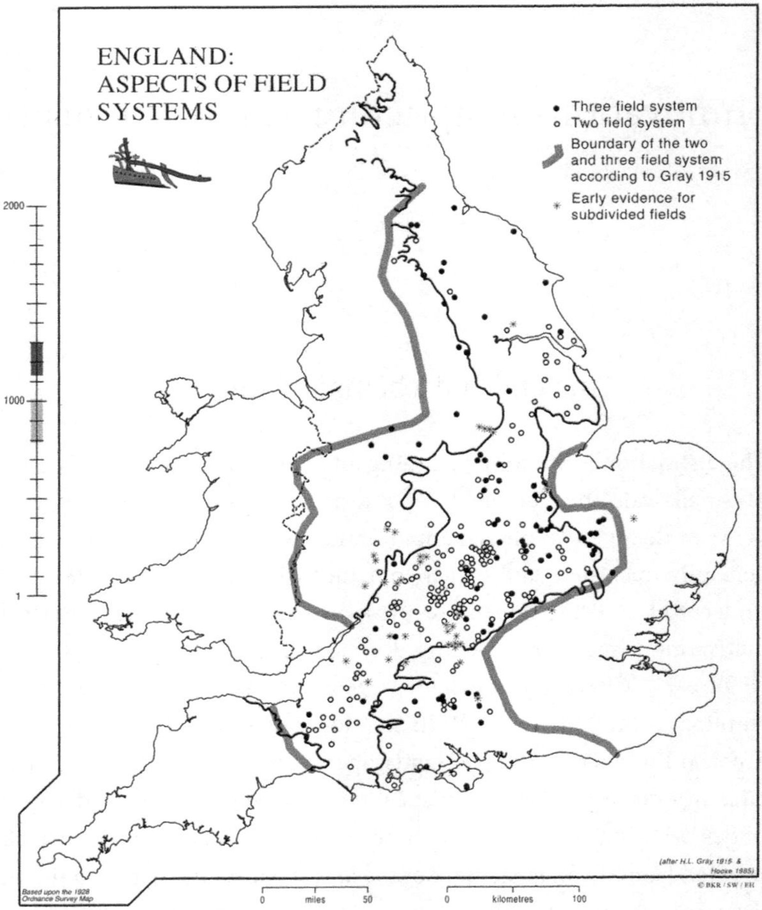

Figure 5. Open fields under wide CPrRs before about 1350. (Reproduced with permission from Roberts and Wrathmell 2002).

who described the countryside 'diuided into champaigne ground and woodland', while his contemporary, Thomas Tusser trenchantly proclaimed that it was 'the countrie enclosed I praise, the tother delighteth not me'.[2] More recently, Oliver Rackham has lyrically described the contrast between 'ancient'

> hamlets, medieval farms in hollows of the hills, lonely moats and great barns in the clay-lands, pollards and ancient trees, cavernous holloways and many footpaths, fords, irregularly shaped groves with thick hedges colourful with maple, dogwood and spindle

and (with markedly less enthusiasm) the 'big villages, few, busy roads, thin hawthorn hedges, windswept brick farms and ivied clumps of trees in corners of fields' of champion countryside.[3] Similar contrasts were already being noted by the eleventh century on the other side of the Channel between the open arable fields of *champagne* country in the Paris basin and northern France, subdivided into strips with scattered holdings and in which the settlement of each community was consolidated in a single nucleation and the small enclosed fields of the wooded landscapes of the *bocage* further west, east and south, fields frequently held in severalty, interspersed with scattered farms and hamlets.

Both Pounds and Verhulst have argued that *champagne* landscapes were the physical expression of the implementation on the vast, new estates of the aristocratic and ecclesiastical elite in the core areas of the Carolingian empire of strategies for the more intensive exploitation of their demesnes.[4] A similar proposition can be inferred from Campbell's observation that 'central and southern counties (the heartland of the old Anglo-Saxon state) appear to have been characterised by a higher incidence of vills of undivided lordship and a lower incidence of freemen, than the eastern and south-western counties (where the continuity of lordship was disrupted by the Scandinavian incursions of the ninth and tenth centuries' – that is, that the origins of champion landscapes can be found on the extensive estates of the long eighth century.[5] At first sight, the substantial similarities in the distribution of nucleated settlements and large open-field systems on either side of the Channel immediately present the possibility that they may have resulted from a common process. There is, however, a serious problem with a question posed in such terms. This is because the classification of English 'champion' landscapes is based on different criteria from those used to characterise the *champagne pays* of France. The difficulty is that open fields managed under a narrow CPrR were found across medieval England not just in the champion Central Province, while similarly governed open fields were only found in the *champagne pays* of Francia. The Central Province was distinguished not by the presence as opposed to the absence of open-field layouts, as in France, but by the distinctive distribution of highly regular open-field systems managed under wide CPrRs compared with the more general distribution of irregular open-field systems managed under narrow CPrRs, which were found across medieval England.

If a Carolingian context has any relevance to the origin of champion landscapes in England then the importance of the distinction between open fields managed under narrow and wide CPrRs needs first to be assessed. If open-field systems governed under wide CPrRs were laid out within the Central Province in the long eighth century, then a comparison with *champagne* France becomes irrelevant, because there is no evidence that open fields managed under similarly wide CPrRs could be found on the European mainland before the thirteenth century.[6] Even though champion and *champagne* might share superficial similarities in their open-ness, they may – in this case – have had quite different origins: the former from the introduction of open-field systems over which there were wide common property rights and the latter from the introduction of open-field systems over which there were narrow common property rights.[7]

The distribution of nucleated settlement provides a second focus for comparison. It is particularly dominant in the landscape of the Central Province (see Figure 9) and in the Carolingian heartlands. If planned settlements were laid out on the estates of the Carolingian *and* middle Anglo-Saxon ecclesiastical and secular elite in the long eighth century, in areas later characterised as *champagne* and champion, then Pounds' and Verhulst's conclusions might have a relevance to Anglo-Saxon England.

The origins of English open-field system managed under wide CPrRs: historiography

The historiography of English open-field systems was outlined in the previous chapter and provides the immediate context for research on the differentiation between open-field systems managed under narrow and wide CPrRs. Gray provided the first scholarly demonstration of the restricted occurrence of open fields governed within wide CPrRs in his map showing the 'Boundary of the Two- and Three-Field System'.[8] By the early 1980s the association between this distribution and the English Midlands had led to the characterisation of the former as 'the Midland system', also referred to as 'regular common-field systems'.[9] More recently, the area in which both open fields under wide CPrRs and nucleated settlements can principally be found has been more tightly quantified as the 'Central Province'.[10] The distinction between arable regulated within narrow and wide CPrRs was first analysed in detail in two seminal papers, which proposed that the latter had evolved from the former in the post-Conquest period.[11] With some notable exceptions, the proposition has not been taken very much further, principally because (as discussed above) the origins of open-field systems themselves remain contentious and because the terminology which distinguishes the two forms of governance remains confused not least by an emphasis on their respective irregular and regular morphologies.[12] Thirsk and, later, Fox argued that the introduction of a fallow season into crop rotations was forced on cultivators by the encroachment of arable on pasture and led inevitably to the imposition of wide CPrRs over all aspects of the management of arable crops.[13] Rights of common grazing on the fallows compensated right-holders for the loss of all, or almost all, their common pasture – that is, the former replaced the latter as a non-arable common pool resource. Because grazing could only be allowed on the stubbles once the harvest was in, because the area of grazing required each year did not vary a great deal (as such open fields tended to be fairly equitably subdivided), and because rights to grazing on stubbles and fallows was exercised under a system of common rights, equity of access to grazing by cultivators could only be achieved if the arable itself was also managed as a common pool resource.

The period of introduction of open-field systems managed under wide CPrRs thus indicated the tipping point in the balance between pasture and fallows in supporting the animals of the vill, and its date remains contentious. Thirsk and Fox agreed that there is no satisfactory documentary evidence for the communal regulation of fallowing before the Norman Conquest.[14] Their conclusion appears to be confirmed by recent analyses of arable land in 1086, which indicate that the proportion of ploughed land in each vill had reached only between 30 and 40 per cent in many parts of the Central Province by the end of the eleventh century.[15] The implication of these results is that there was still plenty of grazing available to stock in vills later characterised by common-field systems and it is therefore unlikely that the cropping and fallowing of open fields required communal regulation by that date. These conclusions appear to be confirmed by patterns of manuring, which suggest large open fields in the same areas were still being managed on the basis of infield/outfield cultivation in the late Anglo-Saxon period rather than in two or three large open fields.[16]

On the other hand, archaeological field-walking over extensive areas of Northamptonshire has found evidence for the imposition of the strips of large-scale open fields over most of the area of each vill. Sherds of broken pottery scattered across the new fields during manuring could reliably be shown to post-date the abandoned middle Anglo-Saxon farmsteads and hamlets that the strips overlay.[17] Early open-field layouts in Holderness (Yorks.) appear to be of roughly the same, or perhaps slightly later, date.[18] This substantial body of data is widely interpreted as the result of the comprehensive introduction from the late eighth century onwards of open-field layouts managed under wide CPrRs. Yet in central Germany, two or three large open fields divided into very long strips were laid out in the early eighth century by Frankish colonists, and where all aspects of cultivation on each holding were undertaken in severalty even though each holding was subdivided into strips equally distributed between the two or three large fields of the vill.[19] That is, the fields were large in scale, open in layout and subdivided into strips, but they were operated within a narrow rather than a wide CPrR. All that can safely be concluded in Northamptonshire and Holderness, then, is that large open fields, divided into strips, were laid out in the middle Anglo-Saxon period. They *may* have been managed within a wide CPrR, but there is at least an equal chance that each strip was instead cultivated in severalty and that they were, rather, managed within a narrow CPrR.

It might, notwithstanding, be argued that there is documentary corroboration for the introduction of wide CPrRs over arable from the tenth century onwards. That evidence is, however, more ambiguous than it may seem at first sight. Take, for example, the charter for Cudley (Worcs.) which recorded that 30 acres lay 'in two fields' in 974 or that for Adlestrop (Glos.), which referred to *Rahulfes furlong quae est in campo de Evenlode* ('Rahulf's furlong which is in the field of Evenlode').[20] It is true that in each case the arable lay in more than one 'field', but there is no certainty of the total number of fields or, indeed, whether 'field' or 'furlong' was the intended meaning. As late as the mid-thirteenth century, it was still possible for furlongs to be referred to as '*feld*' or '*campus*' and a record of two or three fields in the tenth or eleventh centuries cannot be taken as establishing the existence of the subdivision of open arable into two or three equal divisions between which holdings were equitably distributed.[21] Nor is the evidence of the charters sufficient to establish with certainty the communal regulation of all aspects of crop management or – most importantly – the exercise of common rights of pasture on the fallows.

Although open-field layouts, sometimes divided into strips (but almost certainly managed under narrow CPrRs), appear to have been familiar elements in the English landscape for at least two millennia before the end of Roman administration in Britain, it seems unlikely that anyone could have been able to remark on the special character of the landscape of the Central Province at any point in the pre-Conquest period if the regular open-field landscapes of arable cultivated within wide CPrRs were the criterion for the observation. That is, the management of open-field arable landscapes of champion England and *champagne* Francia during the long eighth century may each have tended to the narrow end of the spectrum of CPrRs and thus have been more similar than dissimilar. The medieval and later distinction between the two may not have been relevant in the period of their origin.

Nucleation and the Central Province

Another stumbling block to the investigation of a common origin for English and Carolingian open-field landscapes lies in that other defining characteristic of the Central Province: nucleated settlement. It is generally believed that dispersed settlements were replaced by nucleated settlements from the late eighth century onwards, as part of the same process in which large-scale open fields, subdivided into strips, were laid over the deserted earthworks of middle Anglo-Saxon farms and hamlets in Northamptonshire and Yorkshire (and, it is argued by extension, beyond). Settlement nucleation was, it is suggested, an essential part of the process of introduction of wide CPrRs over arable, since it allowed the agricultural labour-force to be mobilised at short notice when brief windows of opportunity presented themselves for ploughing, mowing or harvesting the heavy clay soils of the Central Province.[22] If nucleated settlement is both a defining characteristic of the Central Province and an essential component of wide CPrRs, then once again, any comparison with the open-field landscapes of Carolingian Francia becomes redundant because wide CPrRs do not appear to have been introduced in England until the later Anglo-Saxon period nor – it follows – could nucleated settlements. However, if settlement nucleation in England were not a fundamental component in the introduction of wide CPrRs over arable, then it might just be possible that there were some commonalities in the origins of champion landscapes in middle Anglo-Saxon England and *champagne* landscapes in Carolingian France.

For much of the twentieth century scholars have taken it as read that 'the medieval village' was nucleated and that it was integrated with open-field systems.[23] Maitland concurred with Seebohm, adding a description of the process that he believed to underlie that association: 'The outlines of our nucleated villages may have been drawn for us by Germanic settlers, whereas in the land of hamlets and scattered steads old Celtic arrangements may never have been thoroughly effaced'.[24] Stenton followed Maitland, arguing that open fields and nucleated settlement were examples of the 'ways in which the Anglo-Saxons in England adhered to their own native [i.e. Germanic] traditions'.[25] The Orwins, too, depicted an 'open-field system' which 'consisted of communities living in what, today, are termed nucleated villages'.[26] Hoskins, in his masterpiece the *Making of the English Landscape*, explained that 'compact villages, of varying size, are to be found in all counties, dating for the most part from Anglo-Saxon times. Everywhere they were accompanied originally by the open-field system'.[27] Large-scale archaeological field-walking in Northamptonshire in the 1970s and 1980s appeared to confirm that a single period and process lay behind the introduction of nucleated settlements and open fields:

> In Northamptonshire … there are two problems. On the one hand the small early Saxon sites were deserted to form the present nucleated villages and on the other the landscape was divided up on a massive scale into strips. Did these two operations occur together, each necessitated by the other? The precise date of such a change in settlement patterns is unknown, but the early Saxon sites produce no Saxo-Norman wares and so were presumably deserted before that pottery was introduced in the ninth century … It seems unlikely that such a remarkable re-planning of the landscape would occur before there was a considerable settled population exerting pressure on land, so that a late eighth-century date is suggested for both the desertion of the Saxon sites and the first formation of strip fields.[28]

Hall's work has been a formative influence on landscape historians over the succeeding 25 years. A major study of Midland England, for example, concluded on the basis of his and other work that 'nucleated villages were a product of a development in agrarian methods' and 'is strengthened by the likelihood that [fields and villages] came into existence at the same time', between about 850 and 1200.[29] Although it was acknowledged that the orderliness of planned settlements and regular field systems managed under wide CPrRs could be the result of later restructuring, the consistent degree of regularity in both fields and settlements suggested that 'it seems likely that the nucleated village was really a by-product of the agricultural changes that encouraged the formation of the fields'.[30] The view that 'by the late ninth and tenth centuries nucleated settlements at the core of several large open arable fields were gradually replacing earlier scattered farmsteads' continues to form the generally accepted view of medieval landscape origins and explanations for their development.[31]

A shared origin for common fields and nucleated settlement has not, however, been universally accepted. As long ago as 1983, Taylor observed that 'the open field could and in some places certainly did, operate successfully without a nucleated village at its centre'.[32] Other chronologies of nucleation have emerged which are independent of those for the development of open and common fields. Foard suggested, also on the basis of fieldwork in Northamptonshire, that settlement nucleation was preceded by irregular polyfocal settlements which gradually coalesced into full nucleation.[33] A further study agreed that 'whether the process of nucleation was associated with a fundamental reorganisation of the decayed late Roman landscape is unclear', as 'the creation of regular settlements was not the inevitable corollary of the laying out of planned field systems'.[34] Instead, the authors suggested, the initial formation of nucleated settlements might have occurred in the middle Anglo-Saxon period, predating the introduction of regular open-field systems under wide CPrRs – which, they suggested, had emerged from the tenth century onwards in a process during which many settlements were formally replanned.[35] Brown and Foard instead proposed a two-phase period of landscape formation in which nucleation and regular open-field systems under CPrRs had separate origins: in the first phase, middle Anglo-Saxon nucleated settlements were established in association with royal vills, leading to the desertion of smaller hamlets and farmsteads; in the second phase, in the ninth and tenth centuries, large open arable fields managed under wide CPrRs were imposed over 'whole townships' regardless of the degree of nucleation achieved within them.[36]

Taylor agreed that nucleation might have been a phased process which followed a different developmental trajectory from that of regular open fields managed under wide CPrRs. He suggested that irregular middle and late Anglo-Saxon settlement gradually began to cluster around the edges of areas of pasture at about the same time that the first open fields began to appear and that, in the late eleventh or early twelfth centuries, such irregular foci were replaced by planned settlements at places like Whittlesford and Pampisford (both Cambs.).[37] Similar explanations have been offered for Great Doddington (Northants.) and the Bourn Valley (Cambs.), where loose, informal nucleations appear to have preceded the planned settlements of the eleventh century, themselves continuing to co-exist with dispersed farms and hamlets.[38] Such conclusions about the separate evolution of wide CPrRs over arable and nucleated settlement have recently been revivified by the Whittlewood Project, which concluded that 'what cannot be substantiated anywhere but in a few special cases, either because the evidence remains too vague or because it simply did not happen, is a link between nucleation and abandonment of outlying farmsteads, the freeing-up of the countryside and the laying out of open fields [managed under a wide system of common rights]'.[39]

Were nucleated settlements a contemporary and related aspect of the process in which wide CPrRs over open-field arable emerged in England, perhaps in the post-Conquest period? If they were not and if nucleations appeared simultaneously in the champion/*champagne* landscapes of England and France three hundred years or more earlier, then the possibility that elites on either side of the Channel developed and implemented common strategies for the economic exploitation of their estates remains a viable question for research. (Explanations for the origin of wide and narrow CPrRs over arable will be explored in the next chapter.)

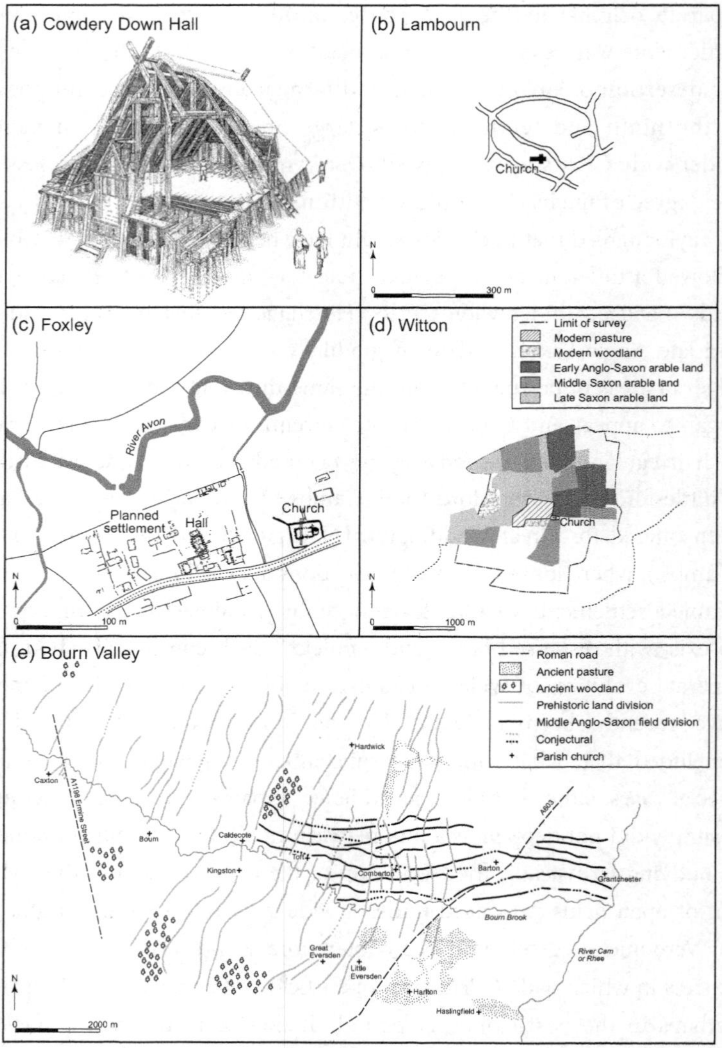

Figure 6. Innovation in the Anglo-Saxon landscape (a) Reconstruction of the palatial middle Anglo-Saxon hall at Cowdery's Down (Hants.) (reproduced with permission from Millett and James 1983). (b) Curvilinear manorial centre including an early church at Lambourn (Berks.) (after Draper 2009). (c) Planned middle Anglo-Saxon nucleated settlement at Foxley (Wilts.), with associated apsidal church (after Hunchliffe 1986). (d) The expansion of Anglo-Saxon arable cultivation at Witton, Norfolk (after Lawson 1983). (e) Large middle Anglo-Saxon field system imposed on the north slopes of the Bourn Valley, Cambridgeshire.

Figure 7. Medieval cultivation remains at Baggrave, Leicestershire. (Reproduced with permission, Cambridge University Committee for Aerial Photography, BLC57, 1972).

The origins of nucleated settlement in England: the evidence[40]

There are innumerable places across the Central Province where nucleated settlements overlie the aratral curves of medieval ploughing which are fossilised in property boundaries, and/or where the remains of ridge and furrow are preserved within later crofts.[41] Such evidence is widespread, from Somerset, across Wiltshire, Oxfordshire and Leicestershire, to

Cambridgeshire, Norfolk, Yorkshire, County Durham and beyond.[42] In Northamptonshire and Lincolnshire, for example, most medieval planned nucleated settlements were laid out in the eleventh or twelfth centuries in a context in which open-field layouts already existed.[43] Yet planned nucleations were not new in the post-Conquest landscape of central, southern England. There is growing evidence mostly in the Central Province for rectilinear, planned nucleations laid out in the late sixth or seventh centuries.[44] Almost all had some connection with the estate centres of the elite: some were royal, like those associated with the complexes at Yeavering and Milfield (Northumb.) and that at Wicken Bonhunt (Essex), where a large, deliberately planned, eighth-century settlement replaced an earlier nucleation; others were ecclesiastical like the planned towns set out alongside the newly founded royal abbeys at Whitby (Yorks.) and Hartlepool (Cleve.) in the late seventh century.[45] A large regular, planned settlement was laid out in about 720 at North Elmham (Norf.) around the episcopal centre of the Bishops of East Anglia.[46] Other high-status nucleations of the same period include the planned settlements of the sixth and seventh centuries focused on a substantial hall at Cowdery's Down (Hants.), and at Foxleys (Wilts.), where there was an apsidal church (Figures 6(a) and (c)).[47] In Northamptonshire, high-status sites with good evidence for middle Anglo-Saxon nucleation include Raunds, Brixworth, Higham Ferrers and Irthlingborough.[48] A nucleated settlement was laid out at Chalton (Hants.) in the seventh century, its houses set out 'in rows running across the ridge of the down and at a slight angle to its true axis'.[49] A huge, planned village covering 40 acres, flourished at West Heslerton (Yorks.) between the mid-fifth and mid-ninth centuries and a similar settlement of the early seventh to the early eleventh centuries at Flixborough (Lincs.) underwent several phases of replanning before it was finally abandoned.[50] At Wharram Percy (Yorks.) an eighth- or ninth-century nucleated settlement that may have included an estate centre and other buildings was inserted into a pre-existing layout provided by Romano-British fields.[51]

Similar planning was undertaken on estates' subsidiary manors. The Abbey at Ely may have been responsible for a substantial planned settlement at its berewick at Brandon (Suff.), formally divided between a large industrial quarter for the weaving, dyeing and export of cloth and the church and other buildings of the monks.[52] A planned nucleation was laid out at the stock-rearing settlement at Pennyland (Bucks.) in the late sixth or early seventh century and at other 'peasant' settlements where renders were collected, like those at Cottenham (Cambs.), Thwing (E. Yorks.), Bramford (Suff.) and Wormegay (Norf.).[53] Renders were collected at the middle Anglo-Saxon complex at Higham Ferrers, which included an enclosure for stock, storehouses and barns, on behalf of the royal estate centred on Irthlingborough (both Northants.); renders may also have been collected at the royal vill at Wicken Bonhunt (Essex).[54] A planned seventh-century settlement at Sempringham in Lincolnshire might be that of the berewick whose render to the Abbey at Peterborough was recorded in an agreement of 852.[55] Fieldwork on the eastern fringes of the Central Province at places like Horningtoft, Wellingham, Longham, Mileham and Weasenham All Saints (all Norf.) indicate a middle Anglo-Saxon origin for settlement nucleations.[56] Zoning of industrial or artisanal areas was also a feature of Frankish estates, of which well-known examples include Karlburg and Soest (both Germany).

The apparent significance of settlement nucleation at aristocratic estate centres or their berewicks, many within the Central Province, is underscored by their absence from low status sites. Most middle Anglo-Saxon settlements from Lincolnshire to Northamptonshire and Staffordshire were unplanned, and their boundaries bore no relation to those of the medieval settlements which succeeded them at some point between the ninth and the eleventh or twelfth centuries.[57] A unique insight into contemporary middle Anglo-Saxon perceptions of what a minor settlement 'should' look like, untrammeled by inheritance of past boundaries and land-use, can be found on the Norfolk silt fens, on the eastern edge of Midland England. The region only became available for settlement in the middle Anglo-Saxon period by which time any remains of earlier landscapes had been buried under metres of sub-Roman silt. It may be significant, then, that seventh-, eighth- and ninth-century settlements on the silt fens were generally unplanned, irregular and polyfocal in character.[58]

In conclusion, then, the first post-Roman nucleated settlements in England were laid out on high-status demesnes or their dependent settlements over the course of the long eighth century, particularly on royal and monastic estates. They appear to have predated the introduction of wide CPrRs over open-field arable by several centuries. Yet they cannot have been an integral aspect of the emergence of open-field systems managed under narrow CPrRs which had a much older history (and which could be found across medieval England, far beyond the Central Province). If nucleated settlements were a shared attribute of English champion and Frankish *champagne pays*, how accurate are Pounds' and Verhulst's conclusions that they appeared on high-status estates in the Carolingian heartlands at more or less at the same time that they were introduced in England?[59]

Settlement nucleation in Francia

Nucleation was not a new phenomenon in the Carolingian world. Late Roman and Merovingian planned settlements have been identified, for example, at Bielefeld-Sieker (Germany), at Vorbasse (Jutland) and Wijster (Netherlands).[60] What *was* new over the course of the long eighth century was the striking growth in numbers of planned settlements in the heartlands of Francia, on Carolingian royal demesnes and vast newly granted estates belonging to the ecclesiastical and secular elite in northern France, the Paris basin, in Friesland and around Ghent.[61] Dispersed farms and hamlets at Dommelen and Geldrop (both Netherlands) were replaced between 650 and 720 by nucleated settlements in just the same period in which estates there were granted to Willibrord; the nucleation of settlement around 700 in the Kempen region between the Meuse, Demer and Scheldt (also Netherlands) has similarly been ascribed to 'part of an organisation of the cultural landscape and hence of the landed property and the agrarian production'.[62] An informal seventh-century settlement at Odoorn was replanned in about 700 on a grid plan based on track ways, like those at Kootwijk and Gasselte (all Netherlands).[63] Planned nucleations also proliferated in on high-status sites in Carolingian Germany. A substantial estate at Lauchheim may have belonged to and been managed by 'leading members' of a plutocratic aristocratic dynasty who laid out a planned nucleated settlement there in the mid-seventh century.[64] The Abbey of Lorsch seems to have laid out at least two large planned settlements near its estate centre in the ninth century, and further planned settlements appeared at Vöhingen in the south-west; a nucleation of about 12 farms was laid out along a north-south track way at mid-seventh century Kirchheim near Munich, while a planned settlement – including a church – was set out not far away at Aschheim.[65] Nitz has argued that the Carolingian conquest of the Hassegau was consolidated in a planned reorganisation of the landscape that included the imposition of planned, nucleated settlement at places like Bischdorf, Underregenbach and Körbisdorf.[66]

Nucleated settlement, apparently a key attribute of open landscapes on either side of the Channel, appears to have emerged in both regions in the long eighth century. Is the coincidence accidental or deliberate? The remainder of this chapter explores the possibility that they were just one facet of common approaches adopted by middle Anglo-Saxon and Frankish elites to improving the productive efficiency of their demesnes, including which some of the characteristics that were much later to develop into wide CPrRs over English open-field arable. That possibility is investigated through four sub-questions:

1 To what extent did Carolingian and middle Anglo-Saxon elites share the same cultural values and how easily could ideas be communicated between them? If the underlying values of the two groups were quite different and/or it was difficult for them to communicate with each other, then the likelihood that any similarities were deliberate rather than accidental becomes more remote.
2 How much commonality was there between royal and aristocratic elites on either side of the Channel in motive, opportunity

and means for improving the productivity of their extensive estates over the course of the long eighth century? Even if both groups shared the same values and could share ideas quite straightforwardly, they would be less likely to implement the same strategies on their respective landholdings unless such innovations were focused on similar aims and unless they had the appropriate skills to implement them.

3 On the other hand, commonality between both groups may not have been translated into action on extensive estates either in Francia or in middle Anglo-Saxon England. Is there any evidence that that agricultural productivity was actually improved on the estates of the elite in each region?

4 And finally, what (if any) is the evidence in the landscape on either side of the Channel of the introduction of practical measures aimed at greater control of the management and production of agricultural surpluses and of the labour necessary to deliver them?

The kingdom of Mercia over the long eighth century

The major kingdoms of middle Anglo-Saxon England came to their full flowering in the long eighth century between about 670 and 850. Among them, Mercia was pre-eminent in the sophistication of its administrative structure and in its domination of England for nearly two centuries from the late seventh until the later ninth century. At its height, greater Mercia included the Midlands and Middle Anglia, parts of Berkshire, Oxfordshire, Buckinghamshire and Hertfordshire, Lindsey, Elmet and Deira, and eastern, central and south-eastern Wales (Figure 8).[67] Further afield, the kingdoms and sub-kingdoms of Wessex, Surrey, Sussex, Kent, Middlesex, Essex and East Anglia all recognised Mercian overlordship.

Grants of enormous estates by charter – principally to members of the royal families and to high-ranking churchmen, but also to ealdormen, and initially almost exclusively for the foundation of

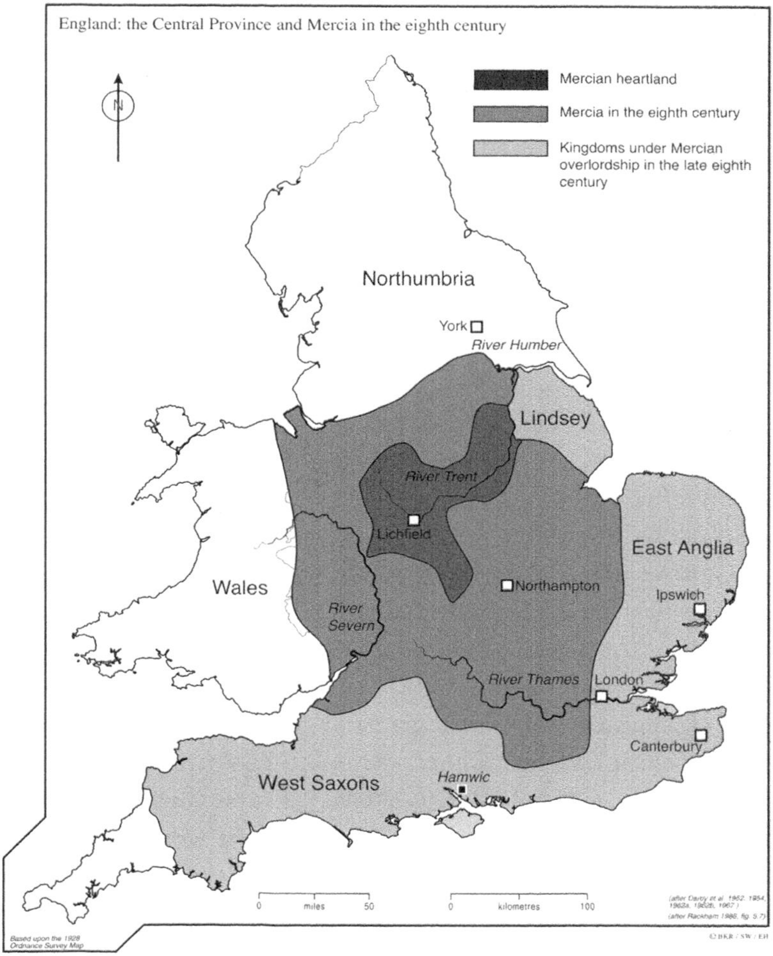

Figure 8. The Mercian hegemony at its greatest extent, about 800.

ecclesiastical houses – were creatively used by middle Anglo-Saxon kings, especially in Mercia, in the construction and consolidation of their kingdoms. As Bassett has observed, such grants offered at least a partial solution to 'one of the hardest problems which faced a successful early medieval ruler – how to hold the kingdom together once it had outgrown what he and those around him could control in person'.[68]

The vast estates and the charters that accompanied them performed this role in a number of ways. First, their dynastic and secular connections enabled middle Anglo-Saxon kings to achieve long-term 'power and wealth based on the exclusive control of land' for their kinfolk, the founders and/or abbots/abbesses of many of the ecclesiastical houses (generally minsters) that received grants of vast estates in this period.[69] The inalienability of such estates was reinforced by the development of saintly cults focused on a (frequently royal) member of the founder's family like Æbbe (died 694), the Abbess of Minster-in-Thanet, who was the 'daughter of King Eormenred of Kent, sister of three saints ... and mother of four others'.[70] The monastic house at Wenlock (Salop.) is another typical example: 'It was founded in the mid- to late seventh century by Merewalh, a son of Penda, whose daughter Mildburg later became abbess, part of 'a branch of the Mercian royal family, characterised by distinctive alliterating names, which established a dynastic monastery in its own province, and entrusted to it one of its own members, quickly recognised as a saint'.[71] The estate eventually swelled to 220 hides, receiving further grants from Mildburg's two brothers, Merchelm and Mildfrith, and her relation, King Ceolred. Second, kings could use such grants of land by charter as a means to 'insert their own men within, and assert their own authority over, the kingdoms that bordered their own'.[72] In this way, for example, previously peripheral regions like Middle Anglia were brought into greater Mercia at various times over the long eighth century, and Mercian overlordship was extended over the kingdoms of Kent, the Hwicce and the South Saxons. Third, the innovative requirement from the mid-eighth century for the owners of large 'bookland' estates, particularly those in Mercia, to contribute to the three 'common burdens' (provision of men for the *ffyrd*, and for the construction and repair of public fortifications, and of roads and bridges) provided a vested interest for private estates in maintaining their public obligations since they also benefited from the protection of the local armies they helped to maintain at regional defended *burhs*, which included bridges and markets, at nodal intersections of major roads and rivers such as Hereford, Tamworth, Winchcombe, Nottingham and, perhaps, Stamford, Gloucester, Worcester and Chester.[73] The safeguards of state authority and commercial activity therefore became at least partially embedded in the interests of privatised landed property.[74]

An integrated hierarchy of trading networks developed within a 'highly active' internal economy that linked the great *emporia* at *Hamwic*, London, Ipswich and York with defended *burhs*, high-status estate centres and their 'productive' berewicks, and temporary markets or fairs set up in fields for a few days a year, each with its own greater or smaller hinterland.[75] The network of *burhs* almost certainly constructed across greater Mercia in the long eighth century may have generated demand for agricultural surpluses, at very least to feed the labour provided for the construction and maintenance of their defences; it is probable that they also acted as locally and regionally important markets and centres for trade, protected within the walls of the *burh*.[76] At Hereford, for example, the *burh* included an industrial and trading centre; almost all the other Mercian *burhs* have survived as county towns drawing produce in from and distributing goods within their hinterlands, and connecting local and regional markets with national (and international) trading networks.[77] Ecclesiastical estates, too, integrated lordship and economy, offering 'estate and production centres, markets, protected zones, shrines, mausolea of the great, and sources of charity'.[78] At the same time, the first known post-Roman investment in roads and bridges sustained by the great estates through the 'common burden' of bridge-work created a transport infrastructure that offered access to trade by river and sea within the security offered by the *ffyrd*.[79] Rapid economic innovation and growth was further stimulated by royal control of the production and value of a coinage which was 'not only integrated regionally, with the *wic* as the focal point, but … also displayed the free movement of currency between regions (and between kingdoms)' in a complex trading system operating through a hierarchy of economic centres at local, regional, national and international level.[80]

The transition during the long eighth century from a predominantly pastoral to a predominantly arable rural economy occurred within the context of increasingly specialised agricultural production and rural industry on minster and other estates, especially those owned or controlled by royal kin, high-ranking churchmen, and the secular aristocracy.[81] Enormous ecclesiastical estates, whose piously drafted charters may have underplayed their commercial potential, and those of the secular elite acted as collecting centres for agricultural surpluses and provided foci for trade and exchange.[82] The link between estate centres and the wider economy has been concisely expressed by Moreland: 'By the beginning of the eighth century (at the latest) central places had emerged in the English countryside in and through which secular and ecclesiastical elites channelled the fruits of regional production *and* long-distance trade'.[83] By the middle of the eighth century, there was a growing group of kings, nobles and churchmen, many connected by kinship and sharing a common religious and classical culture, who had an interest in managing and extending the economic efficiency and profitability of their newly acquired vast estates and especially of their core demesnes. Royal, ecclesiastical and secular owners seem to have sought common solutions to the challenges of ensuring the agricultural profitability and efficiency of their extensive estates over the long eighth century. They did not do so in insular isolation.

The commonalities between Carolingian and Middle Anglo-Saxon elites

The substantial cultural values and other commonalities between Carolingian and middle Anglo-Saxon kings and their aristocratic and ecclesiastical elites, now owners of vast estates, were largely derived from the long shadow cast by the Roman empire over its former provinces. Nelson, for example, has argued that in Francia parents and teachers perpetuated Roman traditions within their families and estates, even though the structures of Roman administration and government had largely withered and disappeared.[84] The late fifth-century leadership of

Ambrosius Aurelianus embodies these characteristics: his Latin name, his high rank, his kinship and his landownership were each important signifiers of his authority and legitimacy.[85] Similar evocations influenced Anglo-Saxon kings and aristocracy, like the sixth-century kings buried at Sutton Hoo who 'seem to have been dressing up as Romans – claiming a right to rule as the spiritual descendants of the Roman emperors'.[86] Henig has gone so far as to suggest that England 'can still be regarded as culturally late Roman' in the seventh and eighth centuries even though Romano-British material culture had disappeared with remarkable swiftness.[87]

Such values were not developed in isolation. Charlemagne and Offa were active participants in diplomatic linkages connecting them with the eastern empire and beyond. Charlemagne received legations from Byzantium and was sufficiently prominent for the caliph of Baghdad to send an elephant to him at Aachen in 801–802, while Offa modelled one of his coins on an Arab dinar, as goods from all over Europe, the Middle and Far East found their way into Frankish and English ports and into the graves of the elite.[88] Some Byzantine coins, spoons and other artefacts excavated in sixth- and early seventh-century graves may have been diplomatic gifts sent by Emperors in Constantinople to subordinate kings around the periphery of their empire. Harris has proposed that, across western Europe, 'indigenous political authority grew out of a relationship with the East in which the Emperor in Constantinople was seen as legitimizing the rule of western elites'.[89] While this conclusion might be a little more emphatic than the evidence allows, it would nonetheless not have injured any English ruler (or those aspiring to his throne) to be able to demonstrate to both his peers and his subjects that he was an influential, well-connected (and more or less equal) member of a royal network that stretched across the late Roman empire. The hegemony of the Mercian kings over most of England south (and, occasionally, north) of the Humber was such that, 'although the ruling elite of other Anglo-Saxon kingdoms ... had independent connections with the Carolingians, much of the Frankish response to them was conditioned by the state of Frankish diplomacy with Mercia'.[90]

Diplomacy, trade and travel throughout the long eighth century were underpinned by 'interlocking networks of personal friendships, kin groups and political ties'.[91] Synods in Italy, Germany and England were attended by British and European churchmen and Offa and Charlemagne frequently corresponded with each other and with churchmen and aristocrats at each other's courts.[92] Churchmen, kings and aristocrats moved between England and mainland Europe on business, to trade, as missionaries, to marry, or to found or enter monastic houses. Benedict Biscop frequently travelled between Jarrow and Rome in the seventh century; Cuthwine, Bishop of East Anglia and Willibald of Wessex and his family followed him in the eighth; Augustine and Felix of Burgundy, Theodore of Tarsus in Asia Minor and Hadrian, a Latin-speaking African, all took up senior roles in the British church in the seventh century; English missionaries worked in Frisia in the late seventh century and in Germany in the eighth century, while Alcuin, 'the last great scholar of Bede's school', held a prominent place at Charlemagne's court for 14 years between 781 and 795.[93] English kings and aristocrats who travelled to Gaul in the seventh century included Sigeberht, later King of East Anglia, Æthelburh, Queen of Northumbria and Egbert of Wessex (and also, perhaps in the last decades of the eighth, Eadburh, Offa's daughter).[94] Seventh-century Kentish, East Anglian and Northumbrian princesses entered monastic houses at Faremoutier-en-Brie and Chelles (both France), while others married into royal families across the Channel, like Bertha, the Frankish princess who married Æthelbert of Kent in the late sixth century or Charlemagne's granddaughter Judith who married Æthelwulf of Wessex in 856.[95]

Across western Europe the legitimacy, authority, and grandeur of rulers and their elites were demonstrated through deliberately constructed references to Rome.[96] Offa, Charlemagne and Coenwulf minted coins based on late Roman or Byzantine models and their recognition of the strategic value of the iconography of coinage shows a sophisticated understanding of its contribution as a visible reminder of royal power and authority when 'even the poorest might have a coin or two in their purse'.[97] The Roman *imperium* was explicitly referenced in high-status architecture for which Roman ruins were plundered by priests and kings in constructing churches such as those at Brixworth (Northants.) and Hexham (Northumb.), or the Carolingian palaces at Paderborn, Ingelheim or Iphofen (all Germany).[98] The re-use of Roman building materials was accompanied by a renaissance of classical architectural forms, the combination offering powerful 'new symbols of imperial aspirations'.[99] The plans of St John Lateran and St Peter's in Rome were the models for churches constructed by Augustine at Canterbury and Boniface in Germany; the layout of mausolea closely associated with the development of royal saintly cults like those at Repton (Derbys.) and Werden (Germany) was also based on Roman buildings.[100] Even construction techniques were shared: the large cement mixers found at Northampton, Wearmouth and Duxford, all from high-status sites and with dates ranging from the late seventh to the tenth centuries, are exactly like the 14 excavated at Wellin (Belgium), Mönchengladbach, Schüttern, Paderborn and Tilleda (all Germany) and Lindenhof (Switzerland).[101] The designs of most surviving Anglo-Saxon sculpted stone are based on late antique or Byzantine forms, such as those at Breedon-on-the-Hill, the Lichfield Angel (apparently carved in the late eighth century for Offa's new cathedral), or the warrior horseman of the Repton stone (perhaps a portrait of Æthelbald of Mercia).[102] The English revival of classical styles in decorative art was paralleled on the continent where the walls of the palace built by Louis the Pious at Ingelheim were decorated with paintings of the emperors Constantine and Theodosius.[103]

Nor was it only materials that were re-used: rebuilding on Roman sites sometimes incorporated the remains of earlier structures. Early Anglo-Saxon mausolea and chapels were constructed within the Roman cemeteries at St Albans, the Bapistry and Cathedral at Aix-en-Provence (France) lie on the site of the forum, while the Baptistry and chapel at Seviac (France) and at Tholey (Germany) were each built on the ruins of a Roman villa.[104] Cramp has vividly described how the architecture and materials of the seventh-century monastery at Jarrow deliberately referenced that of the Roman world: tall stone buildings whose walls were plastered and painted, floored with red concrete, roofed with stone slate – perhaps leaded – and whose windows held coloured glass, all produced by skilled, peripatetic craftsmen who moved from site to site across Europe.[105]

A shared conceptual vocabulary is also visible in the overall similarities in form to Roman law-codes (rather than detailed content) in charters used by kings in Francia and in England and, later, by the church for grants of land. Charters provided a legal form on both sides of the Channel for the transfer of perpetual rights in land to families and away from communities, while the Theodosian code formed the basis in both eighth-century Mercia and in ninth-century Francia for the imposition of the 'three universal obligations': military service, the construction of public defences and the maintenance of roads and bridges.[106] The development and regulation of new, more restricted rights over property and the imposition of public duties were legitimated in both England and Francia through references to Roman practice.[107]

The commonality of values and attitudes that underpinned such references to the Roman empire were deliberately fostered by the church, based in Rome, communicating across polyglot Europe through the medium of a single language – Latin. The works of classical authors were widely disseminated through the church and contributed to an active pan-European community of scholarship. Manuscripts like Penitentials and Canons moved between libraries and individuals over wide distances, like the fifth-century manuscript of Jerome's commentary on *Ecclesiastes* which belonged to the abbess of a royal Mercian nunnery in about AD 700 and had reached Germany by the end of the eighth century.[108] Church and kings colluded in manipulating divine authority to legitimate their claims to their crowns: Pope Stephen II anointed Pippin and his sons in 754; Pope Leo III astonished Europe by crowning Charlemagne as Holy Roman Emperor in 814; and Offa attempted to establish an archbishopric in Mercia as part of his plans for the consecration of his son Ecgfrith in 781.[109]

Dedications of royal churches to St Peter, annual payments to Rome and the foundation of royal saintly cults further reinforced constructed connections between kingship and godliness.[110]

Such commonalities were not the result of the diffusion or transmission of ideas from one side of the Channel to another, or derived from the dominant influence of one kingdom or the other, but evolved from 'a universal basis', a shared *Romanitas*.[111] As Helen Cam noted almost century ago, 'the resemblances are found to be numerous, yet in no case [are they] so strong as to suggest the direct indebtedness of one country to another'.[112] Almost a century later, this conclusion still holds in, to take just one example, Story's description of the 'dynamic political and cultural relationship between the Anglo-Saxon kingdoms and Charlemagne's Francia'.[113] This is not, of course, to argue for uniformity in elite culture on either side of the Channel. What is suggested is that Anglo-Saxon and Carolingian kings and aristocracies shared the same underlying values, the detail of whose expression varied depending on place, context and date. Yet a coincidence of values could only be useful in the development of common strategies for the management of extensive estates if their Frankish and middle Anglo-Saxon owners were not only influenced by similar motives and opportunities, but also shared the same means for their implementation. How many of the changes introduced in the landscapes at the centres of extensive estates during the long eighth century might be attributed to the implementation of new strategies for their management and exploitation?

Opportunities, motives, and means

Extensive estates granted by early medieval kings to their kin or high-status members of their courts were found on both sides of the Channel, similar in extent, origin and structure, providing Carolingian and Anglo-Saxon elites with similar opportunities for economic exploitation. The ecclesiastical estate originally belonging to a seventh- or eighth-century monastic house at Hanbury (Worcs.) and described in detail in a charter of 836, for example, was made up of at least 11 contiguous vills, while St Cuthbert received an estate called Cartmell in the mid-seventh century which included townships at Holker, Allithwaite, Brouth, Staveley and Cartmell Fell.[114] The extensive estate granted by Charlemagne to his newly founded abbey at Lorsch (Germany) in 773 included the whole of the 'mark' of Heppenheim, while his own estate at Annappes (France) held over 2,000 hectares.[115] Not all were consolidated in this way; some were made up of dispersed parcels, like the demesnes of the seventh-century monastic house at Peterborough which included not only the enormous region around the abbey, now called the soke of Peterborough, but also land at Brixworth (Northants.) and Breedon-on-the-Hill (Leics.). The royal estates around Carolingian Maastricht (Netherlands) and those of the seventh-century Abbey of Wissembourg (Germany) were similarly scattered.[116]

At its most reductive, agricultural production on extensive estates was focused on requirements for the day-to-day support of estate owners and their households. Food renders appear to have been more or less universal across western Europe in the long eighth century, even if their expression may at times have been more normative than real. In 852 the Abbey at Peterborough expected their estate at Sempringham (Lincs.) to deliver '60 fothers of wood … and 12 fothers of brushwood and 6 fothers of faggots …., 2 casks of clear ale and 2 cattle for slaughter and 600 loaves and 10 mittan of Welsh ale'; in addition, they required 'every year a horse and 30 shillings and … one day's food-rent – 15 mittan of clear ale and 5 mittan of Welsh ale and 15 sesters of mild ale'.[117] The normative expectations of Charlemagne's *Capitulare de Villis* of about the same period were similar: two-thirds of tenants' production of 'vegetables, fish, cheese, butter, honey, mustard, vinegar, millet, panic, dried and green herbs, radishes and, in addition, of the wax, [and] soap'.[118] Both are very like those of estate centres in eighth-century Ireland which required the delivery of 'live animals, meat, grain, malt, bread, milk, cheese, butter, vegetables'.[119]

Aristocratic and ecclesiastical lords needed their estates to produce agricultural surpluses too. They had to be of sufficient quantity and quality to satisfy more structured and more intensive demands for renders and manpower from the state, as well as to satisfy the requirements of the conspicuous consumption that gave material expression to their own status. Surpluses could also be invested in the extensive trade in a wide range of luxury and everyday goods that blossomed across Europe in the same period, generating investment capital and providing another means of supporting an expensive lifestyle.

Kings deliberately focused on building and sustaining carefully regulated infrastructures to stimulate and support the development of stable trading conditions. Charlemagne and Offa each developed trading standards, imposed tolls, created a single currency under royal control (in 771 and 792 respectively) and standardised the weight and design of coins. They established commercial centres (*emporia*) and centres for secondary production at places such as Dorestad (Netherlands) and Quentovic (France), or *Hamwic* (Hants.), Ipswich (Suff.), London and York (Yorks.), as well as formally controlled markets in defended *burhs*.[120] Hodges has suggested that it was Offa's capture of London and Kent and the extensive trading networks that they controlled that put him on an equal footing with Charlemagne.[121] They profited, too, from the collection of tolls and the maintenance of monopolies. The estate-owning elites within their kingdoms benefited from secure trading conditions within which their surpluses could be exchanged for capital or goods; both were increasingly bound together in common economic and political interests.[122]

An integrated hierarchy of local, regional and national markets across Anglo-Saxon England provided outlets for the 'surpluses sold by minsters [which] would mainly have comprised agrarian bulk goods', while international trade was made up of 'small volume, high value' goods such as cloth, weapons, pottery, glassware and millstones.[123] Slaves and textiles, grain and fish, Rhenish querns, and Frankish and German pottery were widely traded between England, Francia, the lower Rhine and Meuse, Jutland and Scandinavia.[124] The minor port at Sandtun in Kent sent and received ships to and from the Meuse valley, western Belgium and Picardy throughout the eighth century.[125] A letter from Einhard to one of his deputies in 828 asking for 'flour, grain for brewing, wine, cheese and other things' to be sent to Charlemagne's palace at Aachen and for cattle to be taken the 6.4 km from Maastricht to Lanaeken for slaughter before being brought the additional 44 km to Aachen, vividly illuminates the ways in which estate centres might stimulate, contribute to and benefit directly from purchase and exchange.[126]

The scale of the surpluses produced through intensification of arable production on monastic and secular estates could be considerable: just 22 of the 84 mills on the estates of the Abbey of St Germain-des-Prés (France), for example, produced enough grain to feed the abbey – the output of the other 62 contributed to the abbey's disposable income.[127] There was a growing emphasis, too, on animal husbandry with a clear aim of developing specialised, industrialised production of animal commodities'.[128] Large quantities of pork were produced at royal centres at St Albans (Herts.) and Wicken Bonhunt (Essex), perhaps preserved as bacon and/or ham; Quarrington (Lincs.), Brandon and Bloodmoor Hill (both Suff.) and Yarnton (Oxon.) focused on the production of wool (and, perhaps, mutton), the latter possibly as a berewick of the Abbey at Eynsham.[129] Extensive estates in the Carolingian heartlands of northern France specialised in wool production, while the monastic site at Wandgries-Homage and the royal estate at Lille (both France) also focused on pork and its secondary products – the herds of swine at Lille contained over a thousand pigs, and it was not unusual for the meat from over 600 carcasses each year to be preserved through salting.[130]

The sale and exchange of such surpluses generated capital that paid for the import of, or supported the production of, luxury goods. Imported glassware graced the tables of middle Anglo-Saxon Flixborough where the hunt contributed part of the menu for high-status feasts, just like the ecclesiastical elite at Wandgries-Homage (France) who fed on large quantities of pork, sturgeon and 'exotic imported species'.[131] A late sixth- or early seventh-century Byzantine silk cloth was buried with St Cuthbert at Lindisfarne in 687, while the 157 calf-skins required for the production of the Gospels there required the maintenance of a herd of cattle large enough to graze 1,500 acres of pasture (and even more cows would have been needed to produce the female calves needed to renew the milch-herd and sufficient male calves for use as oxen).[132] The scale of what was involved can be gathered from the management of the Abbey of Peterborough's cattle herds in the early fourteenth century, when around half the animals were immature at any one time.[133]

Intensified production on this scale, involving the complex integration of estate output with household requirements, the industrialised manufacture of secondary goods and the requirements of trade demanded sophisticated methods of accounting to plan, keep track of and record the organisation and management of inputs (including labour services and renders) and outputs (yields of stock and milled and unthreshed grain), income (tolls, profits from trade), and expenditure.[134] Such innovations in managerial oversight could not have been undertaken without literate administrators. That monastic houses, so many of which were founded in this period, took the lead in responding to the new conditions seems to have been true both in Ireland, where 'it is likely that a number of agricultural innovations spread from Church farms' and in the heartlands of Carolingian Europe.[135] They had particular motives for making money – in the numbers of unproductive religious that they housed, in that they were not peripatetic so could not move from one estate to another as resources were exhausted, in their requirements for capital for investment in churches and monastic buildings, against possible future dearth, and in their needs for the luxury goods through which devotion was expressed. The monasteries also had the means, since they trained and supported a class of men who were literate enough to keep records, familiar with the administrative structures of the church and may well have been drawing information from classical texts.

The scale of the intensification of agricultural production on aristocratic estates in Francia and middle Anglo-Saxon England over the course of the long eighth century must have required sound, standardised administrative processes for 'accounting, inventorying and payment of renders [and revenues] to the court', ensuring and tracking a sufficient volume of labour and managing the logistical problems of moving goods across estates and between their centres and the royal court, markets and so on.[136] Whatever their actual purpose, the *polyptyques* from the core of Francia were drawn up on high-status estates which were also the *locus* for the discovery of styli, wax tablets and other evidence for writing just as estates at Flixborough (Lincs.), Brandon (Suff.), St Denis (France) and Paderborn, Corvey and Hamage (all Germany) show evidence for 'writing used both as a medium for record-keeping or other practical uses and as a medium of display'.[137] While it is true that no accounts of rents, income, sales or expenditure survive from this period, Sarris has suggested this may be because the shift from papyrus paper to parchment had not yet been completed; that is, that the absence is not because accounting was not practised, but because the materials on which they were recorded may have been ephemeral.[138]

There is enough evidence, then, to support the contention that aristocratic estate owners on both sides of the Channel were not only in frequent communication with each other and shared the same cultural values, but that they also shared motives, opportunities and means for implementing improvements in the management of their lands. They had a common interest in increasing the productive capacities of their extensive estates – for their own support, for dues owed to the state and for the generation of capital and purchase of luxury goods. A small class of literate men trained in the new monastic houses had the skills to develop sophisticated approaches to estate management. The argument moves on to consider the kinds of evidence which might demonstrate that such general strategies were in fact adopted: intensified agricultural production; strategic location of estate centres to maximise access to trading networks; greater formality in layout and architecture of elite centres; and formalised approaches to the organisation of dependent labour without whom additional arable acres could not be ploughed, sown and harvested.

Strategies for increasing productivity

Intensification of primary and secondary agricultural production

Chapter 3 noted that agricultural surpluses were produced in middle Anglo-Saxon England by expanding the acreage under cultivation, by changing the balance between cereal crops, by extending the use of the heavy plough and by taking a more structured approach to the maintenance of soil fertility. Conditions in the Frankish heartlands were no different. There was large-scale colonisation of new land from Westfriesland in Northern Holland and Saxony in Germany to Languedoc in southern France.[139] The heavy plough, perhaps introduced to Britain in the Roman period, had been used continuously in north-west Europe since the Iron Age and was widely adopted on Frankish estates.[140] As in England, arable cultivation overtook pastoral husbandry in the long eighth century; not only was there was a shift from hulled grains such as emmer and barley to naked grains like rye, oats and (where in appropriate conditions) wheat (although spelt continued to be cultivated in many places), but such crops also enabled the extension of arable cultivation on marginal soils so that 'sandy, sandy-loamy, and limestone soils in the early middle ages came to be used more intensively than the more fertile peat and clay soils'.[141] Surpluses could be substantial: at least a third of the total arable yield produced at Kootwijk (Netherlands) exceeded the needs of subsistence, while the barns at Dalem (Germany) could store far more grain than was required by the local community; similar conditions existed along the Kromme Rijn (Netherlands).[142] Substantial quantities of rye were imported from elsewhere into Feddersen Wierde (Germany), since it was not grown locally.[143] Although rye, barley and oats were the most commonly grown grains in the Rhineland and Germany, there was wide variation from place to place – across central Holland, for example, Odoorn in Drenthe and Dommelen specialised in rye, Kootwijk in oats.[144]

As in England, attention was paid to maintaining soil fertility on the inlands. Manure was augmented with turf before being spread on the sandy *essen* of seventh-century Lower Saxony and eighth-century Kootwijk (Netherlands), a technique that became widespread in north-west Germany and Belgium in the ninth and tenth centuries.[145] Yet evidence for the inclusion of fallowing in European crop rotations is variable and contradictory. The writers of the *polyptyques* seem to have taken fallowing for granted in their prescription for the subdivision of each *cultura* (the 'vast topographical units' which made up the demesne arable) into at least three parts, such that approximately equal proportions carried winter-sown wheat and either spring-sown barley or oats, while a third portion lay fallow.[146] It is just possible that fallowing is indicated by eighth-century treacle mustard pollen (*Erysimum cheiranthoides*) in the Kromme Rijn area of Holland and crop rotations that included fallowing may have been practised at Kootwijk (Netherlands); but the technique appears to have been absent in southern France.[147] As in England, arable productivity was improved not by increases in agricultural efficiency, but through bringing larger areas under the plough, the introduction of new crops, and attention to manuring.[148] A more formal system of crop rotation may have been a uniquely Frankish innovation. (This conclusion may be flawed – there is little or no reliable evidence for formal crop rotations in middle Anglo-Saxon England, perhaps because there is little documentary evidence similar to that of the *polyptiques*. It is a truism that absence of evidence is not evidence of absence.)

There was investment on both sides of the Channel, too, in infrastructure to support the secondary processing of primary products, especially of grain. Watermills proliferated in this period. They were constructed for the large-scale processing of far more grain than was required for subsistence and a number had more than one wheel. They have been excavated at Old Windsor (Berks.), Ebbsfleet and Northfleet (Kent), Nailsworth (Glos.), Wellington (Worcs.), Tamworth (Staffs.) and Corbridge (Northumb.).[149] One of the earliest recorded in place-names, at Mylentun (Kent) was granted by the king to the Archbishop of Canterbury in 822.[150] Those in the Paris basin have already been mentioned and were such an everyday feature of Carolingian estates that 'every valley in Neustria' (France), Flanders and in the Meuse-Demer-Scheldt region of the Netherlands had a watermill in the eighth century, while they were 'neither rare nor isolated' in Carolingian Languedoc.[151]

The production of cloth from wool and/or flax was undertaken at Cottam (Yorks.), Flixborough (Lincs.), Castor (Cambs.), Brandon (Suff.), Barking (Essex) and on estates in the Cotswolds.[152] Flocks and herds at Cottam and Flixborough supported the production of leather goods.[153] Iron-smelting was undertaken at Maxey (Northants.), Romsey (Hants.), Gillingham (Dorset) and Ramsbury (Wilts.). Salt was mined in Droitwich (Worcs.) and manufactured from brine on coastal salt marshes, facilitating the emergence of specialist beef rearing and pork pickling at Walpole St Andrew and Terrington St Clements (both Norf.).[154] In Francia, too, large numbers of immature beasts were brought to elite estate centres like Oost-Souberg (Netherlands), Sugny (Belgium), Paderborn and Karlburg (both Germany).[155] There is also plentiful evidence of interest in other forms of rural industrial production, including textile manufacture at Hessens and Höxter (Germany), huge volumes of flax produced on the estates of the abbeys of Lobbes, St Bertin (both Belgium) and Lorsch (Germany), an international market in Frisian cloth, pottery at Kootwijk and along the Meuse (Netherlands) as well as in the Eifel (Germany), iron-smelting in the Verluwe and at Hoog Buurlo-Braamberg (Netherlands), glass and metalworking at Paderborn Corvey (France), (Germany) and Develier-Courtételle (Switzerland) and salt production along the Friesland coasts and at Soest (Germany).[156]

It is plain, then, that agricultural production of both grain and animal products was intensified on extensive estates across England and Francia over the course of the long eighth century. How was this achieved?

Greater formality on estate centres of the elite

The authority and legitimacy of aristocratic, royal and monastic demands for agricultural surpluses was carefully articulated at estate centres. High-status Carolingian and middle Anglo-Saxon estate centres were deliberately established on, or with easy access to, navigable rivers that offered cost-effective and efficient connections between centre and outlying berewicks, as well as access to regional, national and international markets and trade.[157] Kings, abbots and princes processed and made other ceremonial voyages by boat, a dignified and stately form of transport. The Rhine connected royal palaces at Frankfurt or Ingelheim with the location of royal assemblies at Mainz and Worms and with the major monastic houses at Fulda and Lorsch – the royal mausoleum at the latter emerging as a 'special place of royal charisma', just as the Thames connected Westminster and Windsor, or the Trent (and its tributaries) Tamworth and Repton.[158] Ethelthryth's monastic house at Ely, for example, was built on the Cambridge Ouse which (at that time) flowed into the Wash through Wisbech linking Ely not only with the coastal ports of eastern England and the European mainland but also with large areas of central and eastern England along the Lark, Nene and Bedfordshire Ouse.[159] Similar geographies can be identified at most monastic houses of the period and at royal centres like Winchester or Northampton. Carolingian palaces at Frankfurt, Paderborn and Thionville (all Germany) were situated on major rivers (the Main, Lippe and Moselle) and monastic houses in the Paris basin with access to the Seine included St Denis and St Germain-des-Prés (France).[160] Access to hythes at the major ports was also in demand. The charter to Chertsey Abbey (Surrey) in 672–4 famously included land at the 'port of London, where ships come to land' and the port at Sandtun (Kent) was granted to Lyminge minster in 732, while a number of Frankish monasteries held land at the port of Quentovic (France), whose procurator was the abbot of Fontenelle.[161] Royal trading centres were established or refounded at Rijnsburg, which controlled access to and from the Rhine delta and at Medemblik on the Ijselmeer, as well as at Dorestad (all Netherlands) and Quentovic (France).[162]

Formal attention was paid to the layout of estate centres, both in the details of their construction and in careful zoning which separated the domestic and official structures of estate owners from those of the home farm and workshops.[163] The centre itself was frequently bounded by a grand ditch and, sometimes, a bank like that of the *Capitulare de Villis* which stipulated a geography for 'the buildings inside our demesnes, together with the fences around them'.[164] Many survive in the large oval *burhs* of eighth-century royal and monastic estate centres which lay within 'an imposing ditched (and probably also fenced)' enclosure like those at Lambourn (Berks.), Whittlebury (Northants.) and Kingsteighton (Wilts.), Compiègne (France) and Soest (Germany) (Figure 6(b)). The church and hall at a secular estate centre at Petegem on the Scheldt and at Thier d'Olne on the Meuse (both Belgium) were rebuilt in stone in the ninth century within a formally designed landscape bounded by ditches 7 m wide.[165]

The palace complexes of the Middle Anglo-Saxon kings at Yeavering (Northumb.), Cheddar (Som.) and Cowdery's Down (Hants.) included assembly places.[166] Clauses in the *Lex Baiuvariorum*, a compilation of sixth- to eighth-century Bavarian laws, imply that estate centres of Carolingian noblemen also held spaces intended for public assemblies, and examples have been identified at Carolingian royal centres like Paderborn, Frankfurt and Ingelheim (all Germany).[167] Their design was strikingly similar to the *airlisc* of contemporary Irish kings and monasteries whose boundaries also encompassed places of assembly and a green (*faithche*) for communal activities like horse-racing and ball-games.[168]

The religious connotations of political power were expressed in close connection between great hall and church and can be seen at the royal palaces at Yeavering (Northumb.) and Cowdery's Down (Hants.) as well as at Northampton (Northants.) and Wicken Bonhunt (Essex); Carolingian churches were integrated into secular centres at places such as Petegem (Belgium) and Thier d'Olne (France) mentioned above, and at palaces like that at Aachen (Germany), where church and palace were integrated by architecture and alignment: 'the palace complex consisted of a hall and church, both oriented on an east-west axis and connected at their western ends by an elevated gallery'.[169]

Monumentality and formality in the architecture of halls and palaces further expressed and displayed the power and status of their royal and aristocratic owners. The enormous eighth-century stone hall at Northampton was modelled on similarly large late eighth-century Carolingian palaces at St Denis and Compiègne (both France), Mellier (Belgium), Aachen, Ingelheim, Frankfurt, Paderborn, Tilleda (all Germany) and Lindenhof (Switzerland).[170] Royal and aristocratic 'great halls', often more than 100m^2 in area, were constructed in wood like those at Yeavering (Northumb.), Cowdery's Down (Hants.) and Cheddar (Som.), the timbers used for their construction becoming heavier and their architecture more imposing and monumental, reflecting the growing complexity in the number, use and organisation of the subordinate structures surrounding them.[171] The average area of most Anglo-Saxon buildings was around 5m by 10m; by contrast, the royal and aristocratic halls at Cheddar, Cowdery's Down, Doon Hill, Thirlings, Yeavering, Atcham, Malmesbury, Milfield and Sprouston were over 7.5m wide and most were over 15m long.[172] The contemporary description of the early ninth-century Carolingian palace at Ingelheim (Germany) demonstrates how architecture, layout and materials were combined not only to make a vivid statement of the owner's power, status and wealth, but also to provide a visual metaphor for the formal control, organisation and management of the wider kingdom and estate:

> A royal house, well built of stone, with three chambers; the whole house surrounded by galleries, with 11 rooms for women; underneath, one cellar; two porches; 17 other houses inside the courtyard, built of wood, with as many rooms and with the other amenities all in good order; one stable, one kitchen, one bakehouse, two barns, three haylofts. A courtyard with a strong palisade and a stone gateway with a gallery above from which to make distributions. A smaller courtyard similarly enclosed with a palisade, well ordered and planted with various kinds of trees.[173]

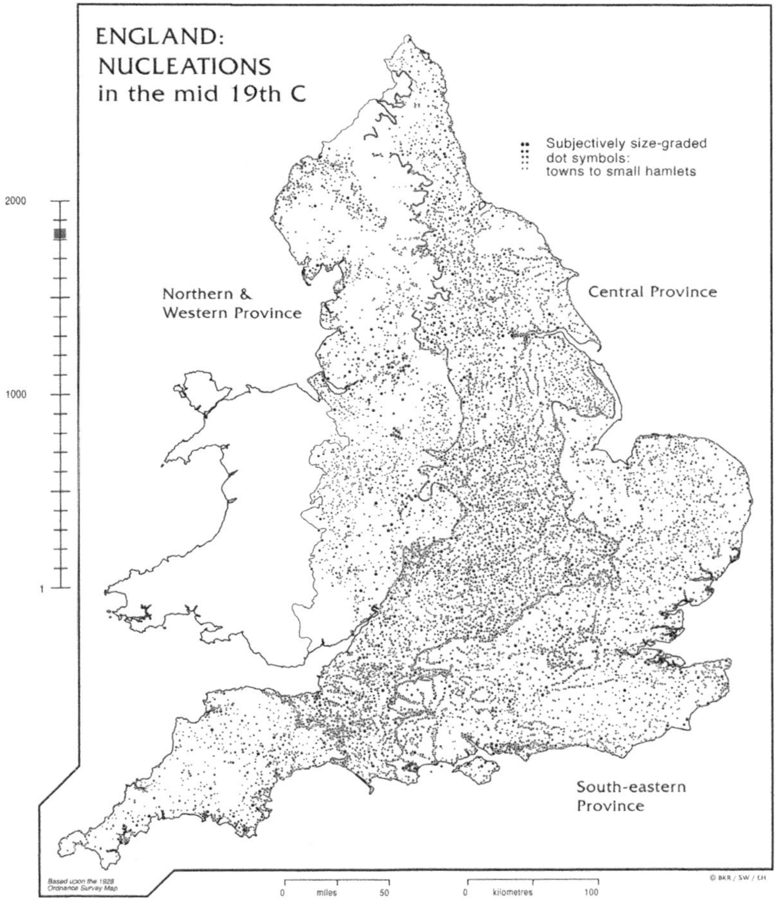

Figure 9. Nucleated settlement in England in the nineteenth century. (Reproduced with permission from Roberts and Wrathmell 2002).

Greater formality in the organisation of dependent labour

Estate managers could approach the practical challenges of increasing the volume of agricultural surpluses in two ways: either by taking greater control of the direction of cultivation on the demesnes, or by 'outsourcing' the problem to tenants on the demesnes whose responsibility it then became to produce greater quantities of primary goods in any way they saw fit. They seem to have adopted both approaches.

There are clauses in the late seventh-century laws of King Ine that appear to differentiate between two methods for managing the arable demesne. The criterion that later seventh-century men seem to have used was whether or not such arable was '*gesette*'. Aston interpreted the difference as being between those parts of the demesne that were directly cultivated by the estate (also called 'inlands') and those parts of the demesne that were leased to tenants ('*gesette*').[174] An eighth-century charter for Talton and Newbold in Tredington (Warwicks.) seems to be based on the same distinction, recording that 'the inland [was] in addition' to the land cultivated by tenants, while at Tidenham (Glos.) a tenth-century charter distinguished between '9 hides of *inlandes* and 21 hides of *gesettes landes* [tenanted land]'.[175] Similar distinctions between the *mansus indominicatus*, the directly cultivated inlands of high-status royal and monastic estates of the Carolingian empire and demesnes leased to peasants are visible in the *polyptyques*.[176] Nevertheless, there was substantial variation between estates in the proportion of land that they held in demesne and the ratios of inland to leased land. On some estates, there was little or no inland and all surpluses were produced by tenants from land held on a lease, as happened in parts of Northumbria and on some of the later ninth-century manors of the abbey of Prüm (Germany) in the Ardennes and on the Meuse, as well as in Flanders.[177] On others, a large area of inland might dominate the estate.

Much of the labour on directly cultivated inland was provided by groups of dependent tenants who were housed on the demesne and received some support in food and other goods in return for labour services.[178] These populations were found across Francia, middle Anglo-Saxon England – where they survived long enough to be called *inmanni* ('the people of the inland') in thirteenth-century Kent – and Wales.[179] They received food and other goods from the *curia* since, as Faith has argued, the small gardens or plots attached to their cottages 'were of a size well calculated to prevent them from becoming independent'.[180] In early medieval Wales, for example, their shared holdings were 'gardens' of about an acre rather than arable field lands and 'appear to have been arranged in a radial fashion around a nucleus of some kind, such as that containing a church'.[181] Whether the imposition of labour services on the inland was an innovation of the long eighth century remains controversial, although there is little contention about their intensification 'all over the northern half of the Carolingian empire from the Seine to the Danube' in that period.[182] Sarris has suggested that demesnes cultivated by the labour services of a specialised, unfree group of inland tenants might be 'identifiable in Gaul and Francia from the early fifth century through to the late seventh', in an organisational form that may have been inherited from late Roman estate structures.[183] Barnwell too has explored the similarities between dependent tenants, described as *hlafæta* in early sixth-century Kent, *farae* in sixth-century Burgundy and Lombardy, and late Roman *bucellarii* ('bread-eaters') who were supported by a lord's estate in return for services.[184]

Such forms of unfree labour service had been common on late Roman villa estates in Britain and may have been long-lived institutions: by the later eleventh century dependent tenants whose labour was specifically focused on the cultivation of the inland could be found in the *bordarii* of Domesday Book whose name derived from the lord's '*bord*' or table and share a common linguistic origin with the medieval *bordiers* of northern France – 'smallholders holding small allotments of land by particularly servile tenure'.[185] On the other hand, a model of direct linear development from late Roman to early medieval estate administration is certainly too simplistic. More likely is the gradual, if uneven, evolution from a combination of inherited and new conditions – existing servile labour on inland demesnes, the imposition of new labour services on both free and unfree tenantry, and the negotiated absorption of free smallholders into recently granted estates.[186]

The labour services of inland populations were unlikely to have been sufficient to produce the higher volumes of agricultural surpluses required by their new middle Anglo-Saxon lords. Additional labour inputs could have been achieved by leasing the remaining demesne on both middle Anglo-Saxon England and Frankish estates to tenants in return for a range of renders and services presaging, but not identical to, those of the eleventh century.[187] Labour services were attached to measured plots of arable land where the lease also included a house: the late seventh-century laws of King Ine specified that

> if anyone covenants for a yardland or more at a fixed rent and ploughs it, if the lord wishes to increase for him the [rent of the] land by demanding service as well as rent, he need not accept it, if he does not give him a dwelling; and he is to forfeit the crops.[188]

The significance of Ine's law is the connection it makes between a lord's right to demand labour services and the provision of a dwelling with leased arable land.[189] In early medieval Wales, too, the holdings of hereditary, unfree bond tenants included both a house and arable lands in open fields.[190] Yardlands, as Faith has pointed out, are measured units of land about a rod in width and about a furlong in length, approximately a quarter of an acre in area and sufficient to provide for the support of a household over the course of a year.[191]

The leased farms lying outside the inlands of high-status Carolingian estates also included both houses and farmbuildings as well as sufficient land for a household's support.[192] A normative statement of the labour services supposed to be provided by 58 leased holdings at Wissembourg (Germany) in the second decade of the ninth century offers an example of what lords had in mind:

> In the months of July and August each one owes service one day a week. After these two months they owe service one day a week and send one man to work in the vineyards; two to plough *iurnales*. Each one pays one hundred poles and one measure of timber, seventeen chickens and fifteen eggs. Above and beyond that they owe a fortnight's service once a year. Once a year they also help make wine in Unkenstein. They supply two horses to the army, give *barefrida* to the servants of the king and likewise owe service to the abbot here and in the neighbouring mansion [at Altenstadt].[193]

If Anglo-Saxon and Carolingian kings, abbots and aristocrats shared common goals of increasing the agricultural efficiency on their extensive estates over the long eighth century, what were the practical strategies that were adopted in each region and to what extent were they similar?

Practical strategies for implementing the drive to great agricultural production

Three innovations can be discerned in the landscapes of Carolingian and middle Anglo-Saxon estates which may have been aimed at improving their productivity: greater supervision of the dependent tenantry in planned, nucleated settlements; formal layouts of inlands; and structured design of the leased demesne.

While inland populations made an important contribution to labour inputs, these were insufficient without the weekwork provided by leaseholding tenants. Both needed careful timetabling and accounting not only to match the number of works and the range of tasks to the needs of the crops on different parts of the estate in different seasons, but also to ensure that sufficient works were being performed and that agricultural buildings and equipment were maintained. The growing acreages of land under the plough in this period could only have been ploughed, sown and harvested (let alone harrowed, weeded and had the birds scared off it) if more people were involved in these activities.

Nucleated settlement was, as has already been seen, introduced almost exclusively on both sides of the Channel over the course of the long eighth century on the centres and berewicks of extensive estates belonging to the secular and ecclesiastical elite. The formalisation and extension of labour services by including dwellings with standardised leased arable holdings may be measured in the emergence of planned nucleations in which houses stood in standardised plots at or near high-status estate centres and their berewicks in the same period in which arable productivity increased. In Wales, for example, 'the characteristic settlement of bond tenants on reckoned [leased] land was a hamlet. The complement of a legal hamlet was given as 'nine buildings and one plough" as well as other appurtenances.[194] The archaeology of the middle Anglo-Saxon episcopal estate centred on Bishopstone (Sussex) also suggests that outlying berewicks at places like Norton 'may have been occupied by servile tenants (and perhaps slaves) tied to the estate centre' perhaps as early as the eighth century.[195] Regular planning in measured plots suggests that dependent tenants were subjected to tighter control of their status and autonomy through their subordination to the process of nucleation, through the proximity of nucleations to the hall complex and through the standardisation of the properties they occupied which emphasised their dependent status. Such visible expressions of subordinate status underscored the fact that differences between tenants were less important than their responsibilities to the lord, and may have facilitated the standardisation and formalisation of the increased labour services that they were expected to perform.

Formalised layouts and management of the inlands

Estate managers developed sophisticated logistical systems for achieving the agricultural surpluses that estates were required to produce and for transporting them to the estate centre and/or to market. As we have already seen, strategic location of estate centres, the layout and architecture of the centres themselves, and greater surveillance and control of inland labour were accompanied by technical innovations aimed at a sustainable increase of the productivity of arable crops. The systematic reordering of agricultural management included restructuring the layout of the inlands and centralised direction of annual patterns of cropping.

Not all owners ran inlands on all their estates, Where they did, inlands sometimes lay in compact blocks and sometimes in discrete 'islands' separated by the holdings of other manors or by tenanted land. On the royal estate in the Bourn Valley (Cambs.), for example, relatively small areas of directly cultivated inland lay in dispersed units, as did that of Frankish demesnes in the Hassegau (Germany).[196] Scattered eighth-century manorial block demesnes have been identified in parcels at Ins near Erlach in Switzerland and at Kirchheim and Lauchheim (both Germany).[197] By contrast, the huge inland at Palaiseau (France) belonging to the abbey of St-Germain de-Prés in the early ninth century lay in a single block covering 396 hectares, just as that of the seventh-century abbey at Winchester (Hants.) is fossilised in the double hundred of Chilcomb, which today includes 28 modern parishes.[198] In Flanders, such directly cultivated demesnes may survive in the single, large, undivided open fields whose names end with the suffix *–kouter*, of which Latemkouter, the principal field of Sint-Martens-Latem near Ghent, is a typical example.[199]

Inlands were frequently laid out within a well-maintained – and sometimes long-lived – enclosure protected by dykes, ditches and/or hedges, like those at Eynsham (Oxon.), Wollaston and Higham Ferrers (both Northants.). Eight hides of inland at Bexhill (Sussex) was defined by 'a boundary ditch (or dyke)' in 772, while 'all that demesne land' at Aston Magna (Glos.) was 'surrounded by a dyke outside' in the tenth-century.[200] Similar layouts are visible at Yadsworthy (Devon), Abbot's Worthy (Hants.), Quarrington (Lincs.), Hinton Hall (Suff.) and Whaddon (Cambs.) perhaps providing a visual demonstration of normative expectations in late-seventh-century Wessex, which indicated that a *ceorl's worthig* (perhaps 'enclosed farmland') 'should be fenced winter and summer'.[201] The author of Charlemagne's great treatise on the management of estates, *Capitulare de Villis*, assumed that the demesne would be fenced, and the same preconceptions informed the Carolingian *polyptyques*, which commented on fencing and hedging of inlands.[202]

Little is known of the detailed layout of middle Anglo-Saxon inlands by comparison with those of the Carolingian heartlands. By the 820s those of the Abbey of St Germain-des-Prés (France) were subdivided into units called '*culturae*' that varied in area from 5 to 88 hectares (that is, from about 12 to 217 acres).[203] Each *cultura* was cultivated as a single open field, with its own sequence of crop rotation; there is no evidence of the grouping of *culturae* into more generally organised field systems.[204] On some demesnes, like those belonging to the abbeys of St-Germain-des-Prés and St Remi de Reims, labour services on specific inland *culturae* were institutionalised in the *lot-corvée*, in which the inland was subdivided into measured units, each allocated to an individual dependent tenant for its cultivation and from which the entire harvest went to the lord.[205] In such places, the inland appears to have been subdivided into intermingled 'parallel long strips', whose length, on the early ninth-century inlands of St Irminio, was between 8 and 25 times their width.[206]

There are some indications that estate managers directed annual patterns of cropping and crop rotations. At the Wissembourg holding at Herxheim, for example, tenants were expected to plough in both winter and spring; while at Varena, held by St-Maur-des-Fossés, just outside Paris, 'each and every one [of the tenants] ploughs 4 perches for the winter wheat and 2 perches for the summer wheat'.[207] Whether or not such directive statements were normative or reflected actual practice, they and the labour services referred to above demonstrate that estate managers ordered the relative proportions of each crop to be planted on the inland and of the timing and number of labour inputs. While crop rotations were centrally directed, the actual organisation of labour of each strip may not have been, since Wickham points out that a Bavarian law code of about 740 anticipated that tenants would arrange the details of how the work was to be completed, even though the estate provided the seed and expected to receive the harvest.[208] It is impossible to know whether the same level of input was also a characteristic of middle Anglo-Saxon estate managers. On the other hand, it is difficult to see how the volume of agricultural surplus that evidently was produced could have been achieved without some direction from the centre. Although there is evidence on high-status estates in the core of the Carolingian empire for fields whose layout was open and which were subdivided into strips, there is no sign in either region of any aspect of the collective management of cultivation to a degree that might imply its organisation within a wide rather than a narrow CPrR.

Structured forms for ordering the leased demesne

Production on those parts of the demesne that were leased to dependent tenants received the same careful attention. In early medieval Wales, 'the great reeve and the royal bailiff' allocated equal areas of arable open-field land among the 'villein men without pedigree' in return for equal renders to the lord.[209] In the Geest region of north-west Germany the reorganisation in the eighth century of older rectilinear fields into single open fields may reflect just this process. The new open field of each settlement, the *esch*, was divided into long, narrow, strip-like holdings between 3–30m wide and between 300–600m long and appears to have been focused on a sub-manorial centre: 'a large isolated farm with compact block field plots separated from the strip fields of the surrounding hamlets'.[210] Hamerow has commented that these new arrangements were 'of considerable importance' because they established a permanent connection 'between the individual household and the land it cultivated'.[211] Intensively manured infields divided into 11m-wide strips were laid out at Dunum and at Gittrup, nr Münster (both Germany) in about 800.[212] Similar peasant strip holdings were held in the ninth-century *essen* of the central Drenthe plain (Netherlands), oval open fields that were 'conglomerate of blocks of parallel parcels', each separately enclosed.[213] Small fields in sixth-century Burgundy were replaced in '*l'expansion des grandes prairies*' in the same way.[214] Large-scale open fields appeared in areas newly colonised by Carolingian armies, where arable fields in Westfalia, Saxony, Lechfeld and the Hassegau (Germany) on areas leased from the demesnes were divided into two or three large fields, in which the intermingled strips of peasant holdings were up to 20–50m wide and up to 3 km long.[215] They are morphologically similar to the long strips into which the arable of Northamptonshire was subdivided from the mid-ninth century onwards. At Wollaston (Northants.) the mid-ninth-century block demesne included the sites of a Roman villa and an early Anglo-Saxon cemetery; beyond, the remaining arable of the vill was divided into long strips and furlongs.[216] The later seventh-century open-field strips at Brent (Som.) and those of the middle Anglo-Saxon field layouts in the Bourn Valley (Cambs.) may reflect similar strategies for integrating patterns of tenanted landholding with methods for arable management (Figures 4(d) and 6(e)).

As in England, there is also a little evidence to suggest that open-field layouts divided into strips were not new in the *champagne* landscapes at the heart of the Carolingian empire. At Döverden (Netherlands) 'a Merovingian/Carolingian cemetery lay within a long narrow parcel of land which closely matched the outlines of a field which appears on a tithe map of 1755', a strip that predated the burials within it.[217] On the other hand, although the early sixth-century *Pactus Legis Salicae* describes damage to crops in open fields where someone 'crosses another man's field (*campo*) where the stalks have already grown with a cart *outside the path or tracks*', there is no knowing whether holdings in such open fields were in strips or in other layouts. All that can be said is that it was possible to move from one unbounded holding to another.[218] As in England, only open-field systems managed under narrow CPrRs can be inferred, as all aspects of crop production remained the prerogative of the cultivator even where tenure was apportioned in strips in open fields. The division in the seventh century of 50 m-wide strips into two equal halves at Vreden and Telgte (both Germany), for example, has been interpreted as evidence of management of open-field strips in severalty and it is important to note that in the many places in the heartlands of Francia – in the Paris basin, between the Meuse-Demer-Scheldt rivers, in the area around Limburg (both Netherlands) and in parts of Germany – there is not 'the slightest indication that this three-field system [that is, arable managed under a wide CPrR] was ever organised on a village-basis, whereby the whole agricultural area of a village was divided into three parts and with cropping regulations' until the thirteenth or fourteenth centuries; several cultivation of individual holdings continued to be the usual practice.[219]

Conclusion

English and Carolingian kings and their secular and ecclesiastical aristocracies were joint authors of strategies for meeting the organisational challenges of producing agricultural surpluses. They met or actively communicated with each other in a range of contexts: family, ecclesiastical, diplomatic and mercantile. They knew about (and copied) each other's contributions to art, architecture, coinage and literature, shared the same values, belonged to the same (international) church and validated their political authority and legitimacy in terms of their shared Roman past. They had common motives, opportunities and means for improving productive efficiency on their vast – sometimes newly acquired – estates. Renders of agricultural surplus supported their households, many members of which were non-productive; and, for the first time in 300 years, stable political and economic infrastructures allowed substantial profits to be made from trade, which could in turn generate capital for investment, luxury goods and noble buildings. The renaissance of interest in classical authors and learning created a small aristocratic literate class which was able to develop complex accounting procedures needed to track production, income and labour within their vast estates and to manage the movement of goods to royal collection centres and within national and international trading networks.

The evidence of the landscape suggests that elites in the Carolingian heartlands and in middle Anglo-Saxon England developed and implemented broadly similar strategies for intensifying agricultural production on their extensive estates across the long eighth century. Estate centres were located in order to maximise communication and transport across the estate as a whole and to integrate production with the wider economy. Architecture and layout of central places and their berewicks were visual statements of authority and legitimacy. Nucleated settlements at estate centres, and at berewicks for the collection and/or processing of renders of grain or stock, all spoke of intensified control over labour services demanded both from unfree tenants on the demesne inlands and semi-free men who leased arable demesnes beyond.[220] The demesne was reorganised into 'fields under permanent cultivation with probable crop rotation', as inlands were managed in consolidated blocks whose outer boundaries were hedged or otherwise differentiated.[221] On the royal and monastic demesnes of the Paris basin and northern France cropping may have been centrally directed and arable divided into strips for greater ease of accounting although there is no evidence for the introduction of the collective management of cropping, fallowing and/or grazing under a wide CPrR. Technical innovations were also adopted: investment in plough technology, extending the area under arable cultivation, changes in the dominance of crops and more structured methods for assuring sustainable soil fertility. There was widespread manufacture of secondary goods through milling, weaving and so on. In some cases, there were tertiary products from industrial processes: salt gained from both mining and boiling brine could be traded not only in its own right, but could also be used in preserving meat and other produce. Such commonality was not an accident nor was it coincidental. The formalisation of managerial techniques was jointly developed and implemented by Anglo-Saxon and Carolingian kings and the monastic and secular elites most closely connected with them and cannot be attributed to one or another. Arrangements for renders and forms of dependent tenure on extensive estates may also have acted as markers of high status for estate owners, referring – like their jewellery and domestic architecture – to a concept of *Romanitas* that they consciously perpetuated as a validation of their status.[222]Envoys who travelled between royal courts, missionaries at foreign courts, or churchmen attending synods may have discussed matters of state or theology by day, but it seems a fair bet to suggest that their informal encounters included conversations about improved techniques for estate management and the efficient production of goods and surpluses.

The problem of a common origin for *champagne* and champion *pays* is, however, only half-resolved. Nucleated settlement is certainly a feature of both landscapes and may well have been introduced on both sides of the Channel by the same kinds of landowners in the same period for the same purposes; some features of the management of arable demesnes on extensive estates may have been adopted in the development of wide CPrRs over arable open fields. Both were introductions in the landscape that reflected new methods for producing substantial agricultural surpluses. Such pressures are visible across England, both within and beyond the Central Province, in extended arable fields, new crops, and the adoption of the heavy plough across. Why did most communities across England outside (but also, sometimes, within) the Central Province continue to manage their open-field holdings under narrow CPrRs into the Middle Ages and beyond? And why did open-field cultivation managed within wide CPrRs only emerge in the Central Province?

Notes

1 Rackham 1986: 5; Roberts and Wrathmell 2002: 1, 61, 144. The distinction was first mapped by Gray in 1915 (1959 edn: frontispiece).

2 Cited in Roberts and Wrathmell 2002: 1; Tusser 1984: 134.

3 Rackham 1986: 4–5.

4 Verhulst 1992, I: 143 and 2002: 17; Pounds 1973: 278–9.

5 Campbell 1981a: 128.

6 Renes 1988: 162–6; Roymans and Gerritsen 2002: 274–5; Slicher von Bath 1963: 56. Verhulst's (2002: 62, my emphasis) perceptive remark says it all: 'the origin of the three-course rotation has been the object of much discussion, especially among German scholars, who unnecessarily complicated the problem by making a connection between three-course rotation and the three-field system'. Although see Baker 1965: 89 'the earliest hints of a mature common field system come from Wetterau, c. 1300' in Germany.

7 Bailey 2010.

8 Gray 1915: frontispiece and 403.

9 Rackham 1986: 178.

10 Roberts and Wrathmel 2002: 10, 124.

11 Thirsk 1964, 1966; for critical responses see, for example, Titow 1965.
12 For a recent elegant critique of the terminological distinctions and of the debate, see Bailey 2010.
13 Thirsk 1964, 1966; Fox 1981.
14 Thirsk 1964: 5–7; Fox 1981. See also Campbell and Godoy 2008: V, 100.
15 Roberts and Wrathmell 2002: 187; Hesse 2000; Oosthuizen 2006: 44.
16 Jones and Page 2006: 93; Taylor and Arbon 2007: 38; Roberts and Wrathmell 2002. See also e.g. Aston 1988: 97; Rippon et al. 2006: 58–64.
17 Addyman 1964: 24; Hall 1988: 108; Hall 1995: 129–30.
18 Harvey 1980, 1983, 1984, 1985. See also Roberts and Wrathmell 2002: 145.
19 Nitz 1988a and 1988b.
20 Hooke 1981a: 190; Anglo-Saxon Charters, S1329 and S1548, accessed August 2011.
21 e.g. Bailey 2007: 17.
22 cf. Williamson 2003.
23 Seebohm 1883: 76.
24 Maitland 1897: 15.
25 Stenton 1971 edn: 15, 280, 286.
26 Orwin and Orwin 1938: 60.
27 Hoskins 1988: 45.
28 Hall 1981: 35–6.
29 Lewis et al. 1997: 202–3, my additions.
30 Ibid.: 204.
31 Hooke 1998: 115. See also Williamson 2003: 181.
32 Taylor 1983: 131.
33 Foard 1978: 370.
34 Brown and Foard 1998: 81, 89.
35 Ibid.: 75–9.
36 Ibid.: 90–1.
37 Taylor 2002: 53–71.
38 Foard 1978: 370; Oosthuizen 2006: 146–7.
39 Jones and Page 2006: 104, my addition.
40 cf. Taylor 1983. The review that follows is hampered both by the paucity of published excavation results. As Hamerow has recently observed of early Anglo-Saxon settlements, 'Fewer than a dozen of the hundreds of

Anglo-Saxon settlements so far investigated have been excavated (and published) on a scale and under conditions which allow for a detailed analysis of their layout and development over time' (2002b: 93). The absence of the 'grey literature' (unpublished construction and other development) from open and peer-reviewed publication is a difficulty which currently bedevils archaeology, which has yet to establish a strategy for dealing with it. It should also be noted that nucleation is not restricted to the Central Province – it is simply the dominant settlement form within it.

41 See Oosthuizen 2010 for a fuller review of the evidence and a more extensive discussion.

42 e.g. Allerston 1970: 97–8; Aston 1985: 87, 89 and 1988: 76–7; Bond 1985; Cessford and Dickens 2004:130, 82; Challis 1995: 22; Dyer 2002: 13; Hayfield 1984, 50; Lewis 2005, 2006; Oosthuizen 1997; Parry 2006: 133, 173–6, 223–4, 229, 236, 275; RCHME 1979: 123; RCHME 1981: 122; RCHME 1982: l, 3–4; Roberts 1978: 297 and 1988; Roberts and Wrathmell 2002: 92–4, 113; Sheppard 1966, 1974 and 1976; Smith 1999: Taylor 1992: 6, 8; Thomas 2006: 34–6; Wade-Martins 1980b: 50–2, 54, 55–7, 65–7.

43 RCHME 1979: xlix; Everson et al. 1991: 14–15.

44 Reynolds 2003: 119.

45 Denison 2002: 4; Cramp and Daniels 1987: 242–6; Loveluck 2001: 108; Wade 1980: 98.

46 Wade-Martins 1980a: 37–40, 94, 103.

47 Millet and James 1983; Hinchliffe 1986.

48 Brown and Foard 1998: 79, 77, 80; Shaw 1991; Boddington 1999: 67.

49 Addyman and Leigh 1972: 17; Cunliffe 1972: 11; Cunliffe 1973: 187.

50 Powlesland 1990: 37–8; Loveluck 1998, 2001.

51 Beresford and Hurst 1979: 68.

52 Carr et al. 1988.

53 Thomas 2011a: 52 and 2011b; Williams 1993; Mortimer 2000: 9; Loveluck 2001: 108; Davies 2010: 110; Reynolds 2003: 119.

54 Thomas 2011: 52; Crabtree 2010: 131.

55 Hayes 1988: 324–5; Hayes and Lane 1992: 215. Anglo-Saxon Charters, S1440, accessed July 2011.

56 Wade-Martins 1980b: 25, 73–5, 39, 42–4, 6, 61.

57 Taylor 1983: 122; Wade-Martins 1980b; Steedman 1994: 221, 295; Losco-Bradley and Kinsley 2002; Parry 2006: 133, 173–6, 223–4, 229, 236, 275; Jones and Page 2006: 89–91, 103–4; Hamerow 2002b: 122; Nitz 1988a, 1988b; Crabtree 2010: 130–1; Taylor 1992, 2002; Everson et al. 1991; Oosthuizen 2006.

58 Silvester 1988: 38–40, 76–9, 69, 95.

59 Hooke 1997: 80.

60 Gerrets 1996: 39; Hamerow 2002b: 68–70.

61 Moreland 2000; Hamerow 2002b: 122–3. Loveluck 2005: 231; Verhulst 2002: 16; Van Bavel 2010: 79.

62 Theuws 1994: 196; also Theuws 1991: 342; Hamerow 2002b: 70–5.

63 Fehring 1991: 167, 169; Gerrets 1996: 39; Hamerow 2002b: 70–5.

64 Heidinga 1987: 44; cited in Hamerow 2002b: 90

65 Bücker and Hoeper 2000: 227–9; Hamerow 2002b: 62, 70–5; Arnold 2000: 286; Nitz 1988b: 253; Loveluck 2005: 231; Eule 1996.

66 Theuws 1994: 198; Randsborg 1991: 76–7; Waterbolk and Harsema 1979: 258; Waterbolk 1995: 1; Hamerow 2002b: 66; Bücker and Hoeper 2000: 227–9; Nitz 1988b: 252–3.

67 Wickham 2005: 303–4. The criteria he proposes are: the centralisation of justice and the army; the development of governmental roles in which the office was permanent and more important than the office-holder; the concept of a public power; independent and stable resources for rulers; and 'a class-based system of surplus extraction and stratification', Wickham 2005: 303. For a critique of Wickham's use of archaeological material, see Hills 2007. Middle Anglia in the late seventh century included a number of *regiones* and small kingdoms in Leicestershire, Northamptonshire, Bedfordshire, Huntingdonshire and west Cambridgeshire, as well as parts of Buckinghamshire, Hertfordshire, Lincolnshire and Derbyshire who recognised the overlordship of, and owed tribute to, Mercia. They had been absorbed into Mercia by the early eighth century.

68 Bassett 2007: 84.

69 Wickham 2005: 303. See also Blair 2005: 85–91.

70 Blair 2005: 144.

71 Thacker 1985: 5.

72 Story 2003: 174.

73 Bassett 2011: 6–10; Haslam 1987.

74 Bassett 2007: 57–8.

75 Naylor 2007: 59, see also 50. See also Palmer 2003: 53–6; Blair 2005: 261. 'Productive' sites are those which are characterised by an unusual volume of Anglo-Saxon coins and metal-work.

76 Bassett 2007: 83.

77 Ibid.: 65, 78–81; he suggests that they included Nottingham, Derby, Leicester, Lincoln, Stamford, Leicester, Lincoln, Northampton, Bedford, Cambridge and Huntingdon.

78 Blair 2005: 261.

79 Bassett 2007: 82; Blair 2005: 256–7. See also Brooks 2000: 11–13, 20–2.

80 Metcalf 2003: 47, my addition.

81 Moreland 2000: 69–104; Hamerow 2002b: 110–12, 152–5, 170; McCormick 2001: 604.

82 e.g. Blinkhorn 1999: 11, 18–19; Hodges 1989: 139–42; Crabtree 1996: 64; Palmer 2003: 49–57; Naylor 2004: 204; Blair 2005: 87, 296, 251–61.

83 Moreland 2000: 102, his emphasis. Wickham 2005: 349 suggests that this did not occur for at least another century, but see the critique in Hills 2007.

84 Nelson 2001b: 126.

85 Millett 1990: 215–19.

86 Newman 2002: 505; Carver 1994: 2.

87 Henig 2004: 11.

88 Dohmen 2010: 84; Huggett 1988; Stenton 1971: 223.

89 Harris 2003: 192.

90 Dumville 1989; Story 2003: 169

91 Story 2005: 198, see also 196–200; Cam 1912: 154.

92 Sherley-Price 1990: 232, 303–4; Parsons 1983: 203. Nelson 2002: 20; Story 2005: 204

93 Sherley-Price 1990: 234; Whitelock 1972: 9; McCormick 2001: 604; Lapidge 1986: 45–6; Parsons 1983: 280–1; Cam 1912: 7.

94 Whitelock 1972: 3–5; Yorke 1990: 39; Cam 1912: 14.

95 Yorke 1990: 39; Whitelock 1972: 8 and 2–3; Gardiner et al. 2001: 276.

96 Carver 1994: 2; Eaton 2001: 19.

97 Coupland 2005: 213; also Yorke 1990: 115; Williams and Bishop 2004: 56.

98 Eaton 2001: 16–18; Zadora-Rio 2003: 8–9; Loveluck 2005: 249; Nelson 1996: 91; Wendehorst 2007; Harris 2003: 140.

99 Loveluck, 2005: 249. See also Parsons 1983: 312.

100 Deliyannis 1995: 114–15; Parsons 1983: 312; Biddle and Kjølbye-Biddle 1985: 235; Taylor 1987: 220.

101 Loveluck 2005; *British Archaeology* 2002a: 7; Williams 1984: 136.

102 Jewell 2001: 262; Hawkes 2001: 245; *British Archaeology* 2006: 7; Biddle and Kjølbye-Biddle 1985.

103 Nelson 1996: 91.

104 Effros 2001.

105 Cramp 1969: 58, 24.

106 Nelson 1996: 95, 2001: 128; Williams 2001: 301.

107 Nelson 1996: 90.

108 Cam 1912: 11. Sims-Williams 1976. See also Pheifer 1987; Herren 1998; McKitterick 2004: 84–119.

109 Hodges 1989: Ch. 5; Nelson 2001b: 134.

110 Yorke 1990: 95; Thacker 1985;

111 Cam 1912: 98.

112 Ibid.: 64, my additions.

113 Story 2005 : 196; see, for example, Nelson 2001b for examples.

114 Bassett 2009; Jolliffe 1926: 2.

115 Innes 2001: 397 and his Fig. 2.; Verhulst 2002: 32.

116 Theuws 2001: 209; University of Leicester Carolingian Polyptyques http://www.le.ac.uk/hi/polyptyques/wissembourg/site.html [accessed August 2011].

117 King's College, London 2010: S1440; http://www.pase.ac.uk/jsp/FactoidDisplay/EventDisplay.jsp?factoidKey=37573 [accessed June 2011]; Lebecq 2000: 148.

118 Loyn and Percival 1975: 70.

119 Kelly 1997: 446.

120 Lebecq 1991; Bassett 2007, 2011; Van Bavel 2010: 103–6. See also Palmer 2003 for more detail and Samson 1999 for a dissenting view.

121 Hodges 1989: 143. Naylor 2004: chapter 6.

122 Samson 1999: 88; Gardiner et al. 2001: 276–7; Nelson 2001b: 132; Coupland 2005 : 211–12 ; Wickham 2000; Moreland 2000.

123 Blair 2005: 258, my addition. This view is supported by Palmer 2003: 55–7; Blinkhorn 1999: 11–16; Moreland 2000: 68–104; Naylor 2004: 129. See also McCormick 2001: 794.

124 Naylor 2004: 116; Loveluck 1997: 9; McCormick 2001: 607.

125 Gardiner et al. 2001: 275.

126 Campbell 2010: 263.

127 Verhulst 2002: 68–9; Lohrman 1989: 401.

128 Crabtree 2010: 131.

129 Ibid.

130 Van Bavel 2010: 125.

131 Crabtree 2010: 129, 130.

132 Hamerow 2002b: 151–2. An adult ox or cow requires an acre of grazing each year.

133 Biddick 1989: 82.

134 Wickham 2005: 289.

135 Kelly 1997: 446; Henning 2007: 17–21, though his view is more nuanced.

136 Campbell 2010: 264.

137 Ibid.: 260, fn 72; Loveluck, 2005: 252; Carr et al. 1988; Moreland 2000: 96; Verhulst 2002: 39–40.

138 Sarris 2004: 303.

139 Besteman 1990: 106; Durand and Leveau 2003: 201. Goffart (2008: 190) has concluded that the *polyptyques* 'are, pre-eminently, tax collectors' books with an official aura', while Campbell (2010: 258) suggested that the managerial purpose of the *Capitulare de Villis* and the *Brevium Exempla* was 'to increase oversight, suppress corruption and enact better accounting practices on royal estates', a view with which Wickham (2005: 290) concurs.

140 Stevens 1966: 111; Brunner 1995: 25; also Van Bavel suggests that the use of the heavy plough only became widespread between the ninth and tenth centuries, 2010: 134.

141 Van Bavel 2010: 131, see also 129–30.

142 Besteman 1990: 106; Durand and Leveau 2003: 201; Kooistra 1996: 79–81.

143 Hamerow 2002b: 137.

144 Groenman-van Wateringen and van Wijngaarden-Bakker 1990: 287; cf. Van Bavel 2010: 126.

145 Gerrets 1996: 39; Hamerow 2002b: 140.

146 Pounds 1973: 204; Verhulst 2002: 17–18, 61, 63. Verhulst 1992: V, 23.

147 Kooistra 1996: 120; Heidinga 1987: 87; Groenman-van Wateringen and van Wijngaarden-Bakker 1990: 285; Gerrets 1996: 39; Durand and Leveau 2003: 203.

148 Van Bavel 2010: 131.

149 Rhatz and Meeson 1992: 156; Jackson 2000; *British Archaeology* 1995; *British Archaeology* 2002b.

150 Hooke 1981a: 267–8; Anglo-Saxon Charters, S186, accessed August 2011.

151 Theuws 1991: 350. See also Van Bavel 2010: 148; Lebecq 1989, 2000: 134; Lohrman 1989.

152 Richards 2003: 165; Naylor 2004: 118; Blinkhorn 1999: 17; MacGowan 1996: 174; Metcalf 2003: 43–4.

153 Ulmschneider 2000: 65; Loveluck 2005: 243, 252–3.

154 Blinkhorn 1999: 11–16, 19; Moreland 2000: 87–96, 98–9; Green 1994: 85; Haslam 1980: 1–68; Maddicott 2005: 24–33.

155 Loveluck 2005: 241.

156 Gerrets 1996: 39; Van Bavel 2010: 147–54; Isenburg 1990: 290–3; Moreland 2000: 96; Groenman-van Waateringe and van Wijngaarden-Bakker 1990: 187; Loveluck 2005: 242, 252; Hamerow 2002b: 183.

157 Blair 1992; Moreland 2000: 103. Lebecq 2000: 127 and 146–7. See also Lebecq 1991; Verhulst 2002: 16.

158 Innes 2001: 423.

159 Whitelock 1979: 479, my emphasis; Gardiner et al. 2001: 166.

160 Samson 1999: 87.

161 Anglo-Saxon Charters, S1165 AD 672 x 674, accessed August 2011; Samson 1999: 87.

162 Bult and Hallewas 1990: 81, 76–7; Moreland 2000; Lebecq 2000.

163 These frequently included corrals for stock, as well as the buildings required for the day-to-day management of the estate – barns for crop storage and equipment, stables, dairies, brewhouses, weaving sheds and so on; Draper 2009: 104; Hamerow 2011: 141–3; Ulmschneider 2011: 159–60; Loveluck 2005: 239; Campbell 2010: 260.

164 Draper 2009: 104; Hamerow 2011: 141–3; Ulmschneider 2011: 159–60; Loveluck 2005: 239; Campbell 2010: 260.

165 Loveluck 2005: 237–8.

166 Hamerow 2011: 138–40; Hardy and Lorrimer 2004: 13–14; Ulmschneider 2011: 159–60; see Marshall and Marshall 1991 for further examples.

167 Nelson 2001a, 2001b; Innes 2001; Loveluck 2005; Hamerow 2002b: 86.

168 Kelly 1997: 364, 369.

169 *Capitulare de Villis*: http://www.le.ac.uk/hi/polyptyques/capitulare/latin2english.html [accessed June 2011]; Campbell 2010: 260; for a plan see Nelson 2001a: 221.

170 Loveluck 2005: 239, 247; Williams 1984: 124–5 and 135–6; Blair has suggested that the site at Northampton may be that of a royal minster, 1996: 104.

171 Theuws 1991: 368–70.

172 Marshall and Marshall 1991: 34, 35, 37.

173 *Brevium Exempla*, 25. Source: http://www.le.ac.uk/hi/polyptyques/brevium/latin2english.html [accessed June 2011].

174 Aston 1958: 65–8; Whitelock 1979: 406. See also Neilson 1929: 736; Faith 1997: 15–55; Hooke 1981a: 207; Sarris 2004: 303. The degree to which there were normative proportions of inland and leased land to which estates were expected to conform is embedded in debates about the 'bi-partite manor' which are discussed in Chapter 5. See also Verhulst (2002: 33–5) and Wickham (2005: 284–5). It should be noted, too, that the interpretation of '*gesett*' also remains contentious. Faith (1997: 103–4) suggests that it refers to land to which a tax burden had been allocated, while McGovern (1971) argued that it was bookland.

175 Hooke 1981a: 348–52.

176 Wickham 2005: 284–5.

177 Aston 1958: 68; Jolliffe 1926: 2; Verhulst 2002: 54–5; Van Bavel 2010: 79. See also Wickham 2005: 284–5.

178 Faith 1997: 59–70.

179 Verhulst 2002: 37, 44: Faith 1997: 56.

180 Faith 1997: 70. See also thirteenth-century cottagers on the Bishop of Ely's estates: 'men with [a customary holding] of a mere acre or so who could not have subsisted entirely on their land' (Miller 1969: 137, my addition).

181 Jones 1981: 207.

182 Wickham 2005: 290, see also 289.

183 Ibid.: 280; Sarris 2004: 310.

184 A person who is dependent on the estate for the provision of his food (lit. 'loaf-eater'): Barnwell 1996: 53–4.

185 Millett 1990: 203; Faith 1997: 71, see also 70–5.

186 Van Bavel 2010: 76.

187 Faith 1997: 49.

188 Whitelock 1979: 406; she adds that 'I assume that the situation considered is when the original agreement has expired and the lord will not renew it on the old terms'.

189 Charles-Edwards 1987: 101–3.

190 Jones 1981: 206.

191 Faith 1997: 78. Measurements varied from place to place by local custom, but by the later Middle Ages a rod was around 5½ yards and a furlong around 220 yards, giving an area of about a quarter of an acre (4840 yards).

192 Verhulst 2002: 17.

193 University of Leicester School of History 2008, accessed June 2011. A *iurnal* is 'a unit of land area' (ibid.).

194 Jones 1981: 209.

195 Thomas 2011a: 44. See also Thomas 2010: 220, 17.

196 Oosthuizen 2006; Nitz 1988a: 157, 155.

197 Reynolds 2003: 110–15; Egli 1988: 97.

198 Verhulst 2002: 41; Faith 1997: 34.

199 Verhulst 2002: 17–20.

200 Aston 1958: 67; Faith 1997: 30 and 173.

201 Loveluck 2005: 239; Hodges 1989: 238; Oosthuizen 1993; Carr et al. 1988; Warner 1987: 30–3; Damminger 1998: 62–4; Hamerow 2002b: 62 and 90–3. Whitelock 1979: 403; Faith 2009; interpretation of *worthig* after Fox 1981: 86.

202 Loyn and Percival 1975: 69; Verhulst 2002: 17.

203 Verhulst 2002: 17. The term will be familiar to historians of medieval agriculture, since it was used in eastern England as a synonym for 'furlong' in irregular field-systems where it might be divided between a number of holders or held in severalty and where it might be cropped individually, e.g. Bailey 2009.

204 Verhulst 2002: 17. See also Roymans and Gerritsen 2002: 280; Nitz 1988a:156; Pounds 1973: 207, 20.

205 'Lot-corvée : parcelle de la réserve mesurée en ansanges, exploitée par un tenancier au profit exclusif de son seigneur', Stéphane Guérault, 'Les Polyptyques Carolingiens, accessed August 2011.

206 Verhulst 2002: 20, 62–3.

207 University of Leicester School of Historical Studies 2008, accessed June 2011. Yet a three-course rotation does not imply a two- or three-field *system*. Rotations were based on *culturae* which varied enormously in area; there is no hint that *culturae* were amalgamated into, or managed as, open fields. Verhulst has definitively summarised how much 'unnecessary' debate has followed from making the unsupported 'connection between three-course rotation and the three-field system' (Verhulst 2002: 62).

208 Wickham 2005: 287.

209 Jones 1981: 208.

210 Matzat 1988: 137–40; Slicher von Bath 1963: 60; Fehring 1991: 174. Verhulst 2002: 18.

211 Hamerow 2002b: 141.

212 Gerrets 1996; Van bavel 2010: 126.

213 Hamerow 2002b: 63, 141; also Waterbolk and Harsema 1979: 258–60; Van Zeist and Palfenier-Vegter 1979.

214 Nitz 1988b: 263; Waterbolk 1995: 1; Besteman 1990: 103; Keen 1984; Cunliffe 1973: 183–8; Escher 2005: 68.

215 Droege 1970: 287; Nitz 1988a: 156, 1988b: 252–62; Matzat 1988: 141 suggests that this interpretation is controversial.

216 Hall 1987: 61.

217 Hamerow 2002b: 63, 141; also Waterbolk and Harsema 1979: 258–260; Van Zeist and Palfenier-Vegter 1979.

218 Eckhardt 1962: 127, XXXIV, 4, accessed June 2011; trans. Drew 1991: 96, my emphasis. It is worth noting that nothing in either of these sources gives any clue to the character of these subdivisions and certainly no evidence that they were strips.

219 Slicher von Bath 1963: 56, my addition; Hamerow 2002b: 142. See also Renes 1988: 164; Matzat 1988: 144; Roymans and Gerritsen 2002: 284.

220 Finberg 1972: 430.

221 Hamerow 2002b: 140.

222 Geake 1999: 205–12.

Part Three

Explaining Continuities and Transformations

5

Continuities in common pasture and open-field systems under narrow CPrRs

The enduring environmental stability of large tracts of open – archaeologically 'empty' – pasture from Bodmin to the Cheviots suggests that the deliberate management of land for pasture may have been practised in Britain since at least the Neolithic. Previous chapters have proposed long-standing continuity in the use of CPrRs from prehistory into the early Middle Ages to structure the collective management of at least some of this pasture and, on occasion, arable too.[1] Yet there is no indication that such longevity was characterised by stasis. The generalised underlying principles of CPrRs ensure their flexibility and adaptability: right-holders need simply from time to time to specify changes in the practical detail of day-to-day management within their understanding of the CPrR's enduring fundamental principles. They might, for instance, agree to amend regulations about *who* is entitled to a right of common, the *boundaries* of the areas to be managed, or the finer details – changing from year to year, and season to season – for the *period* within which the resource may be exploited. Men are more likely to alter the precise date in spring when cattle might be allowed in to graze than to make fundamental changes to the essential principles underpinning the CPrR like the definition of property rights over an environmental resource, the restriction of such rights to a limited number of stakeholders, and their legal status. The consensus required for decision-making within CPrRs moreover results in incremental rather than radical change over the *longue durée*. This chapter explores explanations for such long-term continuities in Anglo-Saxon England.

The historiography

Common property rights first entered the British documentary record in the later seventh century AD at about the same time that the early Anglo-Saxon kingdoms emerged from the obscurity of the previous two centuries. By then, rights of property appear most commonly to have been invested collectively in communities who defined themselves in terms of relationships between kin, and access to such rights seems to have been restricted to those with freeman status in each community. Entitlement to property rights took two inter-connected forms: on the one hand, rights of severalty over an arable holding to which were attached, on the other, rights of common in the non-arable resources of the 'folk'. In early medieval Wales, every *bonheddig* (freeman) had a right of common grazing on the pastures of his clan, just as, in seventh- and eighth-century Ireland (and, perhaps, long before) common land was held by the kin-group – *túath* – such that incursions on it by strangers were offences against the group as a whole, and every freeman within the *túath* had a right to share in its exploitation.[2] Communities across seventh-century England and Ireland were characterised by the expectation that a freeman would hold sufficient arable land to maintain a household and could demonstrate this through his ownership of a full plough-team.[3] In medieval England such early traditions persisted in the attachment to 'ancient' arable holdings of rights of common pasture even when the derivation of such rights from membership of a kin-group had long been forgotten.[4]

Historians are generally agreed that the origins of rights of common property in Britain are 'very ancient' and can, at very least, be traced back to the period of the Anglo-Saxon migrations of the sixth and seventh centuries AD. In the 1920s, for example, Neilson observed that, although rights of intercommon on pasture were obviously influenced by local and regional geography, they 'also corresponded, in some cases at least, with ancient administrative arrangements' which had existed 'time out of mind', and whose 'origin … goes back to the early days of settlement'.[5] Homans concurred: 'the customs of countrymen … are primary and early, probably as old as the Anglo-Saxon invasions' while Hoskins, in one of the few studies of common lands, also concluded that such rights were 'of vast antiquity'.[6] Miller, on the basis of his study of the medieval abbey and bishopric of Ely, agreed: the Isle 'retained a good deal of coherence as a social unit – partly due, perhaps, to the complex of intercommoning rights shared by its inhabitants … as a social unit it has characteristics which may indicate considerable antiquity'.[7]

The 'emergence' between about 400 and 700 of common property regimes over pasture provides a premise for long-standing scholarly models of early Anglo-Saxon political organisation. Neilson was the first to propose that Anglo-Saxon regional identity was based on rights and practices relating to non-arable resources rather than on lordship or kingship.[8] This view has since been re-affirmed, for example, by Davies and Vierck who suggested that 'it is groups and associations of people that form the raw material of early political development, not the carving up of territory', a proposition accepted by and taken further by other scholars.[9] More recent research has made the same judgement. Fowler concluded that for 'much of the [first millennium AD] it seems that pasture was defined as much by the right to feed animals over certain areas of land as by definitions of land itself', while Roberts has written that 'at first [commons] were shared by the whole territory of the shire, but were gradually appropriated to individual parishes or townships. The question is not of the presence of manors or estates in early Anglo-Saxon times, but of the *emergence* of rights in land and rights over land'.[10]

The mechanism for the development of commons is usually explained in terms of expanding control from a core area of settlement over a surrounding periphery. In Shropshire and Herefordshire, for instance, Hooke has vividly described how 'a common characteristic of these minor folk regions seems to have been the presence of a 'heartland' area which was relatively well-developed at an early period and a complementary region which was often less developed but valued as a region of hunting and pastoral activity and which may initially have served as a region of summer pasture', a model also adopted for parts of Oxfordshire and Warwickshire.[11] Later scholarship has agreed, proposing that 'people in neighbouring settlements came to have arrangements over grazing rights and commoning which can only have worked through the recognition of the rights of certain groups to certain places. They also retained long-distance transhumance routes to distant woodland and pasture which are a strikingly enduring feature of early land units'.[12] That is, rights of common are generally explained in terms of two paradigms: first, as one of a nexus of interlocking strategies to assure the stability of continued subsistence and some degree of local political and administrative security in the period *after* Rome withdrew; and second, in terms of territorial conceptions of areas defined as 'core' and 'periphery'.[13]

Such narratives have evolved from the premise that Anglo-Saxon settlers found a landscape relatively empty of Romano-British cultivation and settlement, partly because it was believed that much had not yet been tamed, and partly because it was also believed that what had been colonised had either been abandoned by its sub-Roman occupiers, or forcibly seized from them by Anglo-Saxon migrants.[14] Each Germanic cultivator or small group of 'Anglo-Saxons' was thus free to settle on empty land more or less where he or they wished, bringing a small area around the settlement into cultivation. Some (perhaps most) land remained empty of fields of settlement; the non-arable products (pasture, wood, hay, reeds, etc.) of land that was regarded as unsuitable for ploughing were treated as an open – that is, public – resource. As territories expanded in the sixth and seventh centuries, so resource entitlement became more restricted. Previously unlimited grazing in wood pastures, for example, became confined to members of territorial units the size of modern counties, perhaps connected through kinship or membership of clans. From the seventh to the twelfth centuries AD, as these areas themselves fragmented through subdivision, access to common pastures became increasingly limited. In some places, peasants retained rights to graze their beasts on commons or intercommons distant or administratively detached from their own vills, but more usually, as commons themselves were subdivided between emerging manors and communities, rights over them were gradually restricted to free members of the community within the township or parish in which the pasture lay.[15]

The problems with this model have already been rehearsed. If 'few archaeologists would argue that all, or even the great majority, of the people who lived in 'Anglo-Saxon houses' were in fact Germanic immigrants or the direct descendants of immigrants', it follows that there must have been considerable demographic continuity between about 400 and 700.[16] Prehistoric and, later, Roman husbandmen and women continued to work in their fields and stockyards, day after day, year on year, in peace or anarchy, in wealth and dearth, in health or plague, regardless of changes to lord or king. They drove animals to and from pasture, scared birds off the crops, and processed agricultural products – grinding corn into flour for baking, making cheese or spinning wool. There is little evidence that this pattern of agricultural production changed significantly between the fifth and seventh centuries. If, then, sub-Roman Britons continued to occupy the landscape and to exploit their ancient arable and pasture, whether collectively or in severalty, in traditional ways then at least some continuity in their approaches to social relationships might also be expected – that is, in concepts of how things 'should' be done, and how within those structures people should behave towards one another. That is, the details of their conceptual worlds were adapted to new circumstances over time while maintaining substantial continuity in the framework of underlying values and principles within which they were structured.

A further flaw in the argument for an early medieval origin for CPrRs is that it is based on the assumption that the early or middle Anglo-Saxon documentary evidence of rights to common pasture is contemporary with their introduction; that is, in the belief that the rights were being recorded at the same time that they were first wrought.[17] That premise is not a strong one. By the late seventh or early eighth centuries, for example, Wychwood (the 'wood of the *hwicce*') was already divided from the territory of the Hwicce, hinting that at some earlier time the Hwicce had occupied a much larger region, in which Wychwood was included; the whole of Kent and Sussex already held ancient common rights in the Weald in the same period; and seventh-century Kentish charters took for granted an established relationship between arable landholdings and associated rights of common.[18] Place-names tell the same story: the names of Late British areas of wood pasture survived into the medieval period and beyond, sometimes in areas with a continuous tradition of common rights for which there is evidence from the Neolithic period, if not earlier.[19] In some places 'old tribal boundaries, many of them going back for centuries' were preserved in the foundation of new Roman *civitates*, some of which continued to form the basis of rights and governance for early Anglo-Saxon folk-groups.[20] Most of Herefordshire and Shropshire, for example, was controlled in the early Middle Ages by a group who called themselves *Magonsaēte*, a name which appears to be derived from an indigenous tribal name re-used in the Roman period for a *civitas* focused on the town now called Kenchester; its persistence implies that it 'must have become known to English speakers before 550 AD'.[21] The names of the early medieval kingdoms of south-east Wales were derived from those of the Roman *civitates*, and that of the late Iron Age capital of the Brigantes was formalised in *Isurium Brigantum*, now Aldborough, the region retaining its identity well into the medieval period.[22]

Everything about these territorial rights suggests that they were already old by the early seventh century. In some places, stretches of open or wood pasture were so important that they gave their name to seventh-century folk-groups, most of whom were themselves Late British rather than Anglo-Saxon in origin. The fens of the Gyrwe covered large areas that later belonged to the Abbeys of Peterborough, Crowland and Spalding; part of the *feld* (more like African *veld* than an English 'field') belonging to the Mercians as a whole was preserved at Markfield (Leics.); while the *wold* (wood pasture) of the *Horningas* lay nearby at Horninghold (also Leics.). Other moors, woods or pastures in which freemen from whole shires had rights of common have been identified from Devon to Northumberland, and there is widespread acceptance of the antiquity of the '*public* character' of commons – although 'collective' rather than 'public' is probably more apt.[23] There is no hint in any of the documentary evidence that the common rights of the Gyrwe or the Hwicce were anything but well-accepted by the seventh century – that is, if there were a period in which they had evolved, that period was already long distant. Similarly, the origins of CPrRs over arable in open fields, like those located at the heart of Welsh settlements, might be sought in the 'distant, British past'.[24] In conclusion, before they were first recorded in post-Roman documents, collective territorial rights were already so old as to be considered to have originated time out of mind.

A third flaw in the argument that CPrRs were introduced by Anglo-Saxon migrants lies in the universality across Britain with which they are understood and applied even though these islands have been divided under different political administrations from – at very least – the immediate pre-Roman period: Caesar found Britain already divided between 'tribal' groups; Roman administration barely reached some parts of northern and western Britain; the sub-Roman period was characterised by political fragmentation; and the earliest Anglo-Saxon kingdoms were regional rather than national in their control and even their influence. Indigenous culture evolved in early medieval Ireland without interference from Germanic migration, yet there, too, common land was held by groups of kin among whom every freeman had an equal right to share in its exploitation, just like his counterparts across England and Wales.[25]

The evidence of Chapters 2 and 3 indicated the high probability that CPrRs existed across prehistoric Britain. Their longevity is unsurprising given the flexibility and adaptability that they bring to tradition and innovation in the governance and management of customary individual and collective property rights over land. Tradition may be discerned in inherited expectations of participation, consensus and a 'moral economy', and change in the possibility of minor adjustments to custom and practice introduced by individuals and agreed collectively, in order to meet the changing needs of contemporary groups of right-holders. How might CPrRs, then, express and consolidate social structure and social relationships?

Kinship, status and rights over land

By the time that CPrRs across Anglo-Saxon and Celtic Britain enter the documentary record it is clear that rights of participation in them were expressed in terms of membership of regional communities who defined themselves as kin, a system neatly summarised by Gosden as 'a political system in the idiom of kinship'.[26] Such traditional rights over land were based on two overlapping principles: first, entire clans shared collective rights over large tracts of land from which neither individuals nor individual families/households could alienate parcels without communal consent. Between the fifth and early seventh centuries, for example, the northern part – at very least – of the Cam basin in Cambridgeshire was controlled by the *Grantasaēte*, a community whose *-saēte* suffix proclaimed a real or constructed Late British origin; the *Meonwara* claimed rights over the Meon valley in Hampshire in the same period, while the *Limenweara* of Kent held a marshland territory of 80 'sulungs', a regional version of the hide that, as in other places, included not only a several arable holding but also collective rights to upland grazing.[27] Kinship thus provided a sophisticated means for rationalising and rationing access to communal territorial rights.

But kinship on its own was insufficient. The second criterion for access to CPrRs was based on status: each freeman within the kin-group was entitled to an area of permanent infield for cultivation in severalty (any deficit to be made up by the folk-group as a whole), as well as to outfields, *and* rights of grazing in the common pastures.[28] Freeman status was not, of course, standardised, but a continuum from men of high status whose freedom was undisputed, to those at the other end of the scale, where distinctions were more qualified, and differences between free and unfree less obvious: freemen, for example, who leased land or whose rights of sake and soke over their land were qualified by the rights of their overlord.

The rationale for allocation of rights over land was thus provided by filtering membership of a kin-group through the lens of status. Every free *bonheddig* or *bóaire* in early medieval Wales or Ireland was entitled to 'full rights in a community', whose material expression was that of sufficient arable from which to maintain a household, with concomitant rights of common in the wastes.[29] Households were therefore a nexus for status, landownership and legal responsibilities with complex linkages through which the prestige of the owner was designated, as well as relationships both between the individual members of each household and more generally between households.[30] Such units usually contained between 9 and 12 people, perhaps spread over two or at most three generations; they included not only individuals related by blood but also those who were counted as kin even though they may have been genetically unrelated, together with unrelated dependents of various degrees of unfreedom, like the *hlaf-ætas* in a *ceorlisc* household or the slaves of a *bóaire*.[31]

Like CPrRs, definitions of kinship and status allowed for considerable flexibility in determining whether a man satisfied the dual requirements of being 'kin' and 'free' that entitled him to several rights over a defined area of arable and rights of common over collective non-arable resources. Descent from a common ancestor was determined in terms of agnatic relationships (that is, through the male line) calculated over four generations, which would more or less have covered 'living memory'. Kinship could, however, also be constructed by formalising personal relationships – for example, by adopting an individual into a kin-group through baptism, fostering or marriage, and through rituals such as 'the giving of arms to a boy, the first cutting of an infant's hair and the first cutting of an adolescent's beard'.[32] Other relationships through which kinship might be claimed included membership of specific groups, like the late seventh-century warriors in royal households who 'behaved like a kindred' or, as Davis has argued, in imaginative genealogies such as those constructed for royal Anglo-Saxon kin-groups which provided 'evidence' for their common descent from legendary ancestors like Wōden or Noah.[33] Kinship within the folk-groups of early and middle Anglo-Saxon England could thus have been claimed on almost any grounds, provided that the kin-group in question was prepared to manipulate the detail of local customary practice in order to allow rights of access to an individual who was not a member of their kin-group by birth.[34]

Both philologists and archaeologists agree that such structures were not an Anglo-Saxon development. Charles-Edwards, for example, has concluded that 'a comparative analysis of the words used for kinsmen in Irish, Welsh and Breton shows that as late as the end of the Romano-British period the same kinship system of native Britons was the same as that recorded in the Old Irish laws.[35] The evidence of excavation, too, indicates that Late British social structure was so similar to that of the Anglo-Saxon period that long-term continuities seem very likely, while Gosden cites Tactitus' comments on the similarity between British and Irish social customs in the first century AD.[36] Although Sharples and Cunliffe diverge sharply in their interpretation of social relationships between men of different status in the late Iron Age they, too, agree that late prehistoric Britain was divided between clans within which structural relationships were formalised in personal allegiances based on a nuanced understanding of the complex interplay between status, kinship and rights over land.[37]

The striking universality in structures of kinship and CPrRs across early medieval folk-groups within the British Isles makes it at least possible that they may also have had pre-Roman origins, their customary definitions and practices of kinship, status, relationships and rights passed down in oral traditions.[38] Such structures were generalised enough to allow for adaptability in interpretation and for incremental adjustment. They were strong enough, and (most importantly) flexible enough to provide a long-term, workable and acceptable rationale for access to agricultural resources.

Lordship and several property rights

It is important to reiterate that CPrRs are not in themselves indicative of egalitarian social structures. While the restriction of rights within CPrRs to a limited group of right-holders provided a neat solution to the management of access to environmental resources, such rights were exercised within social and political hierarchies whose depths and rigidity varied over time and place. Many of the medieval peasants who intercommoned their animals on the Somerset Levels were tenants of Glastonbury Abbey, notorious for the rigidity of its manorial regulation; the Verderers of the New Forest exercise their rights of common in a modern Britain which is as strongly hierarchical, albeit in quite different ways.

The relationship between CPrRs and social organisation is nowhere more visible in early medieval Britain than in the renders which were demanded from free households by overlords. Although there is debate about the precise social meaning of these surpluses – whether they represented tribute, renders, taxes, contributions to communal events, or a system of distribution and exchange – of more relevance here is simply their existence, the principle remained unchanged that they were 'transferred from farmers to rulers and other lords, not because lords owned the land but because they ruled the people'.[39]

The laws of King Ine of Wessex demonstrate that the right of kings and lords to demand services and renders from their extensive estates was well-established by the mid to late seventh century. They were still integral to estate management two hundred or so years later, when monks at the Kentish abbey of St Augustine required their estate at Brabourne to deliver each year '40 "ambers"' of malt, a full-grown bullock, 4 wethers, 2240 loaves, a wey of lard and cheese, 4 "fothers"' of wood and 20 hens'.[40] The unit of assessment for the volume of render contributed by each household to the overall render was that normative (and probably variable) area called a hide, as discussed above, notionally sufficient land to support a household from one year to the next. In England, it was the normative unit on which a *ceorl* and his household could nominally be supported, notionally with sufficient arable to be worked by one plough-team; in Ireland, too, a *bóaire* was distinguished by several rights over enough arable to require ownership of a full plough-team.[41] The continuum of status and its internal gradations thus provided visible markers in the landscape in the landholdings of and within each community, and in which land and status were interdependent, complementary indicators of social values and relationships.

The relationship between hides and the contribution of agricultural surplus they made to estates and kings may offer two further reasons to support the proposition that interlocking structures of kinship and rights over land in early medieval Britain had been inherited from the prehistoric past.[42]

The first reason for thinking that the hide might have been a traditional form of measuring the economic potential of an area of land lies in its widespread acceptance by 600, from which there is no evidence of the dissent that might have been expected if it were newly imposed in that period. And if the hide was ancient then so, too, may have been the demands for renders associated with it. Charles-Edwards has persuasively argued that, if the hide was not introduced in the seventh century, then it must predate the political anarchy of the fifth and sixth centuries when rulers were unlikely to have had 'the necessary administrative resources to carry out the task of surveying their kingdoms and creating a unit of assessment for exacting taxes or food-renders'.[43] The logical consequence, if he is right, is that the imposition of the hide as a unit of tax assessment was almost certainly of Roman or prehistoric origin.

The proposition that the hide may have been inherited from Romano-British structures for assessing taxable land values could be tested against evidence for the continuity of Roman estates into the Anglo-Saxon period. If there were no continuity, then it is difficult to see how a unit of taxation based on land could have survived either. That the proposition might have some virtue is indicated by some evidence for the persistence of at least some Roman villa estates into the

Anglo-Saxon period. Among many other examples, Finberg's study of Withington (Glos.) is well-known, as is the example of the conversion of a Roman villa at Lullingstone (Kent) into an Anglo-Saxon estate, while Davies has suggested that the first charters of early medieval Wales transferred 'working estates' on which surpluses were *already* being produced.[44] This conclusion chimes well with Sarris' rhetorical question: 'Is it really the case, for example, that the Roman villa system and associated estate networks left so slight an imprint on the landscape of lowland Britain or on the collective memory of its inhabitants? It is striking, after all, how many early Anglo-Saxon settlements were located on the site of former Roman villas'.[45] There are a number of other similar unusual, but not outlandish, places such as Llandough (Glam.), where a large, continuously occupied Roman villa estate may have become an ecclesiastical estate in the sixth century, or Wollaston (Northants.) where a Roman villa estate continued to function well into the seventh century, when an early Anglo-Saxon prince was buried there with his boar-topped helmet.[46] These arguments suggest that at least some working estates, whose structures included a dependent unfree tenantry labouring on the inlands, survived the uncertainties of the 200 years following the withdrawal of Roman administration and were still identifiable in sixth, seventh or even eighth centuries.

The second reason for suggesting that the hide may already have been a traditional form of land assessment by the early medieval period is that it was found universally across seventh-century Britain – in the law codes of king Ine, in the *cantrefs* of Wales and in early medieval Ireland – despite, as noted above, the administrative subdivision of the islands under different political authorities from the late pre-Roman Iron Age onwards, if not before. Jolliffe and, later, Jones agreed that such similarities in northern England and Wales, separately administered since the early fifth century, were such that 'one is forced to suppose historical continuity' between the institutions of pre-Roman and Anglo-Saxon England.[47] Further support for the possible antiquity of the hide as a unit for calculating renders lies in arguments that the submission of agricultural surpluses to overlords may have originated in prehistory. The storage of large quantities of grain in Iron Age hill forts, for example, has been explained as 'tribute' or 'renders' from local or regional communities to their 'chiefs'.[48] If it is indeed the case that each prehistoric farming unit really was required to submit a render, then it seems likely that assessment of volume was undertaken in such a way as to ensure equity among those producing such goods; and in that case, it seems likely that assessments were imposed on households from above. If each household simply gave what surplus it estimated that it could 'afford' or be seen to 'afford', there would be considerable (and unacceptable) possibilities for evasion and inequity.

How does continuity of Roman, or earlier, estates and the persistent rights of their owners to exact renders fit into a model of common property rights over land vested in regional kin-based communities? If some Anglo-Saxon estates were the direct descendants of Roman or even prehistoric landed units, then two conclusions must follow. The first is that some form of hereditary tenure may reasonably be inferred to have existed at least throughout the millennium before AD 500 as several rights in property passed from one generation to the next. The second is that the common property rights of early medieval folk-groups over territories must have been qualified by several rights over other units of property, even if such other forms of 'private' tenure may have involved no more than the limitation of rights of inheritance to a wider family, for example, an agnatic kin-group of three or four generations' depth. (There is no suggestion in evidence or scholarship that the perpetual, formal individualisation of all rights over specific areas of land that is implied in the modern term 'private property' had yet emerged.)

Is there any evidence for either of these propositions? Reynolds and Millet agree that some form of hereditary rights over land were already ancient by the sixth century AD in long-standing prehistoric customary traditions influenced by Roman law – itself 'more adaptable and less absolute than was traditionally thought'.[49] Imperial legal traditions in Roman provinces did not provide detailed, immutable rules for governing the *minutiae* of social relations, but a normative, flexible structure within which existing forms of several rights over land could be managed and incrementally adapted in response to social and other pressures – a question of traditionally accepted and expected ways of doing things rather than a formal set of rules.[50] Archaeological excavation, too, indicates limited rights of heritability over land during the prehistoric period in indigenous holdings shared between extended families of agnatic kin measured over about four generations, a tradition which persisted well into the early medieval period when similar limited forms of inheritance can be identified on the relatively small share-lands in Ireland, and on the *worthigs* of English *ceorls*.[51] Millett, for example, has argued not only that collective rights over defined units of land might already have become more restricted before the Roman invasion of the mid-first century AD, but that patterns of occupation of some Roman villas reveal that they were estates inherited and occupied by extended family groups, a form of tenure which seems to have been as common as occupation of other villas by 'a single extended family group living in a tradition which continued directly' from the late pre-Roman Iron Age.[52] Such inherited rights in severalty over land may be analogous to custom and practice in southern Africa, where communities allow several rights to units of arable property with associated common rights in pasture to pass from father to sons on the understanding that the land will be returned to the wider kin-group if it is abandoned, poorly managed, or there are no heirs.[53]

Relatively privatised land units, perhaps already subject to restricted rights of inheritance and possibly on which rights to services and renders were already reserved to the estate owner, may thus already have been familiar in fifth- and sixth-century rural landscapes, lying alongside or as islands within large kin-based territories in which all freemen had common property rights. That is, the rights of early medieval freemen to several holdings appear to have been integral to their rights to largely non-arable resources under collective CPrRs. Rights in severalty within hierarchical structures of status and lordship were exercised in synchrony with collective rights in common within CPrRs.

From the early seventh century several property rights were strengthened and extended as kings began to use charters (*boc*) in legal forms legitimated by Roman precedent to grant perpetual, privatised rights over large areas of land to monastic houses headed by their royal kin. With a modern sophistry, royal monastic communities were treated as equivalent to family groups for the purposes of inheritance. This meant that traditional claims of inheritance from wider kin and community were excluded as the limitations to rights of inheritance previously found only on the relatively small share-lands of agnatic kin or the *worthigs* of *ceorls* were now extended over very large land units. Monastic estates were moreover proof against death without an heir, since members of each religious community were defined as a kin-group with collective rights of inheritance. The rights of abbeys and minsters to their estates were furthermore protected by both divine and royal authority, since their leaders could (mostly) be relied on to act in the interests of their wider royal kin. By modelling the inheritance claims of the monastic community on those of the wider kin, kings, abbots and abbesses assured monasteries, nunneries and minsters of an eternal earthly existence.[54] There were now no circumstances in which such an estate might eventually revert to the collective ownership of the clan through dearth of heirs, as ownership was vested not in the abbot or abbess but in the institution of the monastic community. This innovation was explicitly acknowledged in the introduction of grants in perpetuity.

At the same time, grants of bookland confused already-muddled distinctions between public and private obligations, as previously exclusively royal rights to services and renders from folkland were transferred to the new holders of extensive estates whose new lords undertook some functions formerly fulfilled by the state, particularly the three common burdens – maintenance of fortresses and of bridges, and participation in the royal *ffyrd*.[55] A principal innovation of early medieval kings was their normative rationalisation of their adaptation of traditional structures in the interests of strengthening their own authority.

Lordship and the dependent tenantry

The possibility that at least some early medieval estates represented prehistoric or Roman land units held severally by extended family groups with an entitlement to demand renders provides a context for related arguments that groups of unfree dependent tenants, tied to the land, may have formed part of a traditional labour force for such territories.

Groups of unfree tenants were found on estates across early medieval England, Wales and Ireland, in the 'semi-free' *læti* of early seventh-century Kent, the 'semi-freemen' called *fuidir* in early medieval Ireland, the bondmen who were 'tied to the soil' at Caeo in ninth-century Wales, and those of Anglo-Saxon Northumbria.[56] They were not a uniform group, their status ranging from slave to dependent, and Susan Reynolds has engagingly likened their place in the social hierarchy to the components of a trifle, as the 'sherry of accepted values' blurred the distinctions between 'a multiplicity of status and a multitude of gray areas'.[57] The universality with which such men have been identified across Britain in the long eighth century and their fully formed presence in Ine's Wessex led Aston to conclude that there was no indication that they represented the slow decline into tied dependence of former free-holding peasants. Instead, he argued, their dependent status was long-standing and traditional: 'Their tenements and tenure, their customs and even their status, have evolved from the beginning to meet the complex needs, private and public, of great lords from the king downwards'.[58] He pointed out that the documentation of apparently well-developed 'estates, demesnes and tenantry in the forefront of social institutions' in 'a source as early as Ine's laws' is difficult to explain away as a recent development.[59] Similarly, Jones argued that some aspects of the formal organisation of labour and agriculture at the royal court at Aberffraw on Anglesey may already have been present in the mid-sixth century if not before, a suggestion recently supported for lowland Britain by Sarris.[60] If groups of unfree, tied labourers were already an established aspect of landed estates by the early seventh century, what may their origin have been?

It is generally accepted that hereditary groups of unfree tenants, *coloni*, worked the 'demesne' arable of many Romano-British villa estates. More recent scholarship has proposed that, rather than a Roman introduction, they may rather have evolved from groups of dependent labourers on high status households of the Late British Iron Age.[61] For each of these researchers, the social structure of the sixth and seventh centuries has been a major stumbling block to suggestions of the loss of all continuity with Romano-British and Late British estate administration. In Aston's words, 'the organisation of settlement and agriculture … was already old when Ine described it in his laws'.[62] Two conclusions follow from such arguments. The first is that the nucleated settlements laid out at estate centres from the mid-seventh century onwards represents simply the formalised resettlement on early medieval estates of traditionally established groups of dependent tenants. The second is that the introduction of such unfree tenancies on the inlands of newly established estates just represented continuity with existing practices rather than innovations in social relations.

Conclusion

The universality with which open arable cultivated under narrow CPrRs has been identified across almost every part of Britain, from Cornwall to Northumberland, from Kent to Cumbria and into Wales and Scotland makes it difficult to argue that they were an innovation on middle Anglo-Saxon demesnes.[63] Such irregular medieval open fields have been identified across all soil types, in low-lying and high country, in well and poorly drained soils, in all climatic zones, and in wooded and in open countryside. They occurred in areas of early Anglo-Saxon settlement and in areas where Late British populations survived into the seventh or eighth centuries. They cannot be attributed to Romanisation, to one or another of the Anglo-Saxon kingdoms, or to the Scandinavian invasions. They can be found inside and beyond regions of high population. Nor can their comprehensive occurrence be explained by distributions of Anglo-Saxon charters, forms of manorialisation, traditions of inheritance, or distinctions between free and unfree peasants.[64]

Bailey has suggested that open-field arable cultivation managed under narrow CPrRs were particularly likely to be found in areas with a widely diverse social structure and little history of institutional control, basing his argument on their characterisation by a wide variation in the degree of autonomy of individual cultivators to arrange cropping and fallowing in severalty on their own arable holdings.[65] In some parts of Kent or the Lincolnshire fens, for instance, individual holdings were cropped entirely in severalty even though cultivators held rights of common pasture on the wastes that surrounded them. In others, as in many East Anglia vills, while cropping and fallowing was undertaken in severalty, there were limited grazing rights of common grazing over the stubbles. Yet again, there were places in Devon where rights of grazing could be exercised on both stubbles and fallows at certain times of year although the arable was subject to several cultivation.[66] Bailey has cogently argued that this autonomy – expressed in a low level of communal regulation over the arable – was more likely to be found in places in which lordship was 'fragmented, multiple or low status', in which there were a multiplicity of small manorial holdings, and in which there was a preponderance of free tenants.[67] Significantly, all were nonetheless based on principles of equity among all right-holders in the governance, management and regulation of those aspects deemed to require collective organisation, embedded in custom and practice that was recorded in oral traditions framed by concepts of kinship and lordship.

Aspects of the collective organisation of arable cultivation appear to find an echo in the fields of prehistoric and Roman Britain – in particular, in open-field land shared between a number of cultivators but cropped in severalty, in the link between arable holdings and rights of common pasture, in structures for the governance of common property resources, and in traditions for the payment of some surplus to an overlord, whether rationalised as tribute, gift, rent or render.

Together they suggest that generalised structural aspects of kinship, landholding and social relations may have endured across the anarchic years of the fifth and sixth centuries, perpetuated both in collective memory and in the day-to-day agricultural activities and relationships on which the survival of each household was based. These synergies, combined with the almost universal distribution of irregular medieval open fields across Britain and the enormous variety in their detailed regulation suggests that, if middle Anglo-Saxon landowners were formalising production on their extensive estates across large areas of early medieval Britain, many gave local men a pretty free hand in ordering how this was to be achieved. There is little indication of the uniformity that might be expected if lords had imposed a mechanism for achieving their aims.From community to community, responses to demands for increased productivity seem to have been predicated on existing patterns of local land management and continuities in their collective governance.

If it is the case that irregular medieval open fields evolved from older traditions of some arable management under narrow CPrRs, the achievement of the long eighth century may not have been the introduction of open-field systems. Instead, it may have been the adaptation of traditions of collective infield-outfield cultivation managed under narrow CPrRs to demands for increased production. New land was brought into cultivation, the distribution of holdings negotiated, and increased services and renders were delivered to lords by communities with relatively slight lordly input into the means by which these changes were achieved.

Inherited yet evolving expectations about the collective governance of open-field arable under narrow CPrRs, about rights over land based on traditions of kinship and lordship, and perpetuated in strong traditions of customary regulations recollected collectively, may have underlain continuity in the use of ancient structures for the layout and collective management of open-field arable in Britain in the Anglo-Saxon period. Neilson's scholarship may be vindicated in her prescient suggestion of 'the possibility … of a natural development from one agricultural form to another, inherent in processes of husbandry, and underlying and independent of all superficial racial conquest or change'.[68]

Notes

1 O'Connor 2009: 11, my addition.
2 Jones 1981: 202, 207; Davies 1982: 63; Trench 1975: 26; Kelly 1997: 406, 656; also page 407. The *túath* was an early medieval Irish clan-grouping.
3 Charles-Edwards 1972: 17, 14; Kelly 1997: 447.
4 Neilson 1929: 732, 1920: lxxvi.
5 Neilson 1920: xlix.
6 Homans 1953: 39; Hoskins and Stamp 1963: 6.
7 Miller 1969: 13.
8 Neilson 1920: li.
9 Davies and Vierck 1974: 224. See also Davies 1974: 14; Faith 1997: 147, 2; Lewis et al. 1997: 184.
10 Fowler 2002: 224, my emphasis; Roberts 2008: 166, my addition. See also Hamerow 2002b: 129.
11 Hooke 1992: 48; also Ford 1987: 151.
12 Faith 1997: 133.
13 e.g. Neilson 1920: xl and 1928: 4; Hoskins and Stamp 1963: 7; Finberg 1972: 403ff.; Davies and Vierck 1974: 224; Rackham 2004: 45; Ford 1987; Hooke 1998: 144; Faith 1997: 133; Lewis et al. 1997: 184.
14 cf. Hoskins 1988 edn.
15 For examples, see Maitland 1897: 143, 202, 352–5; Rackham 2004: 45; Ford 1987: 148; Hooke 1981a: 48; Lewis et al. 1997: 59; Corcos 2002: 127; Jones and Page 2006: 63, 141.
16 Hamerow 1997: 33.
17 Whitelock 1979: 403–4.
18 Hooke 1978: 335; Neilson 1928: 7, 34, 41. See also Finberg 1972: 404–10, 497; Faith 1997: 30; Everitt 2002: 215.
19 Neilson 1928: 3; Finberg 1957: 37; Hoskins and Stamp 1963: 7, 24; Thirsk 1973: 245–6; Ford 1987: 148; Jones 1987a: 29–30; Costen 1988: 41; Rackham 1988: 25; Gelling 1992: 64; Fleming 1998b: 56; Everitt 2002: 216; Higham 2004: 30.

20 Cunliffe 2010: 604.

21 Hooke 1997: 74.

22 Davies 1978: 20; Jones 1987a: 29–30. Recent archaeological investigation at the site of Aldborough appears to confirm Jones' interpretation: Wainwright 2011. See also Thirsk 1973: 245–6.

23 Lewis et al. 1997: 55, my emphasis. See also Hooke 1981a: 160, 144; Stafford 1985: 8; Hoskins and Stamp 1963: 7–8; Fenton-Thomas 2003: 111; Neilson 1928: 3–7, 34; Finberg 1972: 403–10; Faith 1997: 30.

24 Jones 1981: 222 and 225.

25 Kelly 1997: 407.

26 Gosden 1985: 480.

27 Oosthuizen 2006: 30; Yorke 1995: 40; Jolliffe 1929: 614; Wainwright 2011.

28 Charles-Edwards 1972: 19, 31; Kelly 1997: 402; Jones 1981: 205. See also Härke 1997: 137.

29 Davies 1982: 63; Trench 1975: 26; Jones 1981: 202; Kelly 1997: 406; Gosden 1985: 481.

30 Gosden 1985: 480. See also Jones 1981: 205; Charles-Edwards 1972: 17.

31 Härke 1997: 140; Charles-Edwards 1972: 8–9.

32 Charles-Edwards 1997: 179.

33 Ibid.: 176.

34 Gosden 1985: 482. See also Gosden and Locke 1998: 5; Charles-Edwards 1997. Similar flexibility is provided by the insertion of 'normally' into many modern regulations. Planning regulations noted by the Local Authority Building Control Departments (LABC), for example, explain that 'Construction of a small detached building such as a garden shed or summerhouse in the garden will not normally require Building Regulations if the floor area of the building is less than 15m2.' http://www.labc.uk.com/building-regulation-exemptions (my emphasis).

35 Charles-Edwards 1972: 17. See also Bullough 1969.

36 Härke 1997: 137; Gosden 1985: 485; Jackson 1964. See Sharples 2010: 7–8 for a critique of this view.

37 Sharples 2010: 173; Cunliffe 2010: 605.

38 cf. Charles-Edwards 1972: 14: 'The difference between the Irish and English situations lies not in the social system from which they started, but in the changes which subsequently took place'.

39 Faith 1997: 2.

40 Hooke 2011: 146.

41 Charles-Edwards 1972: 6–9, 14. See also Kelly 1997: 399, 447.

42 Gosden 1985: 480; Gosden 2011.

43 Charles-Edwards 1972: 4, 18.

44 Finberg 1955; Davies 1978: 7–8.

45 Sarris 2006: 12.

46 Knight 2005; Meadows 1997; Meadows 1996.

47 Jolliffe 1926: 40. See also Jones 1987a.

48 e.g. Sharples 2010: 120–3; Jones 2007.

49 Rio 2006: 37. See also Millett 1990: 96–7; Reynolds 1994: 326; Stevens 1966; Davies 1978: 7–20; Millet 1990: 203.

50 Rio 2006: 36.

51 Bullough 1969; Charles-Edwards 1972, 1997; Gosden 1985; Kelly 1997: 412–14; Faith 1997: 129–30.

52 Millett 1990: 201. See also Millett 1990: 96–7 and 197–9.

53 Bennett and Barrett 2007.

54 Faith 1997: 15. See also Vinogradoff 1893; Jolliffe 1935; Bullough 1969.

55 Aston 1958: 68–9.

56 Charles-Edwards 1972: 12; Kelly 1997: 440; Jones 1987: 12; Jolliffe 1926: 39;

57 Reynolds cited in Rio 2006: 34, 38.

58 Aston 1958: 73.

59 Ibid.: 73.

60 Jones 1987a: 13. He has proposed (1987a: 12) that '*maenor*' is the root of '*maenol*', the term for extensive estates in north Wales, and that both are derived from '*maen*', 'stone', suggesting that the word was used to indicate 'the stone girt residence of the king'; Sarris 2009: 12.

61 Millett 1990: 203.

62 Aston 1958: 83.

63 Roberts and Wrathmell 2002: 144; although no open fields are shown in Cornwall on Roberts and Wrathmell's Figure 5.10, areas of open field divided into strips could nonetheless be found in the medieval Cornish landscape: Cornwall County Council, http://www.historic-cornwall.org.uk/flyingpast/medieval.html [accessed August 2011].

64 Roberts and Wrathmell 2002: 144, 19, 22, 32, 34, 38, 69, 74, 78, 79, 125, 126, 127, 142, 178. As late as the fourteenth century, open-field systems still dominated the English landscape, Campbell 1981a: 112.

65 Bailey 2010: 158–9 and 167. See also Campbell 1981a: 114–15; Bailey 2007, 2009; Bishop 1938; Rippon 2008.

66 Campbell 1981a: 114–15.

67 Bailey 2010: 167.

68 Neilson 1929: 726.

6

Transformation into open-field systems under wide CPrRs

The problem of the Central Province

There are three problems consequent on the proposition advanced in earlier chapters that open-field systems cultivated across medieval England under narrow property regimes may have evolved from long-standing traditions of arable management. Each follows from the restricted distribution within the Central Province (at least from the twelfth century onwards) of open-field systems cultivated under wide CPrRs whose central characteristic was the inclusion of full rights of common pasture across the fallows – thus necessitating full collective management of all aspects of cultivation.[1]

The first is that the same strategies for increased arable output were being adopted inside and beyond the Central Province over the long eighth century. Arable fields were being extended, new crops were being grown, there was a greater emphasis on maintaining soil fertility, and the mouldboard plough was more widely used (Figure 6(d)). In each of the middle Anglo-Saxon kingdoms, the owners of royal, ecclesiastical and secular estates were equally integrated into the aristocratic international networks in which such ideas were being developed – such knowledge was not the prerogative of central southern England. Why was it, then, that communities in the Central Province elected to govern both their collective pasture and their open-field arable under wide CPrRs in contrast to those across the rest of Britain who did not?

The second problem is that the Central Province in also the region within which nucleated settlement – apparently introduced on high-status sites in the long eighth century – was dominant. Why were lords (or their representatives) in the Central Province apparently more directive in their organisation of dependent labour, using nucleation to express the greater formalisation (and control) of their relationships with dependent tenants on their extensive estates?

The third problem is one of chronology. Open-field systems under wide CPrRs were first reliably documented in the twelfth century, but we have already seen that settlement nucleation was initiated on high-status estates from the mid-seventh century onwards, that is, up to 500 years earlier. Yet by the high Middle Ages, nucleated settlements and open-field systems managed under wide CPrRs had been combined in 'an extremely stable grain producing machine, with yields secured by the scale of formal rotations and the integration of arable, meadow and pasture'.[2] If open fields managed under wide CPrRs could not be found in middle Anglo-Saxon England, did the interactions between process and stimulus that eventually resulted in their emergence in the medieval landscape nevertheless begin in the rapidly changing political conditions of the long eighth century? That nuanced proposition is explored below.

Current explanations for the origins of wide CPrRs over open-field arable

The most influential explanation for the emergence of wide CPrRs over open-field arable has been that proposed by Thirsk and elaborated by Fox.[3] They argued that the medieval extension of arable cultivation under pressure of population led inevitably to a diminution in the area of available common pasture. As a consequence, there came a tipping point when it became essential to introduce a fallow season in cropping rotations to provide compensatory grazing for the village livestock. The distribution of late eleventh-century population densities, however, suggests that fallow seasons cannot have been more necessary across the Central Province than elsewhere: there were places – like eastern Norfolk – in which there were as many tenants as in the Central Province in 1086 and therefore perhaps as much demand for arable, yet Norfolk tends to be characterised by open-field systems managed within narrow rather than wide CPrRs.[4]

There is a second problem with this proposal. It is in the underlying premise that there will be a paucity of pasture in parishes whose arable is managed under wide CPrRs.[5] While this is very often true, there are also places where medieval open-field systems under wide CPrRs endured well into the nineteenth century and yet where there were also substantial areas of common grazing outside the arable fields. In the contiguous parishes of Willingham and Rampton, for example, along the southern Cambridgeshire fen-edge, there was so much commonable pasture as to dwarf the area of open fields in each parish.[6] Here, there so much available grassland that there was no need to compensate cultivators as grazing was lost to the plough.

It might, of course, be argued that fen pastures were a special case, really only suitable for cattle, being too damp to graze sheep successfully. This is true. Perhaps then, the fallow field in each parish compensated cultivators for the loss of sheep pasture? But there are problems with this position too. Although there were large numbers of sheep, they were 'field sheep', kept for their value in manuring 'as walking dung machines, to transfer nutrients from the permanent pasture … to the arable'.[7] Their wool was not of a commercial quality, and their dairy products could not compete with those from the cows which made the peat fens famous for their cheese, and many medieval peasants had no sheep at all.[8] A determined dissenter might then argue that the agricultural stimulus to the introduction of open-field arable under wide CPrRs in these parishes was the establishment of fallows to receive the benefit of that large 'dunging machine' while the remainder of the crops were under arable. The trouble with this proposition is that open fields managed under wide CPrRs did not emerge in Norfolk, despite highly developed arrangements there for managing sheep in fold-courses.[9] Whatever the reasons for the origins of wide open-field systems, the designation of some arable land as fallows in order to compensate cultivators for pastures lost to arable seems unlikely to have been among them.

All the same, common rights of grazing on the fallows do appear to compensate husbandmen for inadequate areas of pasture or meadow in those many vills where open-field arable did extend over most of the area of a parish. The problem with this proposition as an explanation for the middle or late Saxon emergence of open-field systems under wide CPrRs is that communities inside as well as outside the Central Province still had access to plenty of pasture for grazing the stock of the vill in the late eleventh century: there appear to have been relatively few midland or East Anglian parishes in which arable cultivation had extended over more than around 40 per cent of the available area by 1086.[10] Lack of pasture for whatever reason is unlikely to have been a primary factor in the development of wide CPrRs over open-field arable.

Other explanations have suggested that cultural influences were the driving factor in the emergence of open-field systems under wider CPrRs, especially the influence of late ninth- and tenth-century Scandinavian migrants, arguing that the collective decision-making that underpinned wide common rights over arable was derived from Scandinavian social structures.[11] These views have had difficulty in finding general acceptance and Banham, in a recent review of the evidence, has expressed the objections most clearly: the Scandinavians 'didn't introduce [common-field cultivation] everywhere they lived, and someone must have introduced it into other areas'.[12]

For other scholars, the influence of geography has been the determining factor. Even allowing for the absence of extensive open-field systems from the predominantly pastoral highlands and uplands of northern and western England, however, where the soils are too thin and rocky, slopes are too steep, and/or fields are too high above sea level to allow a sufficient period for grain to grow and ripen, the concentration of open fields under wide CPrRs in the Central Province is puzzling. Good arable land was available far beyond Midland England, and there were as many plough-teams in east Norfolk in 1086 (for example) as there were in parts of the Central Province.[13] The consensus has been that the incidence of common-field systems does not appear to be 'related to any very obvious aspects of the natural environment, such as geology, climate or soils'.[14]

Yet in a new and innovative piece of research, Williamson has directed attention to the influence of soil conditions on the organisation of such field systems, demonstrating that the Central Province is generally coincident with the distribution of particularly difficult clay soils.[15] A combination of the number of days of wet weather that an English farmer might expect each year, combined with the difficulty in working heavy soils that could easily become too wet and clogged, or too dry and hard, put working days at a premium. He has suggested that communities cooperated in ploughing, harvesting and haying on such soils in order to maximise their opportunities for agricultural work. Dispersed settlement, he argued, would result in valuable hours being lost as plough-teams were assembled, or labourers walked to hay meadows or harvest from distant farms and hamlets; nucleated settlement would solve these problems as the tenantry would be immediately to hand when their labour was called for.[16] This is a contentious proposal. It could as straightforwardly be argued that it was more efficient to *retain* dispersed settlement on such soils in order to minimise the distance between homesteads and each area of outlying ploughland and there indeed examples of parishes whose open-field arable lay under wide CPrRs and yet where settlement was never nucleated. The refinement of geological arguments for the distribution of open-field systems under wide CPrRs has received a great deal of attention and further research is awaited to test the proposition in greater detail.

Social structure has provided a central explanatory factor for other scholars who argued that the origins of the distinctive landscape of the Central Province lay in the numbers of free men in each vill: that is, that high proportions of freeholding peasants inhibited the organisational centralisation implied by wide CPrRs over arable because the assent and participation of so many stakeholders would have been required. Hooke, for example, has suggested that the 'essential conservatism of farming communities meant that the introduction of common-field farming in just one vill was unlikely to have been initiated by the community'.[17] Yet the distribution of freemen across eleventh-century England is not demonstrably different across the boundary of the Central Province (although it is true that there were more in eastern England).[18] There are, too, examples of relatively unmanorialised parishes with high proportions of free tenants which by the later eleventh century were also characterised by nucleated settlements and open fields divided into two or three equal parts. North-west Bedfordshire offers a regional example, while that of the Eversdens (Cambs.) a more localised one – the arable being divided into two fields before the Norman Conquest, even though there was no manor, large or small.[19]

On the other hand, the close connection between dominant manorialism and wide CPrRs over open-field arable offers a complementary perspective, suggesting the possibility that it was, rather, strong lordship that played a central role. Aston, for example, has argued that the transfer of personal lordship from the folk to the economic and administrative structures of extensive estates inevitably made for greater homogeneity in the control of their lands by Anglo-Saxon lords.[20] Bailey has pointed out that even in areas of weak lordship wide CPrRs were nonetheless imposed over open-field arable on those manors where lordship was strong and centralised, like those in the Vale of York belonging to the Archbishop of York or the manors of the Abbey of Glastonbury in Somerset.[21] Strong or dominant lordship cannot on its own, however, explain the distinctive landscape of the Central Province. The open-field arable of most of the manors of the Bishop of Ely in 1251, just beyond the eastern boundary of the Central Province, was organised within narrow CPrRs even though the Bishops were stringent, wealthy and powerful lords. While it was perfectly possible for communities to create wide CPrRs for the governance of their open fields, it was probably just more likely that this happened where there was strong lordship. Was there, then, anything distinctive about lordship in the Central Province?

Lordship and the Central Province

Well, yes, there was. More commonly than anywhere else in England the 'well-manorialised midland and southern region' was characterised by manors whose area was coincident with that of the vill – that is, vills in which there was just one manor which controlled all or most of the landholding within it.[22] Campbell has connected that observation with the core of the Anglo-Saxon period by pointing out that this geography was coincident with 'the heartland of the old Anglo-Saxon state' of Mercia.[23] That manorialised 'heartland' was also the area in which there was by far the greatest concentration of medieval open-field systems under wide CPrRs, that is, the Central Province: eastern Warwickshire, southern Leicestershire, Northamptonshire, Huntingdonshire and west Cambridgeshire; Gloucestershire, Oxfordshire, north Buckinghamshire and Bedfordshire with secondary, but less dense, distributions in Somerset, Wiltshire and Hampshire, and in Lincolnshire and parts of Yorkshire.[24] Geography, lordship and political administration appear to overlap in central and eastern Mercia, the kingdom that dominated England throughout the long eighth century (Figure 8).[25]

Innovations in land management within the Central Province may have been the consequence of a deliberate policy aimed at consolidating the authority of the Mercian royal house. Royal minsters provided Mercian kings with opportunities for enhancing their reputations and consolidating their hold on power.[26] Charters endowed seventh- and eighth-century minsters, led by members of the royal kin, with extensive estates many already established administrative units, over which they were granted several rights in perpetuity.[27] The 'boom' in saintly cults from the late seventh century which raised royal abbots and abbesses to sanctity enhanced the status and authority of the wider royal kin-group and, by extension, the Mercian kingdom.[28] Many minsters were established at royal centres and were 'intimately connected with the royal administration', serving as places for the collection of renders, and providing repositories for royal treasure and archives.[29]

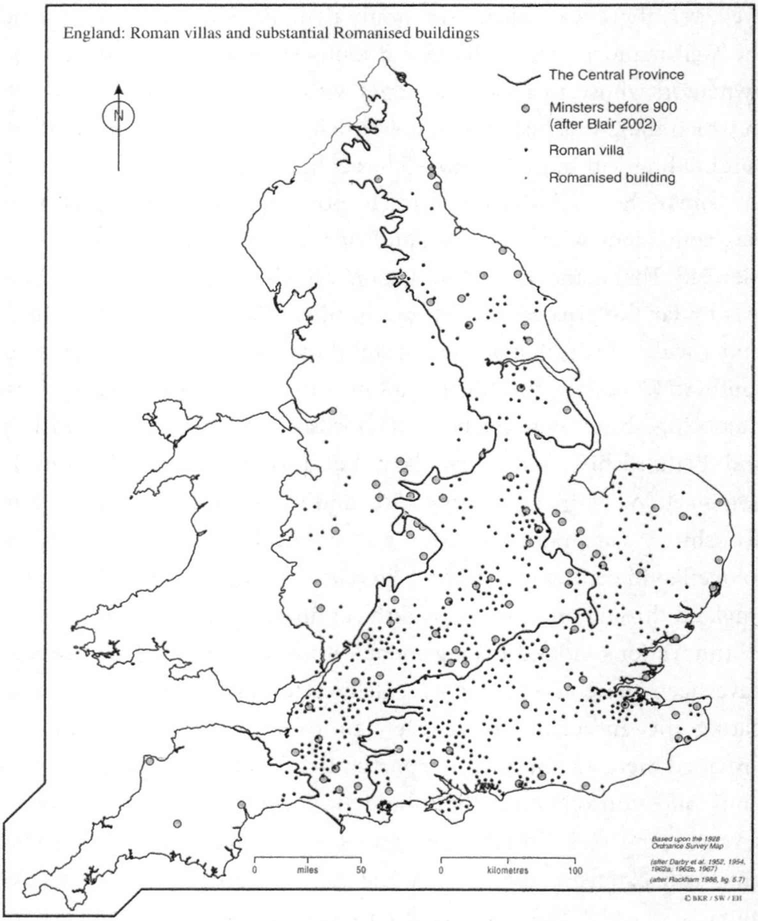

Figure 10. Substantial Romanised buildings and villas in England. (Reproduced with permission from Roberts and Wrathmell 2002).

The possibility that ecclesiastical lordship may have played a catalytic role is suggested by continental research indicating that the most intensive strategies for arable production were introduced on Carolingian royal monastic estates in the heart of the Frankish kingdom. Could similar strategies have been explain the origins of the Central Province in Anglo-Saxon England? By the later tenth century, the wealthiest and most powerful abbeys were located around the periphery of the Central Provence – Glastonbury in the south-west, Winchester, Abingdon and the London houses to the south, Canterbury in the south-east, and the great fenland monasteries along its eastern boundary.[30] That distribution suggests that high-status ecclesiastical lordship in the *late* Anglo-Saxon period was unlikely to be a dominant factor in the origins of the Central Province. If, instead, such innovations were indeed Mercian, and contemporary with Frankish developments, perhaps middle Anglo-Saxon monastic houses may have led innovations in the management of demesnes? There are significant problems in pursuing this line of enquiry. Sources for locating middle Anglo-Saxon minsters before about AD 900 are contentious, relatively few and focused principally on Mercia or Northumbria. Nonetheless, they appear to show a clustering of royal and aristocratic minsters within the boundaries of greater Mercia (Figure 10).[31]

There is, of course, an obvious problem with the proposal, which echoes those made for ethnic origins for open-field systems governed under wide CPrRs: *if* the seeds of wide CPrRs over open-field arable were indeed sown on Mercian ecclesiastical estates, they were not found throughout Mercia and other people must have introduced them beyond the boundaries of the kingdom.[32] That is, if dominant religious lordship provides one limiting lens on the distribution of wide CPrRs over open-field arable, and Mercian leadership of the English renaissance another, other factors must also have played a part.[33]

Other influences on the emergence of wide CPrRs over open-field arable

Three of these influences may be found in Hooke's useful suggestions that 'in general the open fields [under wide CPrRs] appear to have been laid out across land that was already open and cultivated in Roman times and in some valley regions of southern England it seems unlikely that the land which was to remain under cultivation ever went out of use'.[34] That is, that open-field arable governed under wide CPrRs tended to appear where a number of factors combined to produce optimal conditions: Romanised traditions of land-ownership, a long history of grain production, and continuity of cultivation across the fifth, sixth and seventh centuries. The evidence in many places (discussed above) for continuous occupation of field systems across the first millennium tends to support the proposition and, of course, Romanised buildings and villas have been found across the central and southern parts of the Central Province, and across south-east England in general (Figure 12).[35] While there is no particular correlation between Romanised landscapes and the Central Province, there are nevertheless more substantial Roman buildings and villas than elsewhere in Mercia in just those central and eastern areas of the kingdom in which there is the greatest density of wide CPrRs over open-field arable.[36]

Hooke's second suggestion, that such arrangements were particularly focused on areas in which grain production was *already* an important part of the local economy can be tested against initial mapping of the distribution of cleared land between *c.*730 and 1086.[37] These maps are fraught with difficulties in the completeness and interpretation of the evidence used in their construction, since they are based on gaps between areas of known Anglo-Saxon woodland and wood pasture, and the location of mid-twentieth century commons and wastes.[38] Nonetheless, there does seem to have been more open land – whether arable or grass land – and lower densities of woodland inside the Central Province than out (Figure 11). More significantly,

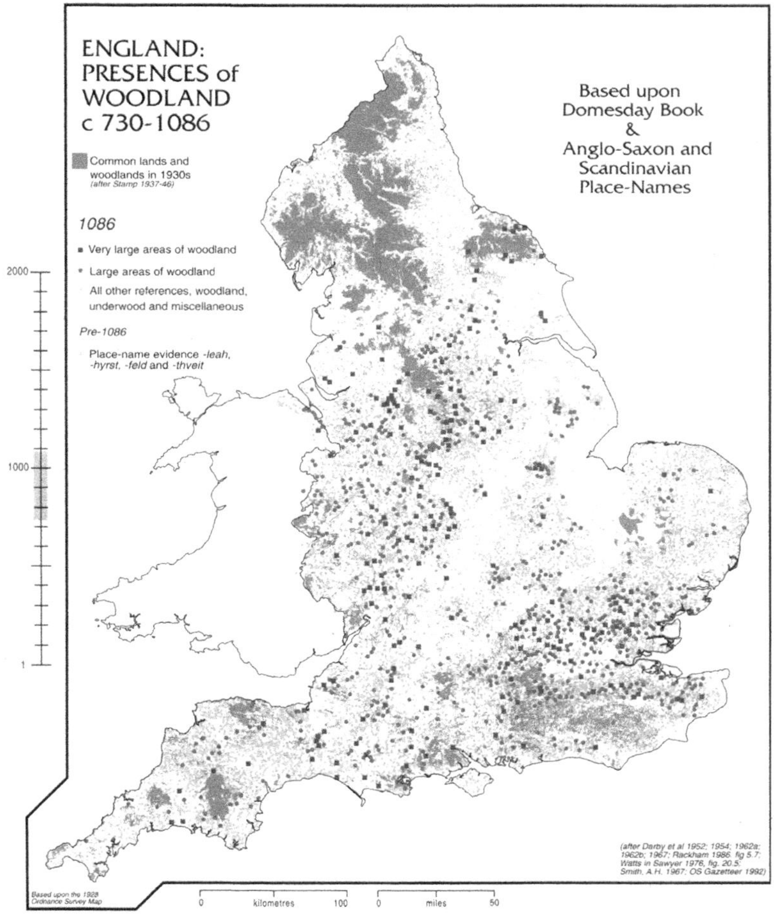

Figure 11. The distribution of Anglo-Saxon woodland. (Reproduced with permission from Roberts and Wrathmell 2002).

the areas with the most clearances appear once more to have been in just those parts of central and eastern Mercia already identified. It is therefore certainly feasible that existing arable was a stimulus to estate owners in central and eastern Mercia for introducing new forms of land and workforce management and arable cultivation on their estates.

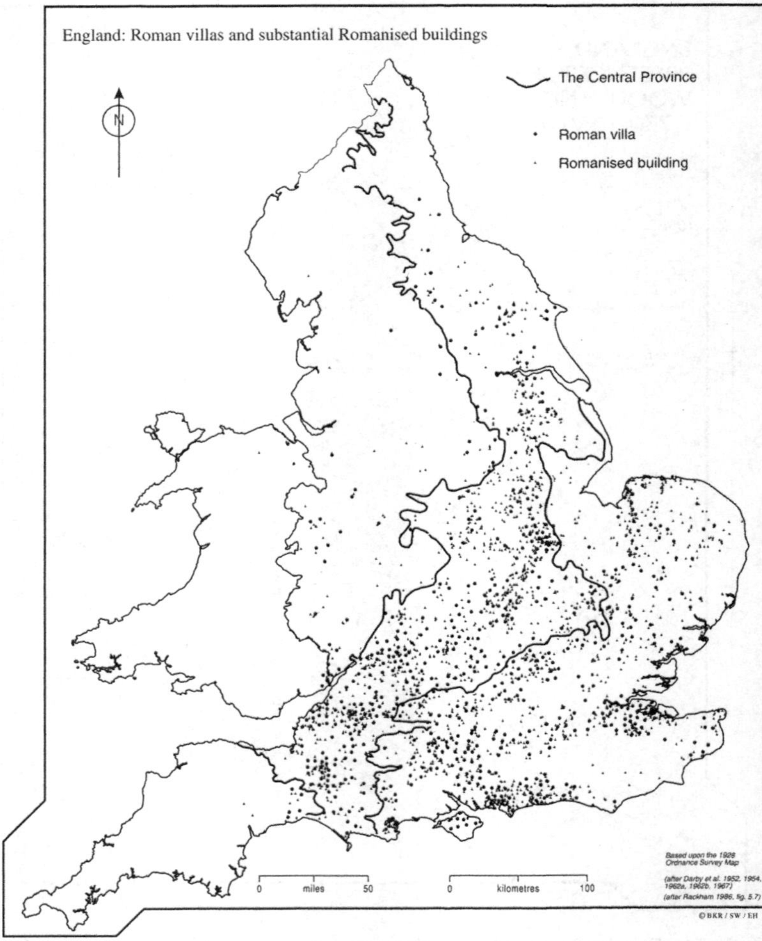

Figure 12. Monastic foundations in England before about 900. (Mapped after Blair 2002b, over Figure 10 above, reproduced with permission from Roberts and Wrathmell 2002).

The implication of Hooke's proposition is that the persistence of cultivation on Romanised estates into the middle Anglo-Saxon period may been accompanied – at least in some places – by the survival of groups of unfree tenants who were tied to the soil, that is, by the presence of a dependent tenantry whose labour was largely focused on the cultivation of the demesne.[39] Hereditary groups of relatively unfree tenants, *coloni*, had worked the arable farms of Roman villa estates. As outlined in the previous chapter, their origins may lie in the prehistoric past.[40] Groups of such unfree or semi-free tenants were widely found across early medieval Britain, and their presence in Ine's Wessex in the later seventh century AD, apparently in a developed form, led Aston to conclude that 'their tenements and tenure, their customs and even their status, have evolved from the beginning to meet the complex needs, private and public, of great lords from the king downwards'.[41] The possibility, then, that classes of unfree tenants survived from the Roman period into the long eighth century AD, at least in some areas of previously intensive Roman arable cultivation, is feasible although contentious. The problem is the familiar one: that they were as easily found outside as inside the Central Province, and their presence on some Mercian extensive estates is insufficient on its own to explain the restrictive distributions of the Central Province.

Perhaps a more useful way forward might be to explore whether *some elements* of arable management and organisation which were introduced on high-status Mercian estates during the long eighth century may had some synergies with those of later wide CPrRs over open-field arable. And if the long eighth century seems too short a period for such innovation, it might be remembered that the period extends over 150 years, while the hold of the 'Mercian supremacy' was even longer, extending to AD 890.[42] This is at least equivalent in length to the period between 850 and AD 1000 to which the origins of wide open-field systems are most commonly ascribed (and far longer than the race for Parliamentary enclosure between about 1770 and 1840 whose impact on the landscape was just as marked).

The Mercian contribution?

The extent to which Mercian kings, nobles and churchmen, innovative in outlook and active participants in a lively north-west European cultural renaissance, developed detailed strategies and techniques over the course of the long eighth century for the arable layout, tenure and cropping on the inlands of their extensive estates has already been discussed in some detail. It would be surprising if such kings – astute enough to establish networks of defensive *burhs*, to provide an infrastructure for national and international trade and exchange, and to exploit the Church to bolster its authority – did not also see strategic political and economic possibilities in the endowment of royal minsters with enormous estates, especially where there was some degree of continuity with the Roman past, where arable cultivation was predominant, where there was already a core of dependent tenants, where there was ready access along the major waterways to national and international markets, and where the religious authority of an ecclesiastical estate might bolster royal administration and control.[43]

The 'apparently innate connection between arable farming and the dominant lordship of the inland' so characteristic of the Central Province was also particularly evident on the royal Carolingian monastic demesnes in the Paris Basin. Here representatives of the landowning elite not only ordered the layout and management of arable on their extensive estates, but appear to have supervised their practical application.[44] Estate managers implemented specific strategies: inlands and tenanted demesnes were divided into measured strips, peasant holdings on the demesne were intermingled, and patterns of crop rotation were ordered by estate managers.[45] Similar strategies appear to have been adopted in central and eastern Mercia on high-status estate centres and their most significant berewicks where planned nucleated settlements were laid out, on which tied dwellings were integrated with arable holdings. That centralised direction of cultivation is visible in the landscape of early medieval England not only in nucleated settlements laid out at high-status estate centres but also in the measured subdivision of inland and leased demesne into strips (perhaps, for example, in Northamptonshire and Holderness) accompanied by the intermingling of tenanted holdings and the enforced regulation of cropping.[46] Aston has drawn attention to the specifically close connection between such manorial organisation and monastic landholdings, writing of 'highly developed dependent tenures on ecclesiastical estates and their spasmodic and almost casual occurrence on lay lordships' and as well as to their 'rigidity and permanence', commenting that 'dependent tenure was deeply embedded in the organisation and external relations and, as it were theory, of an ecclesiastical estate'.[47]

While the division of arable open fields between cultivators and the layout of some holdings in strips were, as we have seen, probably traditional practices across middle Anglo-Saxon England, the intermingling of fractions of holdings and centralised direction of crop rotations will have required a wider CPrR over arable than may then have been customary. Such innovations may have been particularly visible on ecclesiastical estates whose lordship may have provided the catalyst for application of some elements of wide CPrRs to arable cultivation on existing estates with groups of dependent tenants and long traditions of arable cultivation. The autonomy of tenants to cultivate their holdings in severalty would immediately have been compromised by lordly direction about which cereals they should grow each year and on which fraction of their lands. The intermingling of strips affected both individual decisions about several cultivation and about the timetabling for communal grazing on stubbles and fallows, given the risks of allowing stock – whether tethered or penned – onto harvested or fallow strips in open fields where crops on other strips were still growing. The tensions between the two competing demands of the long eighth century – those of interventionist lords for central management of cropping to improve productivity and those of peasants whose holdings were a mnemonic for status, kinship, tradition and collectivity – provided the central problem in land management. How were they to be resolved?

A joint endeavour?

The relative autonomy of early medieval and later peasants in managing the cultivation of their fields under narrow CPrRs is markedly absent from the Central Province. Yet, the most notable feature of wide CPrRs over medieval open-field arable systems was that, by the mid-twelfth century, they integrated two contrasting value systems. On the one hand, dominant lordship was expressed in their regulation of the management of productivity on their inland demesnes by their dependent tenants.[48] On the other hand, wide CPrRs over arable open fields were predicated on the full participation of all cultivators in the governance and management of all aspects of rights of common over arable, including the fallows.[49] So intense was the consequent demand for collectivity that Campbell and Godoy have suggested that the 'complex scheduling problems' of ploughing, sowing and harvesting while also meeting the requirement for full common rights on stubbles and fallows 'places a premium upon the collective management of resources'.[50] This was achieved through enforceable by-laws, recorded in oral traditions of custom and practice at village assemblies in which each cultivator was expected to participate. That is, the efficiency of cultivation on open-field systems in whose management lords took a leading role depended on widening traditional forms of governance over common property resources to include grazing on the fallows and stubbles.

The achievement of manorial lords and local communities in the Central Province over the long eighth century may thus have been the recognition that, if arable cultivation on the demesnes could no longer be undertaken by dependent tenants managing their holdings in severalty, it made sense to harness traditional mechanisms for ensuring collective participation and agreement to the introduction of centrally directed cultivation. That is, innovation and tradition may have been combined on high-status Mercian demesnes in a negotiated solution that allowed the implementation of new managerial approaches to agricultural efficiency while at the same time preserving and respecting traditional forms of governance that assured the participation and agreement of tenants, most of whom were of Late British descent. Even if such innovations were initially restricted to the demesnes, and tenanted strips beyond continued to be cultivated in severalty, the gradual extension of CPrRs to include the management of all agricultural land, whether pasture or arable, eventually became the distinguishing feature of the Central Province.

The evolution over the following centuries of wide CPrRs over open-field arable may have offered early medieval tenants and their successors some real continuities of customary autonomy and status within social hierarchies and conditions of labour which became less advantageous to them over time. The application of a wide CPrR over arable provided a context in which peasant rights to participation in their governance and regulation had an equal standing with those of the lord. Dyer has made a similar point in arguing that, where nucleated settlement and common-field systems occurred in townships divided between several manors, late Anglo-Saxon lords and peasants must have collaborated in setting up common property governance of open-field arable: 'Village communities, which were capable of taking on the management of manors as collective lessees in the eleventh century, may well have been involved in village reorganisation. In which case the regularly planned village is evidence not of close seigniorial control, but of the limitations on the power of manorial lords who had to deal with a strong and cohesive village community'.[51]

Just as the origins of the Anglo-Saxon kingdoms appear to have been rooted in ancient traditions of collective governance over pasture, so too may the extensive estates of the long eighth century have utilised traditional forms of social organisation to achieve highly managerial ends. The tide of remodelling which left 'the English Midlands submerged' may have been an uneven process, initiated on some lordly demesnes and gradually adopted on the lands of free tenants in the same vills, imitated at the same time on the estates of their neighbours and/or by freemen in nearby communities.[52]

Notes

1 Bailey 2010: 158.

2 Roberts and Wrathmell 2002: 136.

3 Thirsk 1973: 648–9; Fox 1981: 65; Campbell 1981a: 115; Campbell and Godoy 2008: V, 107. See Bailey 2010: 161–3 for a cogent critique of this position.
4 Hill 1981: 19; Campbell 1981b. See also Bailey 2010: 159–60.
5 Bailey 2010: 159.
6 Wright and Lewis 1989: 211.
7 Campbell 1981b: 18.
8 Postan 1973: 231, 245; Miller 1969: 41.
9 Campbell 1981b.
10 Oosthuizen 2006: 43–4.
11 Hodges 1989: 154; Hart 2000: 30; Hart 1995: 47. For arguments, no longer accepted, that such field systems were a Germanic introduction, see, for example, Maitland 1897: 365–6 and 515–518; Hoskins 1988 edn: 45–7; Stenton 1971: 280.
12 Banham 2009, my additions. Dr Banham generously gave me a pre-publication copy of the paper.
13 Roberts and Wrathmell 2002: 69.
14 Taylor 2002: 53. See also Roberts and Wrathmell 2002: 32–39, 64.
15 Williamson 2003.
16 Ibid.: 6, 142–3 and 156.
17 Hooke 1998: 119–20. See also Harvey 1989: 36.
18 Roberts and Wrathmell 2002: 127; Williamson 2003: 47.
19 Lewis et al. 1997: 209; Oosthuizen 1997.
20 Aston 2004: 89.
21 Bailey 2010: 167–8.
22 Neilson 1929: 728.
23 Campbell 1981a: 128.
24 Gray 1959: frontispiece; Roberts and Wrathmell 2002: 124; Thirsk 1964: 1966; Fox 1981.
25 Oosthuizen 2007.
26 Thacker 1985.
27 Blair 2002b: 470. There is, as far as I know, no map showing the distribution of early or middle Anglo-Saxon charters; most were produced from the tenth century onwards; see Hill 1981: 22–5.
28 Blair 2002b: 471. See also 468; Rollason 1978: 82.
29 Thacker 1985: 2.

30 Hill 1981: 154–5.
31 Rollason 1978: 82; see Blair 2002b: 467–71 for a critical evaluation of the distribution of early Anglo-Saxon saints' cults, and Blair 2002a.
32 Banham 2009.
33 Bailey 2010: 170.
34 Hooke 1998: 116, my addition.
35 Roberts and Wrathmell 2002: 78–9.
36 Ibid.: 78–9.
37 Ibid.: 28.
38 It cannot always be certain, for example, where woodland attached to a vill may actually have been. In some cases it may have been at some distance from the vill. Nor does the distribution make a distinction between managed stands of woodland, which may have been quite small, and tracts of unmanaged wood or wood pasture.
39 Hooke 1998: 116.
40 Millett 1990: 203.
41 Aston 1958: 73, my addition. See also Charles-Edwards 1972: 12; Kelly 1997: 440; Jones 1987a: 12; Jolliffe 1926: 39.
42 Dumville 1989: 136.
43 Blair 2005: 85–91; Thacker 1985; Bassett 2007.
44 Campbell 1981a: 129.
45 Faith 2009: 37.
46 e.g. Hall 1981, 1982b, 1984, 1988, 1995; Harvey 1980, 1983, 1984, 1985.
47 Aston 2004: 90, 89.
48 Bailey 2010: 167, my addition. See also Faith 2009: 37.
49 Bailey 2010: 159.
50 Campbell and Godoy 2008: V, 111–12, my addition. See also Bailey 2010: 159.
51 Dyer 1996: 306. See also Lewis et al. 1997: 208. Faith has offered a qualification of this observation, pointing out that initiators of change were probably 'neighbouring substantial farming families' as not all inhabitants of a township were holders of land (1997: 147).
52 Rackham 1986, 178, my additions.

Epilogue

The argument presented in the preceding chapters has been based on two related premises. The first is that late British populations survived in many parts of early Anglo-Saxon England to an extent that is more pervasive and substantial than was previously thought. The second is that, in this case, some of the inherited cultural perspectives and attitudes of those sixth- and seventh-century men, women and children are likely, at worst, to have influenced some of the evolving social habits and traditions in the post-Roman centuries and, at best, to have continued to frame Anglo-Saxon society more generally. The evidence underlying these premises has been discussed above and will not be rehearsed again here.

What remains controversial, however, is the *relative* extent of continuity on the one hand and of change on the other. The most important current aspect of that controversy is, perhaps, that it reflects a moment in scholarship in which the dominant discourse for explaining the archaeology and history of Anglo-Saxon England is beginning to shift. For over a century, researchers have 'known', with all the certainty of 'fact', that the 250 years or so between the end of the fifth century and the middle of the seventh represented an almost complete break in almost any terms that might be considered – demographic, cultural, political, linguistic, religious, material. It has until relatively recently been possible to explain any evidence of exceptions to that discourse simply as atypical.

Yet an interdisciplinary array of archaeologists, historians, linguists, art historians and so on – only occasionally aware of work in each others' fields – have for some time now consistently been reporting research results whose growing volume is beginning to represent a challenge to that world view. Their conclusions, which contest accepted explanations, tend not to have been treated synthetically – that is, as a whole – but as a series of isolated case studies, frequently by researchers themselves, with the result that we do not yet have an evaluative overview of all the available evidence for continuity across the early and middle Anglo-Saxon periods.

Debates on the archaeology and history of Anglo-Saxon England tend, then, to be framed as arguments for or against change – that is, as a traditional dichotomy. This means that sometimes discussion and debate may become adversarial as positions are aggressively defended to the point of ideology, while at the same time struggling against the straightjacket of simplicity which such dialectical approaches tend to encourage.

Habitus and the *longue durée* offer a nuanced view of the makings of the Anglo-Saxon landscape as a dynamic collaboration between middle Anglo-Saxon elites and peasant communities, in which tradition and transformation can both be discerned. The complicated question of how Roman Britain evolved or metamorphosed into Anglo-Saxon England remains relatively opaque, and further research is needed into the ways in which such societies might exhibit both cultural continuity *and* change across the full diversity of available evidence. We need to know more about how – from region to region, time to time, and varying from one social context to another – some customs might persist, while others were replaced as if they had never been, and yet others were changed in their interaction with new ideas, structures or habits. The propositions offered here as a contribution to that process are simply that – a series of proposals for further research in the course of which a new discourse may develop for explaining the complicated glory of cultural change.

Bibliography

Abrams, J. and Ingram, D. 2008. 'Farming on the edge: Archaeological evidence from the clay uplands to the west of Cambridge', *East Anglian Archaeology* 123.

Addyman, P. 1964. 'A dark age settlement at Maxey, Northants.', *Medieval Archaeology* 8: 20–73.

—and Leigh, D. 1972. 'The Anglo-Saxon village at Chalton, Hampshire: Second interim report', *Medieval Archaeology* 16: 13–31.

Aitchison, J. and Hughes, E. 1988. 'The common lands of Wales', *Transactions of the Institute of British Geographers* n.s. 13: 96–108.

Allen, M., Leivers, M. and Ellis, C. 2004. 'Neolithic causewayed enclosures and later prehistoric farming: Duality, imposition and the role of predecessors at Kingsborough, Isle of Sheppey, Kent', *Proceedings of the Prehistoric Society* 74: 235–322.

Allerston, P. 1970. 'English village development', *Transactions of the Institute of British Geographers* 51: 95–109.

Anglo-Saxon Charters. n.d. http://ascharters.net/, accessed June-August 2011.

Applebaum, S. 1954. 'The agriculture of the British Early Iron Age as exemplified at Figheldean Down, Wilts.', *Proceedings of the Prehistoric Society* 20: 103–114.

—1966. 'Peasant economy and types of agriculture', in C. Thomas, ed., *Rural Settlement in Roman Britain.* York, Council for British Archaeology: 99–107.

—1972. 'Roman Britain', in H. P. R. Finberg, ed., *The Agrarian History of England and Wales* I, ii, *AD 43–1042.* Cambridge, Cambridge University Press: 5–267.

Arnold, C. J. 1984. *Roman Britain to Saxon England.* London, Croom Helm.

—1988. *An Archaeology of the Early Anglo-Saxon Kingdoms.* London, Routledge.

Arnold, S. 2000. ' 'Nucleated and dispersed' under dem aspect von wüstungsprozessen und damit verbundenen siedlungskonzentrationen an ausgewählten beispielen aus dem südwesten Duetschlands', *Ruralia* III: 273–287.

Aston, M. 1985. 'Rural settlement in Somerset: Some preliminary thoughts', in D. Hooke, ed., *Medieval Villages: A Review of Current Work*. Oxford, Oxford Committee for Archaeology: 81–100.

—1988. 'Land use and field systems', in M. Aston, ed., *Aspects of the Medieval Landscape of Somerset*. Taunton, Somerset County Council: 83–98.

—1999. '"Unique, traditional and charming". The Shapwick Project, Somerset', *Antiquaries Journal* 79: 1–58.

Aston, T. H. 1958. 'The origins of the manor in England', *Transactions of the Royal Historical Society*, Fifth Series 8: 59–83.

—2004. 'The ancestry of English feudalism', in R. Evans, ed., *Lordship and Learning*. Woodbridge, Boydell and Brewer: 79–94.

Atkin, M. A. 1985. 'Some settlement patterns in Lancashire', in D. Hooke, ed., *Medieval Villages: A Review of Current Work*. Oxford, Oxford University Committee for Archaeology: 170–85.

Ault, W. O. 1954. 'Village by-laws by common consent', *Speculum* 29, 2: 378–394.

—1960. 'Village assemblies in medieval England', in *Album Helen Maud Cam*, Volume 1. Louvain, University of Louvain: 13–35.

—1965. 'Open-field husbandry and the village community', *Transactions of the American Philosophical Society* 55, 7: 5–102.

—1972. *Open Field Farming in Medieval England*. London, Allen and Unwin.

Bailey, M. 2007. *Medieval Suffolk*. Woodbridge, Boydell and Brewer.

—2009. 'The form, function and evolution of irregular field systems in Suffolk, 1300–1500', *Agricultural History Review* 57, 1: 34–6.

—2010. 'Beyond the Midland system: The determinants of common rights over the arable in medieval England', *Agricultural History Review* 58, 2: 153–71.

Baker, A. R. H. 1965. 'Howard Levi Gray and "English Field Systems": An evaluation', *Agricultural History* 39, 2: 86–91.

—and Butlin, R., eds. 1973. *Studies of Field Systems in the British Isles*. Cambridge, Cambridge University Press.

Banham, D. 2009. 'Race and tillage: Scandinavian Influence on Anglo-Saxon Agriculture?', in M. Kilpiö, L. Kahlas-Tarkka, J. Roberts and O. Timofeeva, eds., *Anglo-Saxons and the North: Essays Reflecting the Theme of the 10th Meeting of the International Society of Anglo-Saxonists in Helsinki, August 2001*. Tempe, Arizona, ACMRS: 165ff.

Barnwell, P. 1996. '*Hlafæta, ceorl, hid* and *scir*: Celtic, Roman or Germanic?', *Anglo-Saxon Studies in Archaeology and History* 9: 53–61.

Bassett, S. 1980–1. 'Medieval Lichfield: A topographical review', *Transactions of the Staffordshire Archaeological and Historical Society* 22: 93–121.

—1985. 'Beyond the edge of excavation: The topographical context of Goltho', in H. Mayr-Harting and R. I. Moore, eds., *Studies in Medieval History Presented to R. H. C. Davis*. London, Hambledon: 21–39.

—ed. 1989. *The Origins of the Anglo-Saxon Kingdoms*. Leicester, Leicester University Press.

—2007. 'Divide and rule? The military infrastructure of eighth- and ninth-century Mercia', *Early Medieval Europe* 15, 1: 53–85.

—2009. 'The landed endowment of the Anglo-Saxon minster at Hanbury (Worcs.)', *Anglo-Saxon England* 38: 77–100.

—2011. 'Anglo-Saxon fortifications in western Mercia', *Midland History* 36, 1: 1–23.

Bedell, J. 1999. 'Memory and proof of age in England 1272 - 1327', *Past and Present* 162: 3–27.

Bell, M. 1989. 'Environmental archaeology as an index of continuity and change in the medieval landscape', in M. Aston, D. Austin and C. Dyer, eds., *The Rural Settlements of Medieval England*. Oxford, Blackwell: 269–286.

Bennett, J. and Barrett, H. 2007. 'Rangeland as a common property resource: Contrasting insights from communal areas of central Eastern Cape Province, South Africa', *Human Ecology* 35: 97–112.

Beresford, M. 1953. 'The Poll Tax and Census of Sheep, 1549 Part 1', *Agricultural History Review* 1: 9–15.

—and Hurst, J. G. 1979. 'Wharram Percy: A case study in microtopography', in P. Sawyer, ed., *English Medieval Settlement*. London, Arnold: 52–85.

—and St Joseph, J. K. 1979. *Medieval England*. Cambridge, Cambridge University Press.

Berger, J.-F. 2001. 'Évolution des agro-et des hydrosystèmes dans la région médio-Rhodanienne', in P. Ouzalis, C. Pellecuer, C. Raynard, P. Van Ossel and P. Garmy, eds., *Les Campagnes de la Gaule à la Fin de l'Antiquité*. Montpellier, Actes Du Colloque: 369–403.

Berkes, F. 1985. 'The common property resource problem and the creation of limited property rights', *Human Ecology* 13, 2: 187–208.

Besteman, J. C. 1990. 'North Holland AD 400–1200', in J. C. Besteman, J.M. Bos and H. A. Heidinga, eds., *Medieval Archaeology in the Netherlands*. Assen, Van Gorcum: 91–120.

Biddick, K. 1989. *The Other Economy*. Los Angeles, University of California Press.

Biddle, M. and Kjølbye-Biddle, B. 1985. 'The Repton stone', *Anglo-Saxon England* 14: 233–292.

Birrell, J. 1987. 'Common rights in the medieval forest: Disputes and conflict in the thirteenth century', *Past and Present* 117: 22–59.

Birtles, S. 1999. 'Common land, poor relief and enclosure: The use of manorial resources in fulfilling parish obligations', *Past and Present* 165: 74–106.

Bishop, T. A. M. 1935–6. 'Assarting and the growth of open fields', *Economic History Review* 6: 26–40.

—1938. 'The rotation of crops at Westerham, 1297–1350', *Economic History Review* 9, 1: 38–44.

Blair, J. 1992. 'Anglo-Saxon minsters: A topographical review', in J. Blair and R. Sharpe, eds., *Pastoral Care Before the Parish*. London, Leicester University Press: 226–266.

—1994. *Anglo-Saxon Oxfordshire*. Stroud, Sutton.

—1996. 'Palaces or minsters? Northampton and Cheddar reconsidered', *Anglo-Saxon England* 25: 97–122.

—2002a. 'A handlist of Anglo-Saxon saints', in A. Thacker and R. Sharpe, eds., *Local Saints and Local Churches in the Early Medieval West*. Oxford, Oxford University Press: 494–565.

—2002b. 'A saint for every minster? Local cults in Anglo-Saxon England', in A. Thacker and R. Sharpe, eds., *Local Saints and Local Churches in the Early Medieval West*. Oxford, Oxford University Press: 457–494.

—2005. *The Church in Anglo-Saxon Society*. Oxford, Oxford University Press.

Blinkhorn, P. 1999. 'Of cabbages and kings: Production, trade and consumption in middle-Saxon England', in M. Anderton, ed., *Anglo-Saxon Trading Centres Beyond the Emporia*. Glasgow, Cruithne Press: 4–23.

Boddington, A. 1996. *Raunds Furnells The Anglo-Saxon Church and Churchyard*. London, English Heritage.

Boivin, N. 2008. *Material Cultures, Material Minds*. Cambridge, Cambridge University Press.

Bond, C. J. 1985. 'Medieval Oxfordshire villages and their topography: A preliminary discussion', in D. Hooke, ed., *Medieval Villages: A Review of Current Work*. Oxford, Oxford University Committee for Archaeology: 101–23.

Bourdieu, P. 1977. *Outline of a Theory of Practice*. Cambridge, Cambridge University Press.

Bourdillon, J. 1994. 'The animal provisioning of Saxon Southampton', in J. Rackham, ed., *Environment and Economy in Anglo-Saxon England*. York, Council for British Archaeology: 120–125.

Bowden, M., Brown, G. and Smith, N. 2009. *An Archaeology of Town Commons in England*. Swindon, English Heritage.

Bracton *De Legibus et Consuetudinibus Angliae* (Bracton on *The Laws and Customs of England*, attributed to Henry de Bratton, c.1210–1268), Harvard Law School Library. http:www.hlsl5.law.harvard.edu/bracton/, accessed July 2011.

Bradley, J. and Gaimster, M. 2000. 'Medieval Britain and Ireland, 1999', *Medieval Archaeology* 44: 235–354.

—2001. 'Medieval Britain and Ireland, 2000', *Medieval Archaeology* 45: 233–379.

—and Haith, C. 1999. 'Medieval Britain and Ireland, 1998', *Medieval Archaeology* 43: 226–302.

Bradley, R. 1984. *Social Foundations of Prehistoric Britain*. London, Routledge.

—2000. *The Archaeology of Natural* Places. London, Routledge.

—and Fulford, M. 2008. 'The chronology of co-axial field systems', in P. Rainbird, ed., *Monuments in the Landscape*. Stroud, Sutton: 114–122.

Braudel, F. 1981. *The Structures of Everyday Life*. London, Collins.

—1989. *The Identity of France. 1. History and Environment*. London, Fontana.

British Archaeology 1995. 'Anglo-Saxon watermill found on Tyne', *British Archaeology* 11: 5.

—2002a. 'Rare Iron Age temple excavated near Cambridge', *British Archaeology* 66: 7.

—2002b. 'Saxon watermill', *British Archaeology* 66: 6.

—2006. '"Find of several lifetimes" - cathedral archaeologist', *British Archaeology* 88: 7.

Brooks, N. 2000. *Communities and Warfare, 700–1400*. London, Hambledon.

Brown, A. E. 1991. *Early Daventry. An Essay in Early Landscape Planning*. Leicester, University of Leicester and Daventry District Council.

—1996. 'Burton Lazars, Leicestershire: A planned medieval landscape?', *Landscape History* 18: 31–45.

—and Foard, G. 1998. 'The Saxon landscape: A regional perspective', in P. Everson and T. Williamson, eds., *The Archaeology of Landscape*. Manchester, Manchester University Press: 67–94.

—and Taylor, C. C. 1989. 'Dispersed settlements in nucleated areas', *Landscape History* 17: 27–34

—and Taylor, C. C. 1993. 'Chellington field survey', *Bedfordshire Archaeological Journal* 23: 98–110.

Brunner, K. 1995. "Continuity and discontinuity of Roman agricultural knowledge in the early Middle Ages', in D. Sweeney, ed., *Agriculture in the Middle Ages*. Philadelphia, University of Pennsylvania Press: 21–40.

Buck, S. 1989. 'Cultural theory and management of common property resources', *Human Ecology* 12, 1: 101–116.

Bücker, C. and Hoeper, M. 2000. 'Dispersed and nucleated settlements in south-west Germany in Merovingian times', in J. Klâpste, ed., *Ruralia III*. Prague, Institute of Archaeology: 217–232.

Bull, E. J. 1993. 'The bi-axial landscape of prehistoric Buckinghamshire', *Records of Buckinghamshire* 35: 11–27.

Bullough, D. A. 1969. 'Early medieval social groupings: The terminology of kinship', *Past and Present* 45: 3–18.

Bult, E. and Hallewas, D. 1990. 'Archaeological evidence for the early-medieval settlement around the Meuse and Rhine deltas up to ca. AD 1000', in J. C. Besteman, J.M. Bos and H. A. Heidinga, eds., *Medieval Archaeology in the Netherlands*. Assen, Van Gorcum: 71–90.

Cam, H. 1912. *Local Government in* Francia *and England : A Comparison of the Local Administration and Jurisdiction of the Carolingian Empire with that of the West Saxon Kingdom*. London, University of London Press.

Campbell, B. 1980. 'Population change and the genesis of commonfields on a Norfolk manor', *Economic History Review* 33: 174–192.

—1981a. 'Commonfield origins – the regional dimension', in T. Rowley, ed., *The Origins of Open-field Agriculture*. London, Croom Helm: 112–129.

—1981b. 'The regional uniqueness of English field systems? Some evidence from eastern Norfolk', *Agricultural History Review* 29: 16–28.

—1983. 'Agricultural progress in medieval England: some evidence from eastern Norfolk', *Economic History Review*, 2nd series, 36: 26–46.

—2000. *English Seigniorial Agriculture, 1250–1450*. Cambridge, Cambridge University Press.

—and Godoy, R. A. 2008. 'Commonfield agriculture: The Andes and medieval England compared', in B. Campbell, *Field Systems and Farming Systems in Late Medieval England*. Ashgate, Variorum: V.

Campbell, D. 2010. 'The *Capitulare de Villis*, the *Brevium Exempla*, and the Carolingian court at Aachen', *Early Medieval Europe* 18, 3: 243–64.

Campbell, G. 1994. 'The preliminary archaeobotanical results from Anglo-Saxon West Cotton and Raunds', in J. Rackham, ed., *Environment and Economy in Anglo-Saxon England*. York, Council for British Archaeology: 65–82.

Cannell, J. 2005. *The Archaeology of Woodland Exploitation in the Greater Exmoor Area in the Historic Period*. Oxford, British Archaeological Reports British Series 398.

Carr, R., Tester, A. and Murphy, P. 1988. 'The Middle Saxon settlement at Staunch Meadow, Brandon', *Antiquity* 62: 371–7.

Carver, M. 1994. 'Environment and commodity in Anglo-Saxon England', in J. Rackham, ed., *Environment and Economy in Anglo-Saxon England*. York, Council for British Archaeology: 1–6.

—1998. *Sutton Hoo: Burial Ground of Kings*. London, British Museum.

—2010. *The Birth of a Borough: An Archaeological Study of Anglo-Saxon Stafford*. Woodbridge, Boydell and Brewer.

Cessford, C. and Dickens, A. 2004. 'The origins and early development of Chesterton, Cambridge', *Proceedings of the Cambridge Antiquarian Society* 93: 125–142.

Challis, K. 1995. 'Recent excavations at Laxton, Nottinghamshire', *Medieval Settlement Research Group Annual Report* 10: 20–23.

Chapman, J. and André, P. 1777 (reprinted 1960). *A Map of the County of Essex Taken from an Actual Survey*. Chichester, Phillimore.

Charles-Edwards, T. 1987. 'The distinction between land and moveable wealth in Anglo-Saxon England', in P. Sawyer, ed., *English Medieval Settlement*. London, Arnold: 97–104.

—1972. 'Kinship, status and the origins of the hide', *Past and Present* 56: 3–33.

—1997. 'Anglo-Saxon kinship revisited', in J. Hines, ed., *The Anglo-Saxons from the Migration Period to the Eighth Century*. Woodbridge, Boydell and Brewer: 171–210.

—2004. 'The making of nations in Britain and Ireland in the early middle ages', in R. Evans, ed., *Lordship and Learning Studies in Memory of Trevor Aston*. Woodbridge, Boydell and Brewer: 11–38.

Chouquer, G. and Favory, F. 1991. *Les Paysages de l'Antiquité : Terres et Cadastres de l'Occident Romain : IVe s. Avant J.-C./IIIe s. Après J.-C.* Paris, Errance.

Ciriacy-Wantrup, S. and Bishop, R. 1975. ' "Common property" as a concept in natural resources policy', *Natural Resources Journal* 3: 713–727.

Coles, B. and Coles, J. 1986. *Sweet Track to Glastonbury*. London, Thames and Hudson.

Corcos, N. 2002. *The Affinities and Antecedents of Medieval Settlement*. Oxford, British Archaeological Reports British Series 337.

Corney, M. and Cunliffe, B. 2006. *The Wessex Hillforts Project*. Swindon, English Heritage.

Cornwall County Council Historic Environment Service n.d. 'Flying through Cornwall's past – Farms, villages and towns – The medieval countryside'. http://www.historic-cornwall.org.uk/flyingpast/medieval.html, accessed August 2011.

Costen, M. 1988. 'The late Saxon landscape', in M. Aston, ed., *Aspects of the Medieval Landscape of Somerset*. Taunton, Somerset County Council: 33–48.

—1992a. '*Huish* and *worth*: Old English survivals in a later landscape', *Anglo-Saxon Studies in Archaeology and History* 5: 65–83.

—1992b. *The Origins of Somerset*. Manchester, Manchester University Press.

—1994. 'Settlement in Wessex in the tenth-century: The charter evidence', in M. Aston and C. Lewis, eds., *The Medieval Landscape of Wessex*. Oxford, Oxbow: 97–114.

Coupland, S. 2005. 'Charlemagne's coinage: Ideology and economy', in J. Story, ed., *Charlemagne: Empire and Society*. Manchester, Manchester University Press: 211–229.

Crabtree, P. 1989. 'Sheep, horses, swine and kine: A zooarchaeological perspective on the Anglo-Saxon settlement of England', *Journal of Field Archaeology* 16, 2: 205–213.

—1994. 'Animal exploitation in East Anglian villages', in J. Rackham, ed., *Environment and Economy in Anglo-Saxon England*. York, Council for British Archaeology: 40–54.

—1996. 'Production and consumption in an early complex society: Animal use in Middle Saxon East Anglia', *World Archaeology* 28, 1: 58–75.

—2010. 'Agricultural innovation and socio-economic change in early medieval Europe: Evidence from Britain and France', *World Archaeology* 42, 1: 122–136.

Cramp, R. 1969. 'Excavations at the Saxon monastic sites of Wearmouth and Jarrow, co. Durham: An interim report', *Medieval Archaeology* 13: 21–65.

—1991. *Grammar of Anglo-Saxon Ornament. A General Introduction to the Corpus of Anglo-Saxon Stone Sculpture.* Oxford, British Academy.

—and Daniels, R. 1987. 'New finds from the Anglo-Saxon monastery at Hartlepool, Cleveland', *Antiquity* 61: 424–32.

Crawford, O. G. S. 1928. *Wessex from the Air.* Oxford, Clarendon Press.

Cunliffe, B. 1972. 'Saxon and medieval settlement-pattern in the region of Chalton, Hampshire', *Medieval Archaeology* 16: 1–12.

—1973. 'Chalton, Hants: The evolution of a landscape', *Antiquaries Journal* 53, 2: 173–90.

—1993. *Wessex to A.D.1000.* London, Longman.

—2010. *Iron Age Communities in Britain.* London, Routledge.

Dallas, P. 2010. 'Sustainable environments: Common wood pastures in Norfolk', *Landscape History* 31, 1: 23–36.

Damminger, F. 1998. 'Dwellings, settlements and settlement patterns in Merovingian south-west Germany and adjacent areas', in I. Wood, ed., *Franks and Alamanni in the Merovingian Period An Ethnographic Perspective.* Woodbridge, Boydell and Brewer: 33–106.

Darby, H. C. 1974. *The Medieval Fenland.* Cambridge, Cambridge University Press.

Dark, P. 2000. *The Environment of Britain in the First Millennium A.D.* London, Duckworth.

Darvill, T. 1996. *Prehistoric Britain from the Air.* Cambridge, Cambridge University Press.

—and Wainwright, G. 2009. 'Stonehenge excavations 2009', *Antiquaries Journal* 89: 1–19.

Davies, A. and Dixon, P. 2007. 'Reading the pastoral landscape: Palynological and historical evidence for the impacts of long-term grazing on Wether Hill, Ingram, Northumberland', *Landscape History* 29: 35–47.

Davies, G. 2010. 'Early medieval 'rural centres' and west Norfolk: A growing picture of diversity, complexity and changing lifestyles', *Medieval Archaeology* 54: 89–121.

Davies, W. 1978. 'Land and power in early medieval Wales', *Past and Present* 81: 3–23.

—1982. *Wales in the Early Middle Ages*. Leicester, Leicester University Press.

—and Vierck, H. 1974. 'The contexts of the Tribal Hidage: Social aggregates and settlement patterns', *Frühmittelalterliche Studien* 8: 223–293.

Davis, C. R. 1992. 'Cultural assimilation in the Anglo-Saxon genealogies', *Anglo-Saxon England* 21: 23–36.

Davison, A. 1990. 'The evolution of settlement in three parishes in south-east Norfolk', *East Anglian Archaeology* 49.

Dawson, M. 2000. The Iron Age and Romano-British period: A landscape in transition', in M. Dawson, ed., *Prehistoric, Roman and Post-Roman Landscapes of the Great Ouse Valley*. York, Council for British Archaeology: 107–130.

Deegan, A. and Foard, G. 2007. *Mapping Ancient Landscapes in Northamptonshire*. Swindon, English Heritage.

Deliyannis, D. M. 1995. 'Church burial in Anglo-Saxon England: The prerogative of kings', *Frühmittelalterliche Studien* 29: 96–120

DeMarrais, E., Castillo, L. and Earle, T. 1996. 'Ideology, materialization, and power strategies', *Current Anthropology* 37, 1: 15–31 and 68–70.

Denison, S. 2002. 'Anglo-Saxon 'planned town' revealed this month', *British Archaeology* 64: 4.

Denman, D., Roberts, B. K. and Smith, H. 1967. *Commons and Village Greens*. London, Leonard Hill.

Denson, J. 1991. *A Peasant's Voice to Landowners by John Denson of Waterbeach 1930*. Cambridge, Cambridge Record Society.

DeWindt, A. 1991. 'Local government in a small town: A medieval leet jury and its constituents', *Albion* 23, 4: 627–654.

Dobres, M-A. and Robb, J. 2005. '"Doing" agency: Introductory remarks on methodology', *Journal of Archaeological Method and Theory* 12, 3: 159–166.

Dodgshon, R. A. 1975. 'The landholding foundations of the open-field system', *Past and Present* 67: 3–29.

—1980. *The Origin of British Field Systems*. London, Academic Press.

—1981. 'The interpretation of subdivided fields: A study in private or communal interests', in T. Rowley, ed., *The Origins of Open Field Agriculture*. London, Croom Helm: 130–144.

Dohmen, L. 2010. 'Wanderers between two worlds: Irish and Anglo-Saxon scholars at the court of Charlemagne', in M. Cohen and J.

Firnhaber-Baker, eds., *Difference and Identity in Francia and Medieval France*. Farnham, Ashgate: 77–97.

Downer, L. 1972. *Leges Henrici Primi*. Oxford, Clarendon Press.

Draper, S. 2009. 'Burh place-names in Anglo-Saxon England', *Journal of the English Place-Name Society* 41: 103–117.

Drew, K. F. 1991. *The Laws of the Salien Franks*. Philadelphia, University of Pennsylvania Press.

Drewett, P., Rudling, D. and Gardiner, M. 1988. *The South-East to A.D.1000*. London, Longman.

Driver, T. 2007. *Pembrokeshire. Historic Landscapes from the Air*. Aberystwyth, RCHAMW.

Droege, G. 1970. 'Fränkische siedlung in Westfalen', *Frühmittelalterliche Studien* 4: 271–288.

Dumville, D. 1989. 'Essex, Middle Anglia and the expansion of Mercia in the south-east Midlands', in S. Bassett, ed., *Origins of Anglo-Saxon Kingdoms*. Leicester, Leicester University Press: 123–141.

Durand, A. and Leveau, P. 2003. 'Farming in mediterranean France and rural settlement in the Late Roman and early medieval periods : The contribution from archaeology and environmental sciences in the last twenty years', in M. Barceló and F. Sigaut, eds. *The Making of Feudal Agricultures*? Leiden, Brill: 177–253.

Dyer, C. 1991. *Hanbury Settlement and Society in a Woodland Landscape*. Leicester, Leicester University Press.

—1996. 'Lords, peasants and the development of the manor: England, 900–1280', in A. Haverkamp and H. Vollrath, eds., *England and Germany in the High Middle Ages*. London, German Historical Institute and Oxford University Press: 301–315.

—2002. 'Villages and non-villages in the medieval Cotswolds', *Bristol and Gloucestershire Archaeological Society* 120: 11–35.

Earle, T. 2000. 'Archaeology, property, and prehistory', *Annual Review of Anthropology* 29: 39–60.

Eaton, T. 2001. 'Old ruins new world', *British Archaeology* 60: 14–19.

Eckhardt, K. A. 1962. *Pactus Legis Salicae*. Hannover, Hahn. http://gallica.bnf.fr/ark:/12148/bpt6k952357/f170.image.r=XXXIV, accessed June 2011;

Effros, B. 2001. 'Monuments and memory: repossessing ancient remains in early medieval Gaul', in M. de Jong and F. Theuws with C. van Rhijn, eds., *Topographies of Power in the Early Middle Ages*. Leiden, Brill: 93–118.

Egli, H.-R, 1988. 'Some thoughts on the origin of the open field system in Switzerland and its development in the middle ages', *Geografiska Annaler* 70B, 1: 95–104.

Escher, K. 2005. *Genése et Evolution du Deuxième Royaume Burgonde* (4443–534). Oxford, British Archaeological Reports International Series 1402.

Eule, M. 1997. 'Die Frühmittelalterlichen siedlungen in Aschheim, lkr. München, Oberbayern', *Ruralia* II: 25–33.

Evans, C. 1992. 'Commanding gestures in lowlands: The investigation of two Iron Age ringworks', *Fenland Research*. Cambridge, Fenland Research Committee: 16–26.

—2003. 'Power and island communities. Excavations at Wardy Hill Ringwork, Coveney, Ely', *East Anglian Archaeology* 103.

—and Beadsmore, E., Brudenell, M. and Lucas, G. 2009. *Fengate Revisited: Further Fen-Edge Excavations, Bronze Age Field Systems and Settlement and the Wyman Abbott/Leeds Fengate Archives*. Oxford, Oxbow.

—and Serjeantson, D. 1988. 'The backwater economy of a fen-edge community in the Iron Age: The Upper Delphs, Haddenham', *Antiquity* 62: 360–70.

—with Mackay, D. and Webley, L. 2008. *Borderlands. The Archaeology of the Addenbrooke's Environs, South Cambridge*. Cambridge, McDonald Institute.

Everitt, A. 1986. *Continuity and Colonization*. Leicester, Leicester University Press.

—2002. 'Common land', in J. Thirsk, ed., *Rural England: An Illustrated History of the Landscape*. Oxford, Oxford University Press: 210–235.

Everson, P., Taylor, C. and Dunn, C. 1991. *Change and Continuity Rural Settlement in North-West Lincolnshire*. London, HMSO.

Evison, N. 1997. 'Lo, the conquering hero comes (or not)', *British Archaeology* 23: 8–9.

Faith, R. 1997. *The English Peasantry and the Growth of Lordship*. Leicester, Leicester University Press.

—1998. 'Hides and hyde farms in central and southern England: A preliminary report', *Medieval Settlement Research Group Annual Report* 13: 33–8.

—2006. 'Worthys and enclosures', *Medieval Settlement Research Group Annual Report* 21: 9–14.

—2009. 'Forces and relations of production in early medieval England', *Journal of Agrarian Change* 9, 1: 23–41.

—2010. 'Farms and families in ninth-century Provence', *Early Medieval Europe* 18, 2: 175–201.

Feeney, D., Berkes, F., McCay, B. and Acheson, J. 1990. 'The tragedy of the commons: Twenty-two years later', *Human Ecology* 18, 1: 1–19.

Fehring, G. P. 1991. *The Archaeology of Medieval Germany*. London, Routledge.

Fenton-Thomas, C. 2003. *Late Prehistoric and Historic Landscapes on the Yorkshire Chalk*. Oxford, British Archaeological Reports British Series 350.

Finberg, H. P. R. 1955. *Roman and Saxon Withington. A Study in Continuity*. Leicester, Leicester University Press.

—1957. *Gloucestershire Studies*. Leicester, Leicester University Press.

—1972. 'Anglo-Saxon England to 1042', in H. P. R. Finberg, ed., *The Agrarian History of England and Wales* I, ii, AD 43–1042. Cambridge, Cambridge University Press: 385–525.

Fleming, A. 1971. 'Territorial patterns in Bronze Age Wessex', *Proceedings of the Prehistoric Society* 37, 1: 138–66.

—1983. 'The prehistoric landscape of Dartmoor Part 2: North and east Dartmoor', *Proceedings of the Prehistoric Society* 49: 195–241.

—1985. 'Land, tenure, productivity and field systems', in G. Barker and C. Gamble, eds., *Beyond Domestication in Prehistoric Europe*. London, Academic Press: 129–146.

—1998a. *Swaledale: Valley of the Wild River*. Macclesfield, Windgather.

—1998b. 'The quest for territorial pattern', in P. Everson and T. Williamson, eds., *The Archaeology of Landscape*. Manchester, Manchester University Press: 42–66.

—2008. *The Dartmoor Reaves*. Oxford, Windgather.

Foard, G. 1978. 'Systematic fieldwalking and the investigation of Saxon settlement in Northamptonshire', *World Archaeology* 9, 3: 357–374.

—2001. 'Medieval woodland, agriculture and industry in Rockingham Forest, Northamptonshire', *Medieval Archaeology* 45: 41–95.

Ford, W. 1987. 'Some settlement patterns in the central region of the Warwickshire Avon', in P. Sawyer, ed., *English Medieval Settlement*. London, Arnold: 143–163.

Fowler, P. 1975. 'Continuity in the landscape', in P. J. Fowler, ed., *Recent Work in Rural Archaeology*. Bath, Adams and Dart: 123–32.

—1983. *The Farming of Prehistoric Britain*. Cambridge, Cambridge University Press.

—2000. *Landscape Plotted and Pieced: Landscape History and Local Archaeology in Fyfield and Overton, Wiltshire*. London, Society of Antiquaries.

—2002. *Farming in the First Millennium*. Cambridge, Cambridge University Press.

Fox, H. S. A. 1981. 'Approaches to the adoption of the Midland system', in T. Rowley, ed., *The Origins of Open Field Agriculture*. London, Croom Helm: 64–111.

—2012. *Dartmoor's Alluring Uplands*. Exeter University Press.

France, R. S. 1954. 'Two customals of the manor of Cockermouth, 1326 and 1483', *Transactions of the Lancashire and Cheshire Antiquarian Society* 64: 38–54.

Fulford, M., Powell A., Entwhistle, M. and Raymond, F. 2006. *Iron-Age and Romano-British Settlements and Landscape of Salisbury Plain*. Reading, Wessex Archaeology and University of Reading.

Gaimster, M. and Bradley, J. 2001. 'Medieval Britain and Ireland, 2000', *Medieval Archaeology* 45: 233–379.

—2002. 'Medieval Britain and Ireland, 2001', Medieval Archaeology 44: 125–264.

—2003. 'Medieval Britain and Ireland, 2002', *Medieval Archaeology* 47: 199–340.

Gardiner, J., Allen, M., Hamilton-Dyer, S., Laidlaw, M. and Scaife, R. 2002. 'Making the most of it: Late prehistoric pastoralism in the Avon Levels, Severn Estuary', *Proceedings of the Prehistoric Society* 68: 1–40.

Gardiner, M. *et al.* 2001. 'Continental trade and non-urban ports in mid-Anglo-Saxon England: Excavations at Sandtun, West Hythe, Kent', *Archaeological Journal* 158: 161–290.

Geake, H. 1999. 'Invisible kingdoms: The use of grave-goods in seventh-century England', *Anglo-Saxon Studies in Archaeology and History 10*, 203–215.

Gearey, B., Charman, D. and Kent, M. 2000. 'Palaeoecological evidence for the prehistoric settlement of Bodmin Moor, Cornwall, Southwest England. Part II: Land use changes from the Neolithic to the present', *Journal of Archaeological Science* 27: 493–508.

Gearey, P. 1999. 'Land, language and memory in Europe 700–1100', *Transactions of the Royal Historical Society* 9: 169–84.

Gelling, M. 1984. *Place-Names in the Landscape*. London, Dent.

—1992. *The West Midlands in the Early Middle Ages*. Leicester, Leicester University Press.

Gerrets, D. 1996. 'Continuity and change in house construction and the lay-out of rural settlements during the early middle ages in the Netherlands', *Ruralia* I: 33–46.

Giddens, A. 1984. *The Constitution of Society*. London, Polity Press.

Gingell, C. 1992. *The Marlborough Downs: A Later Bronze Age Landscape and Its Origins*. Devizes, Wiltshire Archaeological and Natural History Society.

Goffart, W. 2008. 'Frankish military duty and the fate of Roman taxation', *Early Medieval Europe* 16, 2: 166–90.

Gosden, C. 1985. 'Gifts and kin in early Iron Age Europe', *Man* N.S. 20, 3: 475–93.

—1994. *Social Being and Time*. Oxford, Blackwell.

—2011. 'Anthropology and archaeology', in H. Hamerow, D. Hinton and S. Crawford, eds., *Oxford Handbook of Anglo-Saxon Archaeology*. Oxford, Oxford University Press: 1003–1024.

—and Locke, G. 1998. 'Prehistoric histories', *World Archaeology* 30, 1: 2–12.

Gray, H. 1915, 1959 ed. *English Field Systems*. London, Merlin.

Green, F. 1994. 'Cereals and plant foods: A re-assessment of the Saxon economic evidence from Wessex', in J. Rackham, ed., *Environment and economy in Anglo-Saxon England*. York, Council for British Archaeology: 83–88.

Groenman-van Waateringe, W. and van Wijngaarden-Bakker, L. H. 1990. 'Medieval archaeology and environmental research in the Netherlands', in J. C. Besteman, J. M. Bos and H. A. Heidinga, eds., *Medieval Archaeology in the Netherlands*. Assen, Van Gorcum: 283–291.

Guérault, Stéphane 2009. 'Les polyptyques Carolingiens'. http://polycarolingien.free.fr/POLYPTGLOSSAIRE.php3. accessed August 2011.

Hall, C. and Ravensdale, J. R. 1974. *The West Fields of Cambridge*. Cambridge, Cambridge Record Society.

Hall, D. 1981. 'The origins of open-field agriculture – the archaeological fieldwork evidence', in T. Rowley, ed., *The Origins of Open-field Agriculture*. London, Croom Helm: 22–38.

—1982a. *Medieval Fields*. Aylesbury, Shire Publications.

—1982b. 'The countryside of the south-east Midlands and Cambridgeshire', in D. Miles, ed., *The Romano-British Countryside*. Oxford, British Archaeological Reports British Series 103: 337–350.

—1983. 'Fieldwork and field books, studies in early layout', in B. K. Roberts and R. E. Glasscock, eds., *Villages, Fields and Frontiers*. Oxford, British Archaeological Reports International Series 185: 115–31.

—1984. 'Fieldwork and documentary evidence for the layout and organization of early medieval estates in the English midlands', in K. Biddick, ed., *Archaeological Approaches to Medieval Europe*. Kalamazoo IL, University of Michigan Press: 43–68.

—1987. 'The Fenland Project, Number 2. Cambridgeshire Survey: Peterborough to March', *East Anglian Archaeology* 35.

—1988. 'The late Saxon countryside: Villages and their fields', in D. Hooke, ed., *Anglo-Saxon Settlements*. Oxford, Blackwell: 99–122.

—1995. *The Open Fields of Northamptonshire*. Northampton, Northamptonshire Record Society.

—1996. 'The Fenland Project, Number 10. Cambridgeshire Survey: Isle of Ely and Wisbech', *East Anglian Archaeology* 79.

—and Coles, J. 1994. *Fenland Survey. An Essay in Landscape and Persistence*. London, English Heritage.

Hallam, H. 1963. 'The fen bylaws of Spalding and Pinchbeck', *Lincolnshire Architectural and Archaeological Society Reports and Papers* 10, 1: 40–56.

—1965. *Settlement and Society*. Cambridge, Cambridge University Press.

Halsall, G. 2006. 'Villas, territories and communities in Merovingian northern Gaul', in W. Davies, G. Halsall and A. Reynolds, eds., *People and Space in the Middle Ages, 300–1300*. Brepol, Turnhout: 209–232.

Hamerow, H. 1993. *Excavations at Mucking Volume 2: The Anglo-Saxon Settlement*. Swindon and London, English Heritage and British Museum Press.

—1994. 'Migration theory and the migration period', in B. Vyner, ed., *Building on the Past*. London, Royal Archaeological Institute: 164–177.

—1997. 'Migration theory and the Anglo-Saxon 'identity crisis" in J. Chapman and H. Hamerow, eds., *Migrations and Invasions in Archaeological Explanation*. Oxford, Noyes Press: 33–44.

—2002a. 'Catholme: The development and context of the settlement', in S. Losco-Bradley and G. Kinsley, eds., *Catholme. An Anglo-Saxon Settlement on the Trent Gravels in Staffordshire*. Nottingham, University of Nottingham Department of Archaeology: 123–9.

—2002b. *Early Medieval Settlements: The Archaeology of Rural Communities in North-West Europe: 400–900*. Oxford, Oxford University Press.

—2007. 'Intensification of agrarian production and the emporia of mid Saxon England, ca. AD 650–850', in J. Henning, ed., *Post-Roman Towns, Trade and Settlement in Europe and Byzantium*. Berlin, Walter de Gruyter: 219–232.

—2011. 'Anglo-Saxon timber buildings and their social context', in H. Hamerow, D. Hinton and S. Crawford, eds., *Oxford Handbook of Anglo-Saxon Archaeology*. Oxford, Oxford University Press: 128–155.

—and Hayden, C. and Hey, G. 2008. 'Anglo-Saxon settlement near Drayton Road, Sutton Courtenay, Berkshire', *Archaeological Journal* 164: 109–96.

Hardin, G. 1968. 'The tragedy of the commons', *Science* n.s. 162, 3859: 1243–1248.

Harding, J. 2005. 'Rethinking the great divide: Long-term structural history and the temporality of event', *Norwegian Archaeological Review* 38, 2: 88–101.

—and Healy, F. 2007. *Neolithic and Bronze Age Landscapes in Northamptonshire*. Swindon, English Heritage.

Hardy, A. n.d. *Eynsham. A Village and Its Abbey*. Oxford, Oxford Archaeological Unit.

—and Lorrimer, P. 2004. *Higham Ferrers*. Oxford, Oxford Archaeological Unit.

Härke, H. 1997. 'Early Anglo-Saxon social structure', in J. Hines, ed., *The Anglo-Saxons from the Migration Period to the Eighth Century: An Ethnographic Perspective*. Woodbridge, Boydell and Brewer: 125–60.

Harris, A. 2003. *Byzantium, Britain and the West. The Archaeology of Cultural Identity*. Stroud, Tempus.

Harrison, F., ed. and trans. 1918. *Roman Farm Management. The Treatises of Cato and Varro*. New York, Macmillan.

Harrison, J. 2011. ' Brent's waterways, walls and works, c.twelfth-fourteenth centuries', in Bob Silvester and Sam Turner, eds., *Life in Medieval Landscapes: People and Places in the Middle Ages*. Oxford, Windgather: 50–72.

Hart, C. R. 1995. 'The *Aldewerke* and minster at Shelford, Cambridgeshire', *Anglo-Saxon Studies in Archaeology and History* 8: 43–68.

—2000. 'The Danes', in A. Kirby and S. Oosthuizen, eds., *An Atlas of Cambridgeshire and Huntingdonshire History*. Cambridge, Anglia Polytechnic University: 30.

Hart, E. n.d. (*c.* 2004/5). *Hefting in Practice. The Ancient Craft of Grazing the Open Hills*. Private printing.

Hartley, R. 1983. *The Medieval Earthworks of Rutland*. Leicester, Leicester Museums Archaeological Report No. 7.

—1984. *The Medieval Earthworks of North West Leicestershire*. Leicester, Leicester Museums Archaeological Report No. 9.

—1989. *The Medieval Earthworks of Central Leicestershire*. Leicester, Leicester Museums.

Harvey, M. 1980. 'Regular field and tenurial arrangements in Holderness, Yorkshire', *Journal of Historical Geography* 6, 1: 3–16.

—1983. 'Planned field systems in eastern Yorkshire: Some thoughts on their origin', *Agricultural History Review* 31, 2: 91–103.

—1984. 'Open field structure and landholding arrangements in eastern Yorkshire', *Transactions of the Institute of British Geographers* n.s. 9: 60–74.

—1985. 'The development of open fields in the central Vale of York, a reconsideration', *Geografiska Annaler* 76B: 35–44.

Harvey, P. D. A. 1989. 'Initiative and authority in settlement change', in M. Aston, D. Austin and C. Dyer, eds., *The Rural Settlements of Medieval England*. Oxford, Oxford University Press: 31–43.

Haslam, J. 1980. 'A middle Saxon iron smelting site at Ramsbury, Wiltshire', *Medieval Archaeology* 24: 1–68.

—1987. 'Market and fortress in England in the reign of Offa', *World Archaeology* 19, 1: 76–93.

Hatcher, J. 1983. 'English serfdom and villeinage: Towards a reassessment', *Past and Present* 90: 3–39.

Haughton, C. and Powlesland, D. 1999. *West Heslerton The Anglian Cemetery* Volume 1. Yedingham, Landscape Research Centre.

Hawkes, J. 2001. 'Constructing iconographies: questions of identity in Mercian sculpture', in M. P. Brown and C. A. Farr, eds., *Mercia: An Anglo-Saxon Kingdom in Europe*. Leicester, Leicester University Press: 231–245.

Hayes, P. 1988. 'Roman to Saxon in the south Lincolnshire fens', *Antiquity* 62: 321–6.

—and Lane, T. 1992. 'The Fenland Project Number 5: Lincolnshire survey, The South-West Fens', *East Anglian Archaeology* 55.

Hayfield, C. 1984. 'Wawne, East Riding of Yorkshire: A case study in settlement morphology', *Landscape History* 6: 41–67.

Heidinga, H. 1987. *Medieval Settlement and Economy North of the Lower Rhine*. Assen, Van Gorcum.

Henig, M. 2002. 'Roman Britain after 410', *British Archaeology*, 68: 8–11.

—2004. 'Remaining Roman in Britain, AD 300–700: The evidence of portable art', in R. Collins and J. Gerrard, eds., *Debating Late Antiquity in Britain AD 300–700*. Oxford, British Archaeological Reports British Series 36: 13–23.

Henning, J. 2007. 'Early European towns. The development of the economy in the Frankish realm between dynamism and deceleration AD 500–1100', in J. Henning, ed., *Post-Roman Towns, Trade and Settlement in Europe and Byzantium*. Berlin, Walter de Gruyter: 3–40.

Herren, M. 1998. 'The transmission and reception of Graeco-Roman mythology in Anglo-Saxon England, 670–800', *Anglo-Saxon England* 27: 87–104.

Herring, P. 2008. 'Stepping onto the commons: South-western stone rows', in P. Rainbird, ed., *Monuments in the Landscape*. Stroud, Sutton: 79–88.

Hesse, M. 2000. 'Domesday land measures in Suffolk', *Landscape History* 22: 21–36.

Hey, D. 2002. 'Moorlands', in J. Thirsk, ed., *Rural England: An Illustrated History of the Landscape*. Oxford, Oxford University Press: 188–209.

Hey, G. 2004. *Yarnton: Saxon and Medieval Settlement and Landscape*. Oxford, Oxbow Books.

Higham, N. 2004. *A Frontier Landscape*. Macclesfield, Windgather.

Hill, D. 1981. *An Atlas of Anglo-Saxon England, 700–1066*. Oxford, Blackwell.

—2000. '*Sulh*: the Anglo-Saxon plough', *Landscape History* 22: 5–20.

Hiller, J., Petts, D. and Allen, T. 2002. 'Chapter 5: Discussion of the Anglo-Saxon archaeology', in S. Foreman, J. Hiller and D. Petts, eds., *Gathering the People, Settling the Land*. Oxford, Oxford Archaeology: 57–72.

Hills, C. 2007. 'History and archaeology: The state of play in early medieval Europe', *Antiquity* 81: 191–200.

—and O'Connell, T. 2009. 'New light on the Anglo-Saxon succession: Two cemeteries and their dates', *Antiquity* 83: 1096–1108.

Hinchliffe, J. 1986. 'An early medieval settlement at Cowage Farm, Foxley, near Malmesbury', *Archaeological Journal* 143, 240–259.

Hinton, D. A. 1990. *Archaeology, Economy and Society: England from the Fifth to the Fifteenth Century*. London, Seaby.

Hodges, R. 1989. *The Anglo-Saxon Achievement*. London, Duckworth.

—1991. *Wall-To-Wall History*. London, Duckworth.

Homans, G. 1953. 'The rural sociology of medieval England', *Past and Present* 4: 32–43.

Hooke, D. 1978. 'Early Cotswold woodland', *Journal of Historical Geography* 4: 333–41.

—1981a. *Anglo-Saxon Landscapes of the West Midlands: The Charter Evidence*. Oxford, British Archaeological Reports British Series 95.

—1981b. 'Open-field agriculture – the evidence from the pre-Conquest charters of the West Midlands', in T. Rowley, ed., *The Origins of Open-Field Agriculture*. London, Croom Helm: 39–63.

—1988a. 'Early forms of open field agriculture in England', *Geografiska Annaler* 70B: 121–31.

—1988b. 'Regional variation in southern and central England in the Anglo-Saxon period and its relationship to land units and settlement', in D. Hooke, ed., *Anglo-Saxon Settlements*. Oxford, Blackwell: 123–51.

—1992. 'Early units of government in Herefordshire and Shropshire', *Anglo-Saxon Studies in Archaeology and History* 5: 47–63.

—1996. 'Changing settlement patterns and land use in Midland and southern England in the early medieval and medieval period', *Ruralia* I: 80–89.

—1997. 'The Anglo-Saxons in England in the seventh and eighth centuries: aspects of location in space', in J. Hines, ed., *The Anglo-Saxons from the Migration Period to the Eighth Century An Ethnographic Perspective.* Woodbridge, Boydell and Brewer: 65–84.

—1998. *The Landscape of Anglo-Saxon England*. Leicester, Leicester University Press.

—2001. 'Mercia: landscape and environment', in M. P. Brown and C. A. Farr, eds., *Mercia: An Anglo-Saxon Kingdom in Europe*. Leicester, Leicester University Press: 160–172.

—2011. *Trees in Anglo-Saxon England: Literature, Lore and Landscape*. Woodbridge, Boydell and Brewer.

Hoskins, W. G. 1988 ed. The *Making of the English Landscape*. London, Guild.

—and Stamp, D. 1963. *The Common Lands of England and Wales*. London, Department of the Environment.

Hough, C. 2000. 'Cattle-tracking in the Fonthill letter', *English Historical Review* 115, 463: 864–92.

Huggett, J. W. 1988. 'Imported grave goods and the early Anglo-Saxon economy', *Medieval Archaeology* 32: 63–96.

Hunter, J. 2003. *Field systems in Essex*. Colchester, Essex County Council.

—and Ralston, I., eds. 2009. *The Archaeology of Britain*. London, Routledge.

Huntingford, G. W. B. 1957. 'The scouring of the White Horse', *Journal of the Royal Anthropological Institute of Great Britain* 87, 1: 105–114.

Hurst, J. G. 1984. 'The Wharram Research Project: Results to 1983', *Medieval Archaeology* 28 : 77–111,

—1998. 'Memory, orality and literacy in an early medieval society', *Past and Present* 158: 3–36.

—2001. 'People, places and power in Carolingian society', in M. de Jong and F. Theuws with C. van Rhijn, eds., *Topographies of Power in the Early Middle Ages*. Leiden, Brill: 397–438.

—2009. 'Framing the Carolingian economy', *Journal of Agrarian Change* 9, 1: 42–58.

Isenburg, I. 1990. 'Salzsleder in Soest', in H. Hellenberger and H. G. Horn, eds., *Archäologie in Nordrhein-Westfalen*. Köln, Romisch-Germanisches Museum: 282–285.

Jackson, K. H. 1964. *The Oldest Irish Tradition. A Window on the Iron Age.* Cambridge, Cambridge University Press.

Jackson, R. 2000. 'An Anglo-Saxon watermill at Wellington', *Historic Environment Today* 3, 1. http://www.herefordshire.gov.uk/htt/docs/HET_Vol3_Issue3_Oct2000.pdf, accessed August 2011. The original, fuller report was available for a time on http://www.smr.herefordshire.gov.uk/saxon_viking/mill_wellington.htm, accessed July 2006, and the HER record (51636) can currently be found on http://www.herefordshire.gov.uk/htt/smrSearch/Monuments/Monument_Item.aspx?ID=51636, accessed August 2011.

Jewell, R. 2001. 'Classicism of Southumbrian sculpture', in M. P. Brown and C. A. Farr, eds., *Mercia: An Anglo-Saxon Kingdom in Europe*. Leicester, Leicester University Press: 247–262.

Jolliffe, J. E. 1926. 'Northumbrian institutions', *English Historical Review* 41, 161: 1–42.

—1929. 'The hidation of Kent', *English Historical Review* 44, 176: 612–618.

—1935. 'English book-right', *English Historical Review* 50, 197: 1–21.

Jones, G. 1981. 'Early customary tenures in Wales and open-field agriculture', in T. Rowley, ed., *The Origins of Open-Field Agriculture*. London, Croom Helm: 202–225.

—1987a. 'Multiple estates and early settlement', in P. Sawyer, ed., *English Medieval Settlement.* London, Arnold: 9–34.

—1987b. 'The portrayal of land settlement in Domesday Book', in J. Holt, ed., *Domesday Studies.* Woodbridge, Boydell and Brewer: 183–200.

Jones, M. 2007. 'A feast of Beltane? Reflections on the rich Danebury harvests', in C. Gosden, H. Hamerow, P. de Jersey and G. Lock, eds., *Communities and Connections: Essays in Honour of Barry Cunliffe*. Oxford, Oxford University Press: 142–153.

Jones, R. and Page, M. 2006. *Medieval Villages in an English Landscape. Beginnings and Ends*. Macclesfield, Windgather.

Kamash, A., Gosden, C. and Lock, G. 2010. 'Continuity and religious practices in Roman Britain: The case of the rural religious complex at Marcham/Frilford, Oxfordshire', *Britannia* 41: 95–210.

Keen, L. 1984. 'The towns of Dorset', in J. Haslam, ed., *Anglo-Saxon Towns in Southern England*. Chichester, Phillimore: 203–48.

Kelly, F. 1988. *A Guide to Early Irish Law*. Dublin, Dublin Institute for Advanced Studies.

—1997. *Early Irish Farming*. Dublin, Dublin Institute for Advanced Studies.

Kings College, London, Department of History and Centre for Computing in the Humanities 2010. 'Prosopography of Anglo-Saxon England'. http://www.pase.ac.uk/index.html, accessed June-August 2011.

Kissock, J. and Anthony, M. 2009. 'The early landscapes of Llandewi and Henllys, Gower', *Medieval Settlement Research Group Annual Report* 24: 70–77.

Knight, J. 2005. 'From villa to monastery: Llandough in context', *Medieval Archaeology* 40: 93–107.

Kooistra, L. I. 1996. *Borderland Farming*. Assen, Van Gorcum.

Laing, L. 2007. 'Romano-British metalworking and the Anglo-Saxons', in N. Higham, ed., *Britons in Anglo-Saxon England*. Woodbridge, Boydell and Brewer: 42–56.

Langdon, J. 1988. 'Agricultural equipment', in G. Astill and A. Grant, eds., *The Countryside of Medieval England*. Oxford, Blackwell: 86–107.

Lapidge, M. 1986. 'The school of Theodore and Hadrian', *Anglo-Saxon England* 15: 45–72.

Last, J. 2005. 'Life by the river: A prehistoric landscape at Grendon, Northamptonshire', *Proceedings of the Prehistoric Society* 71: 333–360;

Lawson, A. 1983. 'The archaeology of Witton, near North Walsham, Norfolk', *East Anglian Archaeology* 18.

Lebecq, S. 1989. 'La Neustrie et la mer', in H. Atsma, ed., *Neustrie: Les Pays au Nord de la Loire de 650 à 850*, 1. Sigmaringen, J. Thorbecke: 367–404.

—1991. 'Pour une histoire parallèle de Quentovic et Dorestad', in J.-M. Duvosquel and A. Dierkens, eds., *Villes et Campagnes au Moyen* Âge. Liege, Editions du Perron: 415–428.

—2000. 'The role of monasteries in the systems of production and exchange of the Frankish world between the seventh and the beginning of the ninth centuries', in I. L. Hansen and C. Wickham, eds., *The Long Eighth Century*. Leiden, Brill: 121–148.

Lewis, C. 2005. 'Test pit excavation within occupied settlements in East Anglia in 2005', *Medieval Settlement Research Group Annual Report* 20: 9–16.

—2006. 'Test pit excavation within currently occupied rural settlement in East Anglia – results of the HEFA Cors Project in 2006', *Medieval Settlement Research Group Annual Report* 21: 37–44.

—and Mitchell-Fox, P. and Dyer, C. 1997. *Village, Hamlet and Field*. Manchester, Manchester University Press.

Lewis, J. *et al.* 2006. *Landscape Evolution in the Middle Thames Valley*. Oxford, Oxford Archaeology.

Lock, G. 2007. 'Wessex hillforts after Danebury: Exploring boundaries', in C. Gosden, H. Hamerow, P. de Jersey and G. Lock, eds., *Communities and Connections: Essays in Honour of Barry Cunliffe*. Oxford, Oxford University Press: 341–356.

Lohrmann, D. 1989. 'Le moulin à eau dans le cadre de l'économie rurale de la Neustrie (VIIe – IXe)', in H. Atsma, ed., *La Neustrie. Les Pays du Nord de la Loire de 650 à 850, 1*. Sigmaringen, J. Thorbecke: 367–404.

Losco-Bradley, S. and Kinsley, G. 2002. *Catholme: An Anglo-Saxon Settlement on the Trent Gravels in Staffordshire*. Nottingham, Nottingham University Press.

—and Wheeler, H. M. 1984. 'Anglo-Saxon settlement in the Trent valley: Some aspects', in M. Faull, ed., *Studies in Late Anglo-Saxon Settlement*. Oxford, Oxford Department for External Studies: 103–14.

Loveluck, C. P. 1997. 'Uncovering an Anglo-Saxon royal manor – finds from Flixborough shed new light on the Saxon kingdom of Lindsey', *British Archaeology* 28: 8–9.

—1998. 'A high-status Anglo-Saxon settlement at Flixborough, Lincolnshire', *Antiquity* 72: 146–61.

—2001. 'Wealth, waste and conspicuous consumption: Flixborough and its importance for middle and late Saxon rural settlement studies', in H.

Hamerow and A. MacGregor, eds., *Image and Power in the Archaeology of Early Medieval Britain*. Oxford, Oxbow: 79–130.

—2005. 'Rural settlement hierarchy in the age of Charlemagne', in J. Story, ed., *Charlemagne: Empire and Society*. Manchester, Manchester University Press: 230–258.

Loyn, H. R. and Percival, J. 1975. *The Reign of Charlemagne: Documents on Carolingian Government and Administration*. London, Edward Arnold.

Lu, F. 2001. 'The common property regime of the Huaorani Indians of Ecuador: implications and challenges to conservation', *Human Ecology* 29, 4: 425–447.

Luke, M. 2008. 'Life in the loop: Investigation of a prehistoric and Roman landscape at Biddenham Loop, Bedfordshire', *East Anglian Archaeology* 125.

MacGowan, K. 1996. 'Barking Abbey', *Current Archaeology* 149: 172–8.

Maddicott, J. R. 2005. 'London and Droitwich, c.650–750: Trade, industry and the rise of Mercia', *Anglo-Saxon England* 34: 7–58.

Maitland, F. 1897. *Domesday Book and Beyond*. Cambridge, Cambridge University Press.

Marshall, A. and Marshall, G. 1991. 'A survey and analysis of the buildings of early and middle Anglo-Saxon England', *Medieval Archaeology* 35: 29–43.

Matzat, W. 1988. 'Long strip field layouts and their later subdivisions', *Geografiska Annaler* 70B, 1: 133–147

McCormick, M. 2001. *Origins of the European Economy*. Cambridge, Cambridge University Press.

McGovern, J. F. 1971. 'The meaning of 'gesette land' in Anglo-Saxon land tenure', *Speculum* 46, 4: 589–596.

McKitterick, R. 2004. *History and Memory in the Carolingian World*. Cambridge, Cambridge University Press.

McOmish, D., Field, D. and Brown, G. 2002. *The Field Archaeology of Salisbury Plain*. Swindon, English Heritage.

Meadows, I. 1996. 'Wollaston: The Nene valley a British Moselle?', *Current Archaeology* 150: 212–5.

—1997. 'Wollaston: the 'Pioneer' burial', *Current Archaeology* 154: 391–5.

Meaney, A. 1993. 'Gazetteer of hundred and wapentake meeting-places of the Cambridge region', *Proceedings of the Cambridge Antiquarian Society* 82: 67–92.

Meddens, F. and Beasley, M. 2001. 'Roman seasonal wetland pasture exploitation near Nash on the Gwent Levels, Wales', *Britannia* 32: 143–185.
Mercer, R. 2009. 'Hambledon Hill', *British Archaeology* 107: 38–43.
Metcalf, M. 2003. 'Variations in the composition of the currency at different places in England', in T. Pestell and K. Ülmschneider, eds., *Markets in Early Medieval Europe*. Macclesfield, Windgather: 37–47.
Miles, D. ed., 1984. *Archaeology at Barton Court Farm, Abingdon, Oxon*. Oxford and York, Oxford Archaeological Unit and Council for British Archaeology.
Miller, E. 1969. *The Abbey and Bishopric of Ely*. Cambridge, Cambridge University Press.
Millett, M. 1990. *The Romanization of Britain*. Cambridge, Cambridge University Press.
—and James, S. 1983. 'Excavations at Cowdery's Down Basingstoke, Hampshire, 1978–81', *Archaeological Journal* 140: 151–279.
Milner, N. and Mithen, S. 2009. 'Hunter-gatherers of the Mesolithic', in J. Hunter and I. Ralston, eds., *The Archaeology of Britain*. London, Routledge: 53–77.
Minc, L. 1986. 'Scarcity and survival: The role of oral tradition in mediating subsistence crises', *Journal of Anthropological Archaeology* 5: 39–113.
Moffett, L. 2011. 'Food plants on archaeological sites: the nature of the archaeobotanical record', in H. Hamerow, D. Hinton and S. Crawford, eds., *Oxford Handbook of Anglo-Saxon Archaeology*. Oxford, Oxford University Press: 346–360.
Moorhouse, S. 2003. 'The anatomy of the Yorkshire Dales: Decoding the medieval landscape', in T. Manby, S. Moorhouse and P. Ottaway, eds., *The Archaeology of Yorkshire*. York, Yorkshire Archaeological Society: 293–362.
Moreland, J. 2000. 'The significance of production in eighth-century England', in I. L. Hansen and C. Wickham, eds., *The Long Eighth Century*. Leiden, Brill: 69–104.
Morris, R. 1989. *Churches in the Landscape*. London, Dent.
Mortimer, R. 2000. 'Village development and ceramic sequence: The Middle to Late Saxon village at Lordship Lane, Cottenham, Cambridgeshire', *Proceedings of the Cambridge Antiquarian Society* 89, 5–34.
Murphy, K. 2001. 'A prehistoric field system and related monuments on St David's Head and Carn Llidi, Pembrokeshire', *Proceedings of the Prehistoric Society* 67: 85–99.

Murphy, P. 1983. 'Iron age to late Saxon land use in the Breckland', in M. Jones, ed., *Integrating the Subsistence Economy*. Oxford, British Archaeological Reports International Series 181: 177–210.

—1994. 'The Anglo-Saxon landscape and rural economy: Some results from sites in East Anglia and Essex', in J. Rackham, ed., *Environment and Economy in Anglo-Saxon England*. York, Council for British Archaeology: 25–37.

Nash, A. 1982. 'The medieval fields of Strettington, West Sussex, and the evolution of land division', *Geografiska Annaler* 1982B, 1: 41–9.

Naylor, J. 2004. *An Archaeology of Trade in Middle Saxon England*. Oxford, British Archaeological Reports British Series 376.

—2007. 'The circulation of early-medieval European coinage: A case study from Yorkshire, *c*.650-*c*.867', *Medieval Archaeology* 51: 11–61.

Neilson, N. 1910. 'Customary rents', in P. Vinogradoff, ed., *Oxford Studies in Social and Legal History* 2. Oxford, Clarendon Press.

—1920. *A Terrier of Fleet, Lincolnshire*. London, British Academy.

—1925. 'Custom and the common law in Kent', *Harvard Law Review* 38, 4: 482–498.

—1928. *The Cartulary and Terrier of the Priory of Bilsington Kent*. London, British Academy.

—1929. 'English manorial forms', *American Historical Review* 34, 4: 725–39.

—1942. 'Early English woodland and waste', *Journal of Economic History* 2, 1: 54–62.

—1944. 'The early pattern of the common law', *American Historical Review* 49, 2: 199–212.

Nelson, J. 1986. 'Dispute settlement in Carolingian West Francia', in W. Davies and P. Fouracre, eds., *The Settlement of Disputes in Early Medieval Europe*. Cambridge, Cambridge University Press: 45–64.

—1996. *The Frankish World, 750–900*. London, Hambledon.

—2001a. 'Aachen as a place of power', in M. de Jong and F. Theuws with C. van Rhijn, eds., *Topographies of Power in the Early Middle Ages*. Leiden, Brill: 217–241.

—2001b. 'Carolingian contacts', in M. Brown and C. Farr, eds., *Mercia: An Anglo-Saxon Kingdom in Europe*. Leicester, Leicester University Press: 126–143.

—2002. 'England and the continent in the ninth century: ends and beginnings', *Transactions of the Royal Historical Society* 6th ser. 12: 1–21.

Netting, R. M. 1976. 'What Alpine peasants have in common: Observations on communal tenure in a Swiss village', *Human Ecology* 4, 2: 135–146.

Newman, J. 2002. 'Sutton Hoo before Raedwald', *Current Archaeology* 180: 498–505.

Nitz, H-J. 1988a. 'Introductions from above: Intentional spread of common-field systems by feudal authorities through colonization and re-organisation', *Geografiska Annaler* 70B, 1: 149–159.

—1988b. 'Settlement structures and settlement systems of the Frankish central state in Carolingian and Ottonian times', in D. Hooke, ed., *Anglo-Saxon settlements*. Oxford, Blackwell: 249–273.

O'Connor, T. 1994. '8th–11th century economy and environment in York', in J. Rackham, ed., *Environment and Economy in Anglo-Saxon England*. York, Council for British Archaeology: 136–147.

—2009. 'Culture and environment: Mind the gap', in M. J. Allen, N. Sharples and T. O'Connor, eds., *Land and People*. Oxford, Oxbow: 11–18.

—2011. 'Animal husbandry', in H. Hamerow, D. Hinton and S. Crawford, eds., *Oxford Handbook of Anglo-Saxon Archaeology*. Oxford, Oxford University Press: 361–376.

Ó'Corráin, D. 2005. 'Ireland c.800: Aspects of society', in D. Ó'Cróinín, ed., *A New History of Ireland*. Oxford, Oxford University Press: 549–608.

Oosthuizen, S. 1993. 'Saxon commons in south Cambridgeshire', *Proceedings of the Cambridge Antiquarian Society* 82: 93–100.

—1996. *Cambridgeshire From the Air*. Stroud, Sutton.

—1997. 'Medieval settlement relocation in west Cambridgeshire: Three case studies', *Landscape History* 19, 43–55.

—1998. 'Prehistoric fields into medieval furlongs? Evidence from Caxton, South Cambridgeshire', *Proceedings of the Cambridge Antiquarian Society* 86: 145–52.

—2002a. 'Ancient greens in 'midland' landscapes: Barrington, Cambridgeshire', *Medieval Archaeology* 46: 110–115.

—2002b. 'Unravelling the morphology of Litlington, South Cambridgeshire', *Proceedings of the Cambridge Antiquarian Society* 91: 55–61.

—2003. 'Medieval greens and moats in the Central Province: Evidence from the Bourn Valley, Cambridgeshire', *Landscape History* 24: 73–88.

—2005. 'New light on the origins of open field farming?', *Medieval Archaeology* 49: 165–93.

—2006. *Landscapes Decoded: The Origins and Development of Cambridgeshire's Medieval Fields.* Hatfield, University of Hertfordshire Press.

—2007. 'The Anglo-Saxon kingdom of Mercia and the origins and distribution of common fields'. *Agricultural History Review* 55, 2: 153–80.

—2010. 'Medieval field systems and settlement nucleation: common or separate origins?', in N. Higham, ed., *The Landscapes of Anglo-Saxon England.* Woodbridge, Boydell and Brewer: 108–131.

—2011. 'Anglo-Saxon fields', in H. Hamerow, D. Hinton and S. Crawford, eds., *Oxford Handbook of Anglo-Saxon Archaeology.* Oxford, Oxford University Press: 377–401.

Orwin, C. S. and Orwin, C. S. 1938. *The Open Fields.* Oxford, Clarendon Press.

Östrom, E. 1990. *Governing the Commons.* Cambridge, Cambridge University Press.

Owen-Crocker, G. 2007. 'British wives and slaves? Possible Romano-British techniques in 'women's work', in N. Higham, ed., *Britons in Anglo-Saxon England.* Woodbridge, Boydell and Brewer: 80–90.

Owoc, M. A. 2005. 'From the ground up: Agency, practice, and community in the southwestern British Bronze Age', *Journal of Archaeological Method and Theory* 12, 4: 257–281.

Palmer, B. 2003. 'The hinterlands of three southern England *emporia*: Some common themes', in T. Pestell and K. Ülmschneider, eds., *Markets in Early Medieval Europe.* Macclesfield, Windgather: 48–61.

Pantos, A. 2003. ' "On the edge of things": the boundary location of Anglo-Saxon assembly sites', *Anglo-Saxon Studies in Archaeology and History* 12: 38–49.

Parker Pearson, M. 2008. 'Chieftains and pastoralists in Neolithic and Bronze-Age Wessex', in P. Rainbird, ed., *Monuments in the Landscape.* Stroud, Sutton: 34–53.

—2009. 'The earlier Bronze Age', in J. Hunter and I. Ralston, eds., *The Archaeology of Britain.* London, Routledge: 103–125.

Parry, S. 2006. *Raunds Area Survey.* Oxford, Oxbow Books.

Parsons, D. 1983. 'Sites and monuments of the Anglo-Saxon mission in central Germany', *Archaeological Journal* 140: 280–321.

Payne, A., Corney, M. and Cunliffe, B. 2006. *The Wessex Hillforts Project.* Swindon, English Heritage.

Payne, S. 2007. 'New Insights into climate history', *British Archaeology* 92: 54.

Pheifer, J. D. 1987. 'Early Anglo-Saxon glossaries and the School of Canterbury', *Anglo-Saxon England* 16: 17–44.

Pitts, M. 2007. 'Consumption, deposition and social practice: A ceramic approach to intersite analysis in late Iron Age to Roman Britain', *Internet Archaeology* 21. http://intarch.ac.uk/journal/issue21/pitts_html, accessed June 2011.

—2008. 'Globalising the local in Roman Britain: An anthropological approach to social change', *Journal of Anthropological Archaeology* 27: 493–506.

—2010. 'Artifact suites and social practice: An integrated approach to Roman provincial finds assemblages', *Facta* 4: 125–152.

Pocock, E. A. 1968. 'The first fields in an Oxfordshire parish', *Agricultural History Review* 16, 2: 85–100.

Pollock, F. and Maitland, F. M. 1968. *The History of English Law Before the Time of Edward I*, 2 vols. Cambridge, Cambridge University Press.

Poos, L. and Bonfield, L. 1998. *Select Cases in Manorial Courts 1250–1550*. London, Seldon Society.

Postan, M. 1973. *Essays on Medieval Agriculture and the Problems of the Medieval Economy*. Cambridge, Cambridge University Press.

Postgate, M. R. 1962. 'The field systems of Breckland', *Agricultural History Review* 10, 2: 80–101.

—1973. 'Field systems of East Anglia', in A. R. H. Baker and R. A. Butlin, eds., *Studies of Field Systems in the British Isles*. Cambridge, Cambridge University Press: 281–324.

Pounds, N. J. G. 1973. *An Historical Geography of Europe 450 B.C. - A.D. 1330*. Cambridge, Cambridge University Press.

Powlesland, D. 1986. 'Excavations at Heslerton, North Yorkshire 1978–82', *Archaeological Journal* 143: 53–173.

—1990. 'An interim report on the Anglo-Saxon village at West Heslerton, North Yorkshire', *Medieval Settlement Research Group Annual Report* 5, 36–40.

—ed. 1998.'The West Heslerton assessment', *Internet Archaeology* 5. http://intarch.ac.uk/journal/issue5/westhescd_index.html, accessed June 2011.

Price, E. 2000. *Frocestor: A Romano-British Settlement its Antecedents and Successors*. Gloucester, Gloucester and District Archaeological Research Group.

Pryor, F. 1996. 'Sheep, stockyards and field systems: Bronze Age livestock in the fenlands', *Antiquity* 70: 313–24.

—2002. 'The Welland Valley as a cultural boundary zone: An example of long-term history', in T. Lane and J. Coles, eds., *Through Wet and Dry*. Lincoln, Lincolnshire Archaeology and Heritage Reports Series: 18–32.

Rackham, O. 1986. *The History of the Countryside*. London, Dent.

—1988. 'Woods, hedges and ditches', in M. Aston, ed., *Aspects of the Medieval Landscape of Somerset*. Taunton, Somerset County Council: 13–32.

—1994. 'Trees and woodland in Anglo-Saxon England: The documentary evidence', in J. Rackham, ed., *Environment and Economy in Anglo-Saxon England*. York, Council for British Archaeology: 7–11.

—2004. *Trees and Woodland in the British Landscape*. London, Phoenix.

—2010. *Woodlands*. London, Collins.

Randsborg, K. 1991. *The First Millennium AD in Europe and the Mediterranean: An Archaeological Essay*. Cambridge, Cambridge University Press.

RCHME 1968. *West Cambridgeshire*. London, HMSO.

—1976. *Iron Age and Roman Monuments in the Gloucestershire Cotswolds*. London, HMSO.

—1979. *Archaeological Sites in Central Northamptonshire*. London, HMSO.

—1981. *North-West Northamptonshire*. London, HMSO.

—1982. *South-West Northamptonshire*. London, HMSO.

Renes, J. 1988. 'Some aspects of open fields in the southern part of the province of Limburg (the Netherlands)', *Geografiska Annaler* 70B, 1: 161–167.

Reynolds, A. 2003. 'Boundaries and settlements in later sixth- to eleventh-century England', *Anglo-Saxon Studies in Archaeology and History* 12: 98–136.

Reynolds, S. 1981. 'Law and communities in western Christiandom', *American Journal of Legal History* 25, 3: 205–224.

—1984. *Kingdoms and Communities in Western Europe*. Oxford, Clarendon Press.

—1985. 'What do we mean by 'Anglo-Saxon' and 'Anglo-Saxons'?', *Journal of British Studies* 24, 4: 395–414.

—1994. *Fiefs and Vassals*. Oxford, Clarendon Press.

Rhatz, P. and Meeson, R. 1992. *An Anglo-Saxon Watermill at Tamworth*. York, Council for British Archaeology.

Richards, J. 2003. 'The Anglian and Anglo-Scandinavian sites at Cottam, East Yorkshire', in T. Pestell and K. Ülmschneider, eds., *Markets in Early Medieval Europe*. Macclesfield, Windgather: 155–167.

Richardson, G. 2005. 'The prudent village: Risk pooling institutions in medieval English agriculture', *Journal of Economic History* 65, 2: 386–413.

Riley, H. 2006. *Historic Landscapes of the Quantock Hills*. Swindon, English Heritage.

—and Wilson-North, R. 2001. *The Field Archaeology of Exmoor*. Swindon, English Heritage.

Rio, A. 2006. 'Freedom and unfreedom in early medieval *Francia*: The evidence of the legal formulae', *Past and Present* 193: 7–40.

Rippon, S. 1991. 'Early planned landscapes in south-east Essex', *Essex Archaeology and History* 22: 46–60.

—1994. 'Medieval wetland reclamation in Somerset', in M. Aston and C. Lewis, eds., *The Medieval Landscape of Wessex*. Oxford, Oxbow Books: 239–53.

—1998. 'Medieval settlement on the north Somerset Levels: The third season of survey and excavation at Puxton, 1998', *Archaeology in the Severn Estuary* 9: 69–78.

—2000. 'The historic landscapes of the Severn Estuary Levels', *Archaeology in the Severn Estuary* 11: 145–61.

—2002. 'Infield and outfield: The early stages of marshland colonisation and the evolution of medieval field systems', in T. Lane and J. Coles, eds., *Through Wet and Dry: Essays in Honour of David Hall*. Lincoln, Lincolnshire Archaeology and Heritage Reports Series 5: 54–70.

—2004. 'Making the most of a bad situation? Glastonbury Abbey, Meare, and the medieval exploitation of wetland resources in the Somerset levels', *Medieval Archaeology* 48: 91–130.

—2007. *Landscape, Community and Colonisation. The North Somerset Levels during the 1st to 2nd Millennia AD*. York, Council for British Archaeology.

—2008. *Beyond the Medieval Village: The Diversification of Landscape Character in Southern Britain*. Oxford, Oxford University Press.

—and Fife, R. M. and Brown, A. G. 2006. 'Beyond villages and open fields: The origins and development of a historic landscape characterized by dispersed settlement in south-west England', *Medieval Archaeology* 50: 31–70.

Robb, J. 2010. 'Beyond agency', *World Archaeology* 42, 4: 493–520.

Roberts, B. K. 1978. 'Rural settlement in County Durham: Forms, pattern and system', in D. Green, C. Haselgrove and M. Spriggs, eds., *Social Organisation and Settlement: Contributions from Anthropology, Archaeology and Geography*. Oxford, British Archaeological Reports International Series (Supplement) 47, i: 291–322.

—1981. 'Townfield origins: The case of Cockfield, County Durham', in T. Rowley, ed. *The Origins of Open Field Agriculture*. London, Croom Helm: 145–61.

—1985. 'Village patterns and forms: Some models for discussion', in D. Hooke, ed., *Medieval Villages: A Review of Current Work*. Oxford, Oxford University Committee for Archaeology: 7–25.

—1988. 'Norman village plantations and long strip fields in northern England', *Geografiska Annaler* 70B, 1: 169–177.

—1989. *The Making of the English Village*. London, Longman.

—1993. 'Five Westmoreland settlements: A comparative study', *Transactions of the. Westmoreland and Cumberland Antiquarian and Archaeological Society* 93: 131–43.

—1996. 'The great plough: A hypothesis concerning village genesis and land reclamation in Cumberland and Westmoreland', *Landscape History* 18: 17–30.

—2008. *Landscapes, Documents and Maps*. Oxford, Oxbow.

—and Wrathmell, S. 2002. *Region and Place: A Study of English Rural Settlement*. Swindon, English Heritage.

Rogerson, A., Davison, A., Pritchard, D. and Silvester, R. 1997. 'Barton Bendish and Caldecote: Fieldwork in south-west Norfolk', *East Anglian Archaeology* 80.

Rollason, D. 'Lists of saints' resting places in Anglo-Saxon England', *Anglo-Saxon England* 7: 61–93.

Roymans, N. and Gerritsen, F. 2002. 'Landscape, ecology and mentalités: A long-term perspective on developments in the Meuse-Demer-Scheldt region', *Proceedings of the Prehistoric Society* 68: 257–287.

Ruttan, L. M. 1998. 'Closing the commons: Cooperation for gain or restraint?', *Human Ecology* 26, 1: 43–66.

Samson, R. 1999. 'Illusory emporia and mad economic theories', in M. Anderton, ed., *Anglo-Saxon Trading Centres Beyond the Emporia*. Glasgow, Cruithne Press: 76–90.

Sarris, P. 2004. 'The origins of the manorial economy: New insights from late antiquity', *English Historical Review* 129: 279–311.

—2006. 'Review essay. Continuity and discontinuity in the post-Roman economy', *Journal of Agrarian Change* 6, 3: 400–413.

—2009. 'Introduction: Aristocrats, peasants and the transformation of rural society, *c.*400–800', *Journal of Agrarian Change* 9, 1: 3–22.

Schwyzer, P. 1999. 'The scouring of the White Horse; Archaeology, heritage and 'identity' ', *Representations* 65: 42–62.

Seebohm, F. 1883. *The English Village Community*. London, Longmans.

Sharples, N. 2010. *Social Relations in Later Prehistory*. Oxford, Oxford University Press.

Shaw, M. 1991. 'Saxon and earlier settlement at Higham Ferrers, Northamptonshire', *Medieval Settlement Research Group Annual Report* 6: 15–19.

Sheppard, J. 1966. 'Pre-enclosure field and settlement patterns in an English township', *Geografiska Annaler* 48B: 59–77.

—1974. 'Metrological analysis of regular village plans in Yorkshire', *Agricultural History Review* 22, 2: 118–135.

—1976. 'Medieval village planning in northern England: Some evidence from Yorkshire', *Journal of Historical Geography* 2, 1: 3–20.

—1979. *The Origins and Evolution of Field and Settlement Patterns in the Herefordshire Manor of Marden*. London, Queen Mary College Department of Geography Occasional Paper 15.

Sherley-Price, L., (trans., revised Latham, R.) 1990. *Bede: Ecclesiastical History of the English People*. London, Penguin.

Silvester, R. J. 1988. 'The Fenland Project, Number 3: Norfolk Survey, Marshland and Nar Valley', *East Anglian Archaeology* 45.

Sims-Williams, J. 1976. 'Cuthswith, seventh-century abbess of Inkberrow, near Worcestor, and the Würzburg manuscript of Jerome on Ecclesiastes', *Anglo-Saxon England* 5: 1–22.

Slicher von Bath, B. H. 1963. *The Agrarian History of Western Europe AD 500–1850*. Cambridge, Cambridge University Press.

Smith, C. 1978–9. 'The historical development of the landscape in the parishes of Alrewas, Fisherwick and Whittington: A retrogressive analysis'. *Transactions of the South Staffordshire Archaeological and Historical Society* 20: 1–14.

Smith, G. 1996. 'Archaeology and environment of a Bronze Age cairn and prehistoric and Roman field system at Chysauster, Gulval, nr Penzance, Cornwall', *Proceedings of the Prehistoric Society* 62: 172–4.

Smith, N. 1999. 'Charlton, Wiltshire – the development of a chalkland settlement', in P. Pattison, D. Field and S. Ainsworth, eds., *Patterns of the Past*. Oxford, Oxbow: 77–84.

Spratt, D. A. 1991. 'Recent British research on prehistoric territorial boundaries', *Journal of World Prehistory* 5, 4: 439–480.

Stafford, P. 1985.*The East Midlands in the Early Middle Ages*. Leicester, Leicester University Press.

Steedman, K. 1994. 'Excavation of a Saxon site at Riby Cross Roads, Lincolnshire', *Archaeological Journal* 151: 212–306.

Stenton, F. M. 1918. 'Sokemen and the village waste', *English Historical Review* 33, 131: 344–7.

—1920. *Documents Illustrative of the Social and Economic History of the Danelaw*. London, British Academy.

—1971. *Anglo-Saxon England*. Oxford, Oxford University Press.

Stevens, C. E. 1966. 'The social and economic aspects of rural settlement', in C. Thomas, ed., *Rural Settlement in Roman Britain*. York, Council for British Archaeology: 108–128.

Stoertz, C. 1997. *Ancient Landscapes of the Yorkshire Wolds*. Swindon, RCHME.

Story, J. 2003. *Carolingian Connections*. Aldershot, Ashgate.

—2005. 'Charlemagne and the Anglo-Saxons', in J. Story, ed., *Charlemagne: Empire and Society*. Manchester, Manchester University Press: 195–210.

Swanton, M., ed. 1993. *Anglo-Saxon Prose*. London, Dent.

Taylor, C. C. 1981. 'Archaeology and the origins of open-field agriculture', in T. Rowley, ed., *Origins of Open-Field Agriculture*. London, Croom Helm: 13–21.

—1983. *Village and Farmstead*. London, George Phillip.

—1992. 'Medieval rural settlement: Changing perceptions', *Landscape History* 14: 5–17.

—2000 ed. *Fields in the English Landscape*. Stroud, Sutton.

—2002. 'Nucleated settlement: A view from the frontier', *Landscape History* 24: 53–71.

—and Arbon, A. 2007. 'The Chronicle Hills, Whittlesford, Cambridgeshire', *Proceedings of the Cambridge Antiquarian Society* 96: 21–40.

—and Fowler, P. J. 1978. 'Roman fields into medieval furlongs?', in H. C. Bowen and P. J. Fowler, eds., *Early Land Allotment in the British Isles*. Oxford, British Archaeological Reports British Series 48: 59–62.

Taylor, H. M. 1987. 'St Wystan's church, Repton, Derbyshire: A reconstruction essay', *Archaeological Journal* 144: 205–245.

Thacker, A. 1985. 'Kings, saints and monasteries in pre-Viking Mercia', *Midland History* 10: 1–25.

Theuws, F. 1991. 'Landed property and manorial organisation in northern Austrasia: Some considerations and a case study', in N. Roymans and F. Theuws, eds., *Images of the Past*. Amsterdam, Instituut voor Pre- en Protohistorische Archeologie Albert Egges van Giffen: 299–407.

—1994. 'Elites and the transition from Merovingian to Carolingian', in P. O. Nielsen, K. Randsborg and H. Thrane, eds., *The Archaeology of Gudme and Lundberg*. Copenhagen, Akademisk Forlag: 195–207.

—2001. 'Maastricht as a centre of power in the early middle ages', in M. de Jong and F. Theuws with C. van Rhijn, eds., *Topographies of Power in the Early Middle Ages*. Leiden, Brill: 155–216.

Thirsk, J. 1964. 'The common fields', *Past and Present* 29: 3–25.

—1966. 'The origin of the common fields', *Past and Present* 33: 142–147.

—1973. 'Field systems of the east Midlands', in A. Baker and R. Butlin, eds., *Field Systems of the British Isles*. Cambridge, Cambridge University Press: 232–80.

Thomas, G. 2010. *The Later Anglo-Saxon Settlement at Bishopstone: A Downland Manor in the Making*. York, Council for British Archaeology.

—2011a. 'Bishopstone and Lyminge', *British Archaeology* 119: 42–47.

—2011b. 'The prehistory of medieval farms and villages from Saxons to Scandinavians', in N. Christie and P. Everson, eds. *Rural Britain and Ireland, AD 800–1600: Settlements, Landscapes and Regions*. Oxford, Windgather: 42–62.

Thomas, J. 2006. 'The archaeology of historic/medieval village cores: Evidence from Leicestershire and Rutland', *Medieval Settlement Research Group Annual Report* 21: 34–36.

Thompson, E. P. 1971. 'The moral economy of the English crowd in the eighteenth century', *Past and Present* 50: 76–136.

—1991. *Customs in Common*. London, Merlin Press.

Titow, J. A. 1965. 'Medieval England: the open-field system', *Past and Present* 32: 96–102.

Topping, P. 1989. 'Early cultivation in Northumberland and the Borders', *Proceedings of the Prehistoric Society* 55: 161–179.

—2008. 'Landscape narratives: the South East Cheviots Project', *Proceedings of the Prehistoric Society* 74: 323–364.

Trawick, P. 2001. 'Successfully governing the commons: principles of social organization in an Andean irrigation system', *Human Ecology* 29, 1: 1–25.

Trench, C. 1975. 'Peasant agriculture in medieval Gwynedd', *Folk Life* 13: 24–37.

Tristram, H. 2006. 'Why don't the English speak Welsh?', in N. Higham, ed., *Britons in Anglo-Saxon England*. Woodbridge, Boydell and Brewer: 192–214.

Tusser, T. 1984 ed. *Five Hundred Points of Good Husbandry*. Oxford, Oxford University Press.

Ulmschneider, K. 2000. 'Settlement, economy and the 'productive' site in Anglo-Saxon Lincolnshire, AD 650–780', *Medieval Archaeology* 44: 53–79.

—2011. 'Settlement hierarchy', in H. Hamerow, D. Hinton and S. Crawford, eds., *Oxford Handbook of Anglo-Saxon Archaeology*. Oxford, Oxford University Press: 156–171.

University of Leicester School of Historical Studies 2008. 'Carolingian polyptyches'. http://www.le.ac.uk/hi/polyptyques/, accessed June 2011.

Unwin, P. T. H. 1983. 'Townships and early fields in north Nottinghamshire', *Journal of Historical Geography* 9, 4: 341–346.

Upex, S. 2002. 'Landscape continuity and fossilisation of Roman fields', *Archaeological Journal* 159: 77–108.

Van Bavel, B. 2010. *Manors and Markets: Economy and Society in the Low Countries, 500–1600*. Oxford, Oxford University Press.

Van Zeist, W. and Palfenier-Vegter, R. 1979. 'Agriculture in medieval Gasselte', *Palaeohistoria* 21: 267–300.

Verderers of the New Forest. http://www.verderers.org.uk/, accessed August 2011.

Verhulst, A. 1992. *Rural and Urban Aspects of Early Medieval North-West Europe*. Aldershot, Variorum.

—2002. *The Carolingian Economy*. Cambridge, Cambridge University Press.

Vince, A. 1994. 'Saxon urban economies: An archaeological perspective', in J. Rackham, ed., *Environment and economy in Anglo-Saxon England*. York, Council for British Archaeology: 108–119.

Vinogradoff, P. 1893. 'Folkland', *English Historical Review* 8, 29: 1–17.

—1908. *English Society in the Eleventh Century*. Oxford, Clarendon Press.

Wade, K. 1980. 'A settlement site at Bonhunt Farm, Wicken Bonhunt, Essex', in D. G. Buckley, ed., *Archaeology in Essex to AD1500*. York, Council for British Archaeology: 96–110.

Wade-Martins, P. 1980a. 'Excavations in North Elmham Park 1967 - 1972', *East Anglian Archaeology* 9.

—1980b. 'Village sites in Launditch Hundred', *East Anglian Archaeology* 10.

—ed. 1987. *Norfolk from the Air*. Dereham, Norfolk Archaeological Unit.

Wainwright, M. 2011. 'Archaeologist digs into grandad's tale to uncover lost Yorkshire amphitheatre', *The Guardian*, 17 August 2011. http://www.guardian.co.uk/culture/2011/aug/17/lost-yorkshire-amphitheatre-aldborough, accessed August 2011.

Wake, J. '*Communitas Villae*', *English Historical Review* 37, 147: 406–413.

Warner, P. 1987. *Greens, Commons and Clayland Colonization*. Leicester, Leicester University Press.

—1996. The *Origins of Suffolk*. Manchester, Manchester University Press.

Waterbolk, H. T. 1995. 'Patterns of the peasant landscape', *Proceedings of the Prehistoric Society* 61: 1–36.

—and Harsema, O. H. 1979. 'Medieval farmsteads in Gasselte (Province of Drenthe)', *Palaeohistoria* 21: 227–266.

Weale, M., Weiss, D., Jager, R., Bradman, N. and Thomas, M. 2002. 'Y chromosome evidence for Anglo-Saxon mass migration', *Molecular Biology Evolution* 19, 7: 1008–1021.

Webster, G. 1967. 'Excavations at the Romano-British Villa in Barnsley Park, Cirencester, 1961–1966', *Transactions of the Bristol and Gloucestershire Archaeology Society* 86: 74–83.

Wendehorst, A. 2007. 'Der karolingische Königshof Iphofen', in A. Wendehorst, *Siedlungsgeschichte und Pfarreiorganisation in mittelalterlichen Franken*. Ebern, Gesellschaft für Fränkische Geschichte: 141–148.

Whitelock, D. 1972. 'The pre-Viking age church in East Anglia', *Anglo-Saxon England* 1: 1–22.

—ed. 1979. *English Historical Documents c.500–1042* (hereafter EHD). London, Routledge.

Whittle, A. 2009. 'The Neolithic period, *c*.4000–2400 CAL BC', in J. Hunter and I. Ralston, eds., *The Archaeology of Britain*. London, Routledge: 78–102.

Wickham, C. 1992. 'Problems of comparing rural societies in early medieval western Europe', *Transactions of the Royal Historical Society 6th* ser, 2: 221–246.

—1994. *Land and Power*. London, British School at Rome.

—2000. 'Overview: Production, distribution and demand, II', in I. L. Hansen and C. Wickham, eds., *The Long Eighth Century*. Leiden, Brill: 345–377.

—2005. *Framing the Early Middle Ages*. Oxford, Oxford University Press.

Williams, G. 2001. 'Military institutions and royal power', in M. P. Brown and C. A. Farr, eds., *Mercia: An Anglo-Saxon Kingdom in Europe*. Leicester, Leicester University Press: 295–309.

—and Bishop, R. 2004. 'Coenwulf, king of Mercia', *Current Archaeology* 194: 7

Williams, J. 1984. 'From 'palace', to 'town': Northampton and urban origins', *Anglo-Saxon England* 13: 113–136

Williams, R. J. 1993. *Pennyland and Hartigans*. Buckinghamshire Archaeological Society Monograph Series 4.

Williamson, T. 1984. 'The Roman countryside: Settlement and agriculture in NW Essex', *Britannia* 15: 225–230.

—1986. 'The development of settlement in North-West Essex: The results of a recent field survey', *Essex Archaeology and History* 17: 120–132.

—1987. 'Early co-axial field systems on the East Anglian boulder clays', *Proceedings of the Prehistoric Society* 53: 419–431.

—2003. *Shaping Medieval Landscapes*. Macclesfield, Windgather.

—2010. *The Origins of Hertfordshire*. Hatfield, Hertfordshire University Press.

Winchester, A. 1987. *Landscape and Society in Medieval Cumbria*. Edinburgh, John Donald.

—2000. 'Hill farming landscapes of medieval northern England', in D. Hooke, ed., *Landscape: The Richest Historical Record*. Amesbury, Society for Landscape History: 85–84.

—2006. 'Common land in upland Britain: Tragic unsustainability or utopian community resource?', in F. Bosbach, J. Engels and F. Watson, eds., *Unwelt und Geschichte in Deutschland und Großbritannien: Environment and History in Britain and Germany*. Munich, Saur K.G. Verlag Gmbh : 1–23. http://commons.ncl.ac.uk/?q=system/files/CoburgWinchester.pdf, accessed June 2011.

—and Straughton, E. 2010. 'Stints and sustainability: Managing stock levels on common land in England, c.1600–2006', *Agricultural History Review* 58, 1: 30–48.

Winterbottom, M. 1978. *Gildas. The Ruin of Britain and Other Documents*. Chichester, Phillimore.

Wormald, P. 1986. 'Charters, law and the settlement of disputes in Anglo-Saxon England', in W. Davies and P. Fouracre, eds., *The Settlement of*

Disputes in Early Medieval Europe. Cambridge, Cambridge University Press: 149–168.
—1999. *Legal Culture in the Early Medieval West: Law as Text, Image and Experience*. London, Hambledon.
Wright, A. P. M. and Lewis, C. P. 1989. *Victoria History of the County of Cambridge and the Isle of Ely: Volume IX. Chesterton, Northstowe and Papworth Hundreds*. London, Institute for Historical Research.
Yorke, B. 1990. *Kings and Kingdoms of Early Anglo-Saxon England*. London, Routledge.
—1995. *Wessex in the Early Middle Ages*. Leicester, Leicester University Press.
Zadora-Rio, E. 2003. 'The making of churchyards and parish territories in the early-medieval landscape of France and England in the 7th–12th centuries: A reconsideration', *Medieval Archaeology* 47: 1–19.

Index

Page references in italics indicate a figure